F. Edwards

A - E
inclusive

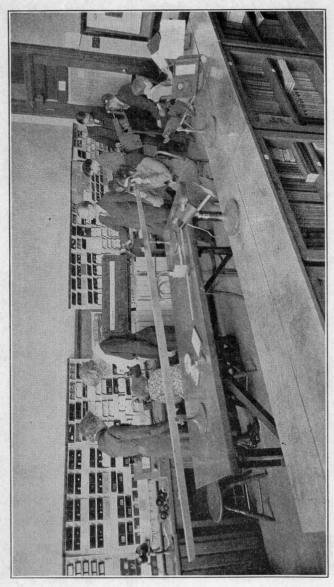

Reading Clinic, State Normal School, Oswego, New York

The Prevention and Correction of Reading Difficulties

By

EMMETT ALBERT BETTS

Director of Teacher Education
State Normal School
Oswego, N. Y.

ROW, PETERSON AND COMPANY
EVANSTON, ILLINOIS
NEW YORK CITY   SAN FRANCISCO

Dedicated to

MISUNDERSTOOD CHILDREN

ACKNOWLEDGMENTS

To the following individuals, organizations, and publishers the writer is grateful for generous permission to quote from published materials. Each quotation in the text is identified by a number keyed to a complete reference to author, title, publisher, and date at the end of the chapter.

American Book Company
D. Appleton-Century Company
Ernest Ashbaugh
Fowler D. Brooks
Leo J. Brueckner
Guy T. Buswell
Cambridge University Press
Hollis L. Caswell
Anna D. Cordts
S. A. Courtis
Prudence Cutright and
   Walter A. Anderson
Helen P. Davidson
Doubleday, Doran & Company
G. B. Duffy
Donald D. Durrell
L. P. Faris
Arthur I. Gates
Ginn & Company
William S. Gray
Ralph Haefner
Alice Hanthorn
Harvard University Press
Gertrude Hildreth
Elizabeth M. Hincks
Ernest Horn
Houghton, Mifflin Company
Edmund B. Huey
Joseph Jastak
H. Jordan
Elizabeth Irwin
Doris M. Lee
Edna B. Liek
J. B. Lippincott Company
Longmans, Green & Company

Howard Y. McCluskey
Macmillan Company
E. F. Mahady Company
W. R. Miles
Marion Monroe
John J. B. Morgan
E. B. Notson
Samuel W. Patterson
George Peabody College
   for Teachers
Walter P. Percival
Professional Press
Public School Publishing Company
Harold Rugg
Scott, Foresman & Company
Ann Shumaker
Silver, Burdett & Company
Nila Banton Smith
George D. Stoddard and
   Beth L. Wellman
Clarence R. Stone
Lorene Teegarden
Lewis M. Terman
Miles A. Tinker
Arthur E. Traxler
Teachers College, Columbia
University of Chicago Press
M. D. Vernon
Guy W. Wagner
John B. Watson
David W. Wells
Margaret L. White
Paul A. Witty
World Book Company
W. D. Zoethout

PREFACE

Teachers everywhere are confronted with the problems of pupils who are retarded in reading. During the past ten years a tremendous and growing interest has been evidenced in this phase of education, which has been reflected in the large number of investigations reported. All teachers are concerned with the problem because reading difficulties retard general educational progress.

Many theories regarding the nature of the problem have been advanced by investigators of high professional standing in their respective fields. Unfortunately many suggestions have been either misinterpreted or too strongly publicized. As a result, confusion has reigned when the problem should have been more clearly defined. The writer has attempted to define certain issues, to discuss them in the light of available evidence, and to integrate the findings from allied research fields for the purpose of "clearing the air" for the classroom teacher.

This book is largely a summary and interpretation of recent research findings. A part of the material has been drawn from the data secured in the writer's reading clinic. The remainder of the book is based on the writer's experience as a teacher, principal, superintendent, and director of research. Most, if not all, of the problems discussed are in need of further experimental appraisal. If American schools are to be learner-centered, there is an urgent need for reducing the time lag between the reporting of research findings and their translation into practice.

It is the writer's point of view that most reading difficulties can be prevented, and that remedial reading procedures should be based on first-teaching techniques. When certain learning conditions are recognized in practice, children will learn to read.

In the main, this book is addressed to able teachers who are interested in making the necessary personal sacrifices to prepare themselves for maximum professional efficiency. There is little hope for qualitative education until a majority of classroom teachers can demonstrate their professional leadership in the communities they serve. It is a truism to state that, other things being equal, no school can rise above the level of the professional imagination of the teaching staff.

Certain problems discussed only briefly in this book will be presented in greater detail in a companion volume entitled *The Reading Program of the Elementary School*. In Chapter I, the nature of the problem has been described. A brief view of the modern reading program is given in Chapter II in order to establish a basis for the discussion of deviations. After the reader is made aware of the nature of the difficulties encountered in a program of reading, the factors underlying reading difficulties are briefly treated in Chapter III. In Chapters IV to XII, inclusive, the discussion is centered largely around the analysis of the symptoms and causes of reading deficiencies. In these chapters an attempt is made to cut away much of the confusing folklore which usually enters most discussions of the subject and to substitute research findings, in so far as possible. As the analysis procedures are evaluated, preventive and remedial measures are also indicated. Chapters XIII, XIV, and XV are summaries of preventive and corrective measures and procedures. A general summary of the entire book is presented in Chapter XVI.

Early inspiration and information relative to this phase of education was derived from the classes of Dr. Charles E. Germane, Dr. Harry A. Greene, Dr. Ernest Horn, and Miss Maude McBroom. Items of merit in this book may be traced to their teachings, but all errors of judgment expressed herein are assumed by the writer.

No book covering the work of a wide range of specialized fields is written without guidance. The writer is especially indebted to R. A. Sherman, manager of the Stereo-Ophthalmic Division of the Keystone View Company, Meadville, Pennsylvania, who made available the research laboratories of his department.

Dr. Carl F. Shepard of Chicago generously contributed his genius for the development of certain forms for the Visual Sensation and Perception Tests. The research work was initiated largely in the schools at Shaker Heights, Ohio. Dr. F. H. Bair, Superintendent of Schools, and Dr. Justin A. Garvin, Head of the Health Department, were the writer's chief sources of encouragement. William Connor, Chief of Research Staff, Board of Education, Cleveland, Ohio, offered many valuable suggestions. Superintendent Harold Maurer and Principal W. Paul Allen of Garfield Heights, Cleveland, Ohio, assisted the writer in standardizing the tests. School people and doctors in the Cleveland area gave full co-operation in the validation of the Betts Ready to Read Tests.

The research work in the Reading Clinic begun at Shaker Heights has been continued at the State Normal School, Oswego, New York. With the constant encouragement and professional interest of Dr. Ralph W. Swetman, Principal, and his staff, the continuation of the investigations is being made possible.

Dr. Guy W. Wagner, Principal of the Campus Elementary School, and Lorin Wheelwright, Director of Music Education, have offered many valuable suggestions which have been incorporated within this book. Special acknowledgments are also due to Lucille Allard, Supervisor, Garden City, New York; Mable Everett, State Normal School, Cheney, Washington; Howard Forsythe, Akron, New York; Frances Rodewald, Director of Reading Clinic, West Hartford, Connecticut; and Grace Stowell, Director of Reading Clinic, Ilion, New York.

Finally, the writer is indebted to his wife, Thelma Marshall Betts, whose encouragement was a constant stimulation.

EMMETT ALBERT BETTS,
Director of Teacher Education.

STATE NORMAL SCHOOL,
OSWEGO, NEW YORK.

TABLE OF CONTENTS

CHAPTER I

Points of View on Retardation

Reading disability is essentially a social disease.—Joseph Jastak (15:259)[1]

The Art and Science of Teaching

Not so long ago, the stern schoolmaster admonished his pupils to mind their p's and q's. Of recent date, research workers have provided enough evidence to relieve us of our sinister feelings and helplessness regarding children who are unadjusted to the reading program. With a background of scientific training, the modern teacher no longer finds it necessary to resort to coercive methods. To her, teaching is still an art, but she finds herself in a position to better understand and anticipate the obstacles which are sure to confront a substantial proportion of the learners in her charge.

Specific Reading Difficulties

Not the least of the perplexities of a modern school are the problems offered by the non-reader or retarded reader. Children who have difficulty in learning to read can conveniently be divided into two classes: (1) those who are below normal on the basis of general ability, i.e., of low

---

[1] Numbers in parentheses throughout the text refer to the numbered references at the end of each chapter. In the case of quotations page references also are given. Students of the problem who are interested in a more nearly complete bibliography on the subject are referred to the writer's *Bibliography on the Problems Related to the Analysis, Prevention, and Correction of Reading Difficulties,* published by the Keystone View Company, Meadville, Pennsylvania.

intelligence, and (2) those who present specific learning disability in reading. If other functions related to reading are adequate, the first class will learn to read to the level of their general ability providing there is sufficient repetition, after a mental age of about six and one-half years is attained. The second group, characterized by a specific learning disability, presents quite a different problem. Their educational profile is radically different. They will usually test high in such subjects as arithmetic and very low in activities where language ability is required.

Incidence of Reading Disabilities

It is usually estimated that from 8 to 15 per cent of the school population is characterized by varying degrees of reading disabilities. In the table below is a summary of the findings of qualified investigators of the problem. The reader should not be confused by the disparity in the conclusions, for the data are modified by many variables. Chief among the factors which may account for such discrepancies is the lack of agreement on the definition of a retarded reader. Among other such factors are administrative policies for admission to the first grade, methods of securing data, and types of population studied.

FREQUENCY OF READING DISABILITIES

Investigator	Percentage of Retarded Readers
Durrell	15.0
Monroe	12.0
Orton	2 to 4
Rauschburg	15.0
Razkaja	12.0
Wallin	4.48

Incidence of Reversals

Deficiencies in reading ability vary in type and degree as do the possible causes. The reversal tendency, i. e., saying *saw* for *was*, *p* for *q* or *d*, etc., has intrigued past investigators to such an extent that other types of major reading difficulties have gone by default. Recent studies (21) have emphasized that not more than 10 per cent of reading troubles can be attributed to reversal tendencies and confusions.

The capacity to read mirror writing and to write in mirrored fashion has been found among retarded readers. Beeley (2) discovered only one mirror writer among every group of 2,500 school children of elementary-school age in Chicago. The possible causes and treatment of such rare cases will be discussed in succeeding chapters.

Reading Ability and Intelligence

According to the definition of a reading disability, the retarded reader usually achieves in activities where reading skills are not of primary importance. Durrell (10) concluded that intelligence tests which involve reading are not a fair measure of the intelligence of such children. In the intermediate grades, Durrell (11) more frequently found retarded readers among the children with normal and superior intelligence than among dull children. Of the retarded readers 25 per cent were found to have intelligence quotients above 110, while only 9 per cent of those with I. Q's below 90 were retarded. Fifteen per cent of the reading cases had normal intelligence. In other words, about 80 per cent of those pupils who were retarded in reading had either normal or superior intelligence. Scientific discovery is gradually re-defining our problems. No longer can the teacher and school administrator account for all learning disabilities on the basis of low intelligence. By the same token, reading readiness cannot be predicted entirely by means of the intelligence tests.

Sex Differences

Among individuals with language difficulties there is a preponderance of boys. From three to four times as many boys as girls are found to stutter. Caswell (8:18) found in all the cities he studied a higher percentage of failures among boys than among girls. He states (8:22): "In grade 5-A in these schools, twenty-three per cent of the boys were not promoted and seven and four-tenths per cent of girls." Stoddard and Wellman (24:156) concluded: "At the preschool ages the girls are clearly in advance of the boys on present day development scales." Brooks (7:22) states: "In oral reading girls do better than boys in all elementary grades."

There is some evidence to show that girls are promoted on lower standards of achievement. Other data, not yet conclusive, indicate that boys mature more slowly than girls. Furthermore, there is the peculiar American tradition that women should teach at the elementary-school level. It is the writer's belief that young men should be encouraged to choose elementary education for their life's work because there is a need for teachers who appreciate the special interests of boys.

Non-Promotions

Percival (20) concluded: "Grade one is the greatest failing grade, being responsible for thirty and two-tenths per cent of the failure in cities and twenty-four and one-tenth per cent of all failures." Furthermore, he found that reading was responsible for 99 per cent of failures in grade one in cities and for 95 per cent of all failures in grade one in the rural schools.

Caswell (8:13) states: "There is a decided tendency for first grade to have a considerably higher rate of non-promotion than other grades." And again (8:15): "Variations in rate of non-promotion for different grades, as revealed by the data here presented, are not significant except in the first grade. The excessive rate in the first grade, as compared with other grades, indicates basic maladjustment in the first-grade work."

Many investigations of number and causes of failure point to the first grade and to reading. Since promotions from first grade are usually made on the basis of reading achievement, all educational policies and teacher and parent attitudes at that grade level need drastic revision.

Reading and Educational Progress

Dr. Dorris Lee (16) investigated the importance of reading ability for achievement in the intermediate grades. To be more than one-tenth of a grade below in reading ability seriously lowered the general achievement index. From this carefully controlled study she concluded that a reading handicap hampered achievement in other school subjects.

At the age of eight or nine most children have interests which are satisfied through reading. From then on the whole educational system both in and out of school requires increasing reading ability for satisfactory social adjustments. *Every child would read if it were in his power to do so.* Social pressure in any community makes it mandatory.

Research workers (16) have found that inability to read blocks general educational progress. The modern primary-school curriculum embraces an increasing amount of science, social science, and literary materials. By the fourth grade, the child who is only slightly below grade on reading achievement has been found to have very few chances for success in other school activities. The problem is real, for many individuals at all levels of education have been carelessly dubbed as dull because a reading inability divorced them from necessary vicarious experiences derived from reading. Hence, reading ability is essential to normal progress in academic subjects.

Individual Differences

That education increases individual differences is a truism. The supercedence of the graded school over the one-room school has aggravated the problem to a degree. Many administrative devices have been resorted to in order to care for the problem of individual differences in the graded school. At present, there appears to be a tendency away from the typical grade and subject-matter achievement classification of children in the primary grades. Several schools are experimenting with plans for the grouping of primary-grade children on the basis of their readiness to read, so that fewer children will experience failure.

Great ranges of individual differences exist before the child is brought under the influence of the school. Children vary in their rate of growth. Anatomists exhibit indisputable evidence of this statement. Working with more subtle and intangible factors, psychologists are finding gross functional differences among children. The emotional or "feeling" make up of each child is a significant variable.

Physiologists are finding that children come to school with physiological differences to challenge the curriculum maker. Some children cannot profit by auditory training which is essential to success with music or certain types of phonetic programs. Others are found to have visual disabilities which impede learnings in activities where these functions are vital.

The teacher is confronted with the necessity of making adjustments to all these physiological, anatomical, and psychological differences. In addition to all the peculiar combinations of these factors, the educator has found that enormous differences exist in the preschool training of pupils. For the student of reading readiness, the range of information possessed by each child has been fruitful for investigation. The background of information is varied according to the social life of the home, the type of community, and the extent to which a foreign language is used in out-of-school activities. Furthermore, the teacher is confronted with the problem of methodology, for the method will be modified by the array of individual differences which characterizes her particular group.

Learnings

Three major types of learning characterize most school activities: namely, intellectual, motor, and emotional. When a child is attempting to master recognition of even the easiest words, he is acquiring a mind set of like or dislike for the process. In this situation, the inexperienced teacher may believe the intellectual learning to be of primary importance, and, therefore, not recognize the emotional learning potentialities. The experienced teacher knows that emotional learnings or feelings which contribute to attitudes

are of prime importance in the learning-to-read process and
that the intellectual learnings are of no more than complementary value. In brief, the child must have a *feeling* of
confidence in the teacher and the interest and curiosity
which will lead him to a genuine desire for investigating
the content of books.

Not of least significance are motor learnings, for the
young learner depends on these as reinforcements to the
others. It is well established that we get a part of this feel
for language through the speech and writing muscles. Here
again individual differences make it mandatory for the
teacher in some cases to resort to a definite program for
motor augmentation of learnings. A detailed discussion of
this aspect of learning may be found in Chapter XIV.

Prognosis

The prognosis, or prediction, of a case of reading disability is becoming increasingly more hopeful. In the early
literature of the subject, about 4 per cent of the school
population were diagnosed as "word blind." Of recent date
the term "word blindness" is rarely used. The tradition of
diagnosis in which a general symptom is designated by a
name is being eclipsed by the development of scientific
analysis techniques. Educators and psychologists are fast
passing through the stage of analyzing *symptoms* and are
now concerning themselves with the study of causes. As a
result, retarded readers are being taught to read.

Feeling Versus Objective Appraisal

In order to care intelligently for this problem of individual differences, the modern teacher finds it necessary to
resort to the use of standardized and informal tests. This

is the scientific way of securing data to appraise her subjective *feeling* regarding the children. As a result of securing more or less objective evidence, many teachers have been caused to change their attitudes toward the problem. Without these data, teachers have been all too ready to dub a child as slow when he experienced little or no learning.

Intelligent insight is, therefore, rapidly displacing snap-judgment feeling for problem children. A teacher imbued with scientific and professional attitude toward her work will substitute "the interpretation of the data lead me to believe thus" for the statement "I feel."

We Create Many Problems

To a degree, we teachers create many of our problem-cases because we do not make practicable adjustments to individual differences. Undoubtedly some types of reading disabilities are caused by requiring a child to engage in reading activities before he is generally ready to participate. In this way children are permitted to practice error. They are taught to dislike reading if they are forced into a situation where failure is sure to result.

A Point of View

The point of view of the writer is that most reading difficulties could be prevented by increasing the entrance age for the first grade, by revising the first-grade program of instruction, by providing a greater quantity of primary-reading material with varied content, by grouping children in terms of general readiness for a given reading program, by beginning instruction with the learner's interest, and by the correction of physical defects. The emphasis in the reading program should be on prevention rather than on correction.

Remedial instruction should be given only after and in terms of a careful analysis of the specific difficulties of the learner. Reading disabilities are usually characterized by a constellation of cumulative difficulties. No one cause and no one remedial procedure should dominate the teacher's philosophy in analyzing and correcting the trouble. Care should be exercised in discriminating between pedagogical and physical handicaps.

Practically all children evidencing specific reading disability can be taught to read for meaning. Present procedures are undoubtedly crude and inefficient, hence much more economical means of teaching children to read will be afforded the teacher of the future. In the meantime, success will usually characterize the venture of the enthusiastic and trained teacher who will give individual and inspired help to the child who has not successfully learned to read.

SUMMARY

1. An individual with a specific reading disability is one who achieves in academic situations where rate of comprehension in reading is not important.

2. Eight to fifteen per cent of the school population evidences specific reading disability.

3. Education increases individual differences. Because traditional education does not make adequate provision for individual differences, there has been too much standardization.

4. Differences in native equipment, environments, and rates of learning are significant variables in the determination of readiness for reading.

5. Teachers should be aware of the inter-relationships of intellectual, emotional, and motor learnings.

6. Both objective data and personal judgment are essential to the complete understanding of the retarded learner.

7. Many cases of reading disability may be prevented by adjusting the school program to the varying readinesses or aptitudes of the pupil.

8. Most of the retarded readers have normal or superior intelligence.

9. Lack of achievement in reading is a contributing cause to non-promotion in the elementary school.

10. Reading difficulties retard and block general educational progress.

11. The prevention of reading difficulties should be the chief concern of educators and parents.

12. Reading difficulties vary in degree and type.

13. Teacher, as well as learner, attitude is a significant factor in the prevention and correction of reading difficulties.

14. Most retarded readers and non-readers can be taught to read.

REFERENCES

1. Baker, Harry J. *Characteristic Differences in Bright and Dull Pupils,* Bloomington, Illinois: Public School Publishing Co., 1927.

2. Beeley, Arthur L. *An Experimental Study in Left-Handedness,* Chicago: University of Chicago Press, 1918.

3. Betts, Emmett A. "Reading Disabilities and their Correction: National Conference on Research in Elementary School English," *Elementary English Review,* XII (March, April, May and June, 1935), 69-73, 106-10, 131-41, 157-65.

4. Betts, Emmett A. "Physiological Approach to the Analysis of Reading Difficulties," *Educational Research Bulletin* (Ohio State University), XIII (September and October, 1934).

5. Betts, Emmett A. "Teacher Analysis of Reading Disabilities," *Elementary English Review,* XI (April, 1934), 99-102.

6. Betts, Emmett A. *Bibliography on the Problem Related to Analysis, Prevention, and Correction of Reading Difficulties.* Meadville, Pennsylvania: Keystone View Co., 1935.

7. Brooks, Fowler D. *The Applied Psychology of Reading,* chap. 1. New York: D. Appleton Co., 1926.

8. Caswell, Hollis L. *Non-Promotion in Elementary Schools,* x-100. Division of Surveys and Field Studies, No. 4. Nashville, Tennessee: George Peabody College for Teachers (1933).

9. Duffy, G. B. "A Diagnostic Study of Reading Difficulties in the Third Grade." Unpublished and filed in Boston University Education Library, 1934.

10. Durrell, Donald D. "The Effect of Special Disability in Reading on Performance on the Stanford Revision of the Binet-Simon Tests." Master's thesis, Department of Education, University of Iowa, 1927.

11. Durrell, Donald D. "Reading Disability in the Intermediate Grades." Unpublished Doctor's dissertation, Graduate School of Education, Harvard University, 1930.

12. Gates, Arthur I. *The Improvement of Reading*, pp. 3-17. New York: Macmillan Company, 1929.

13. Gates, Arthur I. *The Psychology of Reading and Spelling with Special Reference to Disability*. Teachers College Contributions to Education, No. 129. New York: Teachers College, Columbia University, 1922.

14. Gray, William S. *Report of the National Committee on Reading*, pp. 275-89. Twenty-fourth Yearbook of the National Society for the Study of Education, Part I. Bloomington, Illinois: Public School Publishing Co., 1925.

15. Jastak, Joseph. "Interferences in Reading," *Psychological Bulletin*, XXXI (April, 1934).

16. Lee, D. M. *The Importance of Reading for Achieving in Grades Four, Five and Six*. Teachers College Contributions to Education, No. 556. New York: Teachers College, Columbia University, 1933.

17. Lord, Elizabeth, Carmichael, Leonard, and Dearborn, Walter F. *Special Disabilities in Learning to Read and Write*. Harvard Monographs in Education, No. 6. Cambridge, Massachusetts: Harvard University Press, 1925.

18. Monroe, Marion. *Children Who Cannot Read*, pp. xvi-206. Chicago: University of Chicago Press, 1932.

19. Orton, Samuel T. "An Impediment to Learning to Read: a Neurological Explanation of the Reading Disability," *School and Society*, XXVIII (September 8, 1928), 286-90.

20. Percival, Walter P. "A Study of the Causes and Subjects of School Failure." Doctor's dissertation. New York: Teachers College, Columbia University, 1926.

21. Phillips, Albert J. "Relation of Left-Handedness to Reversals in Reading," *Elementary English Review*, XI (April, 1934), 97-98.

22. Smith, Nila Banton. "The Period of Emphasis upon Broadened Objectives in Reading," *American Reading Instruction,* Part VII. New York: Silver, Burdett Company, 1934.

23. Smith, Nila Banton. "Matching Ability as a Factor in First-Grade Reading," *Journal of Educational Psychology,* XIX (November, 1928), 560-71.

24. Stoddard, George D., and Wellman, Beth L. *Child Psychology,* New York: Macmillan Company, 1934.

CHAPTER II
The Reading Program

*More innovations have been effected in reading
instruction during the first thirty years of the present century than during the entire three hundred
years of American history antedating this period.*
—Nila B. Smith (26: 264)

Reading to Learn Versus Learning to Read

In the early history of American-reading instruction,
children were sent to school in order to *learn to read*. Until
recently, the philosophy dominating the thinking of primary teachers has emphasized learning to read as one of
the chief goals. Formal number work is being minimized
rapidly in the first and second grades. The arts, natural
sciences, and social sciences are being given rôles of increasing importance in the entire elementary-school grades. The
upshot of it all is an emphasis on *reading to learn,* even
from the very beginning of reading instruction. If the
philosophy of reading to learn is to be made operative, the
learner must be mature enough to have needs which can be
legitimately satisfied by reading.

As our professional concept of reading readiness has been
enlarged, the program of reading instruction has been modified. This holds true for at least 10 per cent of our American schools. Physical, mental, and emotional readinesses
for reading are now conceded to be essential elements for
real learning situations at all grade levels.

15

The School Program

All teachers are teachers of reading. Arithmetic, social studies, music, and science offer excellent opportunities for the acquisition of reading skills. One of the chief dangers of a departmentalized or platoonized elementary school is that of compartmentalization where subjects are emphasized rather than children. The recent tendency to eliminate so-called school readers has forcefully called attention to the need for a definite program of reading and study in all school activities.

From the point of view of one who studies the reading program, deficiencies in reading may be produced by inadequate provision for: (1) adjustment of the curriculum to individual needs; (2) creation of functional drill situations; (3) coverage of important reading skills at each level of reading rather than in terms of grade level; and (4) reading as a tool subject; that is, achieving in specific reading skills through the content subjects.

The protagonists of the theory of social utility have also sensitized us to the need for learning in socially useful situations. For example, vocabulary building is no longer believed to be the compartmentalized work of the reading period. (Vocabularies are increased through work in the various subject-matter fields.) Ability to select and evaluate material and to use reference materials such as keys, graphs, tables, and the like, is acquired in science and social-studies classes. The emphasis, in other words, is on reading to learn.

Types of Learning Programs

1. **First-teaching.** The initiation of the learner into new skills, informations, or attitudes is called first-teaching.

Efficient learning takes place when the learner is mature enough to profit by the instruction and when the new is presented in an articulate and meaningful fashion. At any grade level, readiness for learning is essential and involves the building of a background and the relating of that background to the new situation. Hence, a third- or a sixth-grade teacher must inventory the background, assist the learner in the acquisition of the missing parts, and stimulate interest, curiosity, anticipation for the new. Other things being equal, the effectiveness of first-teaching is modified by the maturity of the learner. This coupled with the fact that individuals vary widely in their rates of learning necessitates grouping within the classroom. No unit of the curriculum should be left until it is adequately learned.

2. Maintenance drill. After first-teaching, it is frequently necessary to maintain the skills and information by providing varying situations for practice. Maintenance teaching may be necessary for several reasons:

    a) The learning may not be socially significant at that age level. For example, a well-known, fifth-grade arithmetic course of study states: "Strive for automation, not understanding." Because arithmetic processes are introduced before the child has a real need for them, there is a necessity for artificial maintenance in the school. No practice is given in life outside the school. The writer contends that a readjustment of the curriculum in terms of learner requirements would eliminate much of the artificial maintenance drills so common in our schools today.

    b) The learner may have been so immature at the time of the first-teaching that he failed to secure insight for the processes involved. Maintenance teaching provides the

varying situations for the learning which should have
been previously achieved. In this case, maintenance
teaching would provide the perpetual inventory needed
when teaching large groups.

3. Remedial teaching. Remedial or corrective teaching is required when the patient is academically ill. The
complexity of reading difficulties is due to individual differences among learners as well as inefficient first-teaching.
The cause or causes of the difficulty should be analyzed
before prescribing the cure. In some cases the learner may
be totally ignorant of the process and respond with random
errors which are corrected by first-teaching procedures. In
another instance it may be a matter of incorrect learning
which necessitates unlearning or substituting correct responses. These two are the problems of remedial teaching.

When Should Reading Instruction Begin?

Preparation for reading begins long before the child enters school. Ideally, formal reading instruction would not
begin until the child is mentally, physically, and emotionally ready to read eagerly and comfortably. Many eye
specialists would place the beginning age at eight or nine
years. A psychometrist, or mental tester, would probably
suggest a mental age of six and one-half to seven and one-
half. In conformity with blind tradition many parents send
their children to school at five or six years of age to be
taught to read. The scientific answer to the question would
probably be: "Begin reading instruction when the child is
generally mature enough and has a real need for reading."
The compromise is the grouping of the learners and the
education of his contemporaries and parents. This is the
task of the teacher.

Standards of reading readiness are modified largely by the nature of the initial reading program. The modern beginning program, involving the use of charts and pre-primers, probably does not require as much general maturity as did the older type of programs. (Informal teaching becomes possible where teachers are better trained and when sufficient materials and laboratories are available.) Likewise, the informal determination of readiness for pre-primer reading is possible when teachers are familiar with formal tests and with factors which contribute to reading success. Preparatory and chart-building periods in the first grade offer ample opportunity for the teacher to group her pupils in terms of general maturity and rate of maturation in the processes involved. (A child should not be permitted to receive a pre-primer until he can master the elementary word recognition skills, left-to-right rhythmical reading habits, and meaning of the reading-chart contents.) The evidence for postponement or modification of the reading program is being accumulated rapidly. Arguments for the substitution of art, music, science, and other activities for reading instruction in the first grade may be briefly summarized as follows:

1. **Physical immaturity.** Eighty per cent of six-year-old children are normally farsighted; that is, they have short or immature eye-balls. Eye co-ordination required for the noting of fine details in order to discriminate between word forms is not fully developed.

2. **Social immaturity.** Few six-year-old children have needs which require satisfaction through reading. Since there is no real motive for reading, the child should be given an opportunity to have his environment interpreted to him.

3. **Mental immaturity.** Until seven and one-half years of age, some children exhibit a reversal tendency. To place such a child in a reading situation is to permit him to practice confusions. It is also generally believed that a mental age of six and one-half years is essential for beginning reading. According to the statistics of the problem, approximately one-fourth to one-third of first-grade entrants do not even survive the reading ordeal. Of the remainder who do pass, a substantial portion are characterized by poor attitudes, nervous instability, wandering attention, stuttering, and a number of other ailments.

4. **Wasted human effort.** In order to please uninformed and overindulgent parents, the teacher force-feeds the typical child by overstimulation and otherwise artificial motivation. In such a situation, the parent and teacher receive first consideration; the learner is unconsciously conceived to be an automaton. Tradition (at once man's curse, time saver, and inspiration) causes teachers at all grade levels to be placed in a paradoxical situation, with innocent children as the victims. Courses of study in common use call for so much reading in the first grade that there is little time for rhythms, music, art, science, social studies, practical arts, and other activities which can be most profitably offered at that time.

5. **Evolution is slow but inevitable.** To change a curriculum based on adult beliefs to one based upon child interests and needs requires thinking, readjustment of vested interests, and re-appraisals. Regardless of the crudity of the process and the disastrous results, children are still being sent to school at five for the purpose of learning to read. The teacher is, indeed, in a very responsible position.

Parent Education

Parent education must be preceded by teacher education. Patterson (22 : 245) makes a shocking statement: "To cite a fact or two, it has been estimated that more than 40 per cent of our American teacher colleges fail to offer courses in the teaching of reading and that modern methods are in use in fewer than half our classrooms." This statement is amplified when one observes the high percentage of teachers graduated by liberal art schools where the education department is only *tolerated*. Hence, trained teachers must inform their colleagues before the difficulties of the learner can be interpreted to the parents.

American children are in need of teachers who believe in their profession, teachers who have the strong and determined conviction to better prepare themselves for the task at hand. Medical doctors are trained over a regrettably short period of time, yet the period of training for the average teacher in the United States stands out in bold contrast. The teacher should be the educational leader, the pedagogical priest of the community. Until the teacher prepares herself for that high position, her opportunities are negligible.

In order to educate parents, there must be something to educate them about. There must be a definite and intelligent program upon which to confer. The task of educating the parents is more than one of informing. That parents can be interested in contributing and being a part of the school program has been demonstrated many times. Parents believe in education because each community boasts of having the best school. The big job then is one of interesting parents in the legitimate improvement of the educational opportunities for their children.) The reading situation will not be corrected until teachers assume that responsibility. No one else in the community is paid for this purpose. No one else is trained as the teacher is expected to be trained, and no other member of the community has this responsibility.

Stages in the Development of Reading Habits

The Twenty-fourth Yearbook of the National Society for the Study of Education, Part I, still remains a classic in the field of reading. Its publication marked a turning point in instructional materials and methods. The full significance of the profound statements contained therein have not yet been entirely interpreted in the typical public-school situation. Five important divisions of a reading program were distinguished (20: 25): (1) Period of preparation for reading (kindergarten and early part of Grade I). (2) Initial period of reading instruction (Grade I). (3) Period of rapid progress in fundamental attitudes, habits, and skills (Grades II–IV). (4) Period of wide reading to extend and enrich experience and to cultivate important reading attitudes, habits, and tastes (Grades IV–VI). (5) Period of refinement of specific reading attitudes, habits, and tastes (junior and senior high-school grades).

Individual differences, much discussed and given little practical recognition and interpretation in the typical situation, give rise to the need for grouping within the classroom. A teacher of a given grade level who accepts children on their own individual planes of achievement will usually find a range of three or more grades. In other words, a third-grade teacher may have children in all of the first four above mentioned stages of reading.

The periods in the development of a reading program as set up by the Twenty-fourth Yearbook Committee have been extended and revised by the writer in the following discussion.

1. Preparation for reading. Education increases individual differences. In a group of five-year-old children in the kindergarten, individual differences will be manifested in varying abilities to adjust to the group, to follow directions, to learn rhythms, to acquire motor co-ordination, and kindred items. As the hierarchy of functions involved is built, the differences will become greater. After the first few days in the first grade, grouping or an individual plan of instruction becomes imperative if the best interests of the child are given intelligent consideration.

In the past, the work of the kindergarten and the primary teacher have been highly compartmentalized. To the kindergarten teacher has been assigned the task of setting the stage so that the five-year-old can develop into a social being, able to take care of his elementary needs and prepared to participate in a formal reading program. All would have been well had nature only known and co-operated with men in the belief that all children were expected to learn to read after leaving the kindergarten situation. To complicate the problem, teachers, parents, and school administrators have apparently been trained in the belief that all first-grade children at once are to be initiated into a formal reading program. It should be remembered that in spite of traditional beliefs 15 to 35 per cent of first-grade children have been classified as non-promotions.

The Twenty-fourth Yearbook Committee (20) has generously contributed to our professional understanding of the need for an extended period of preparation for reading.

A definite program of experience and training was described as genuine prerequisites for reading. Since the publication of the Twenty-fourth Yearbook in 1925, our concept of reading readiness has been enlarged. The development of reading readiness tests has also greatly contributed to a clearer understanding of the factors contributing to reading success. No longer are activities such as bead stringing countenanced as legitimate reading readiness activities.

Normal children have been found to be physically, mentally, and emotionally ready for reading at ages ranging from five to seven and one-half years. It has been demonstrated that factors other than intelligence contribute to reading aptitude. Many of the children with specific reading disability are of normal or superior intelligence.

A mental age of six and one-half years is conceded to be the minimum age for introduction to the typical first-grade reading program. Frequently children of below normal intelligence have been brought to the writer's clinic for help when they were mentally too immature to profit from instruction. A child with an I. Q. of seventy to seventy-five cannot profit greatly from initial reading instruction until he is nine or ten years old chronologically. Frequently teachers and parents pronounce the case as hopeless at a time just before the child is mature enough to be helped.

When readiness is discussed, the question usually arises, "Readiness for what?" The typical program of reading embraces work with the pre-primer sometime during the first six weeks of the first grade. A modern program of first-grade reading should precede the pre-primer work with a definite preparatory and chart building period. An analysis of reading readiness or aptitude tests shows the following factors to be significant for success with the typical first-grade reading program:

a) A mental age of at least six and one-half years

b) Good two-eyed vision

c) Ability to make visual discrimination between word forms

d) Ability to make auditory discriminations between word sounds

e) Little or no tendency to reverse letter or word forms

f) A wide background of information and experience in science, social science, and literature

g) Ability to perceive simple relationships between ideas

h) Ability to fuse or blend sounds into words

i) A good speaking vocabulary

j) Ability to express thoughts in acceptable language units, sentences, etc.

k) Ability to associate symbols, such as names, signs, etc., with meaning or the thing for which they stand

l) Ability to enunciate and articulate correctly

m) Curiosity, interest, anticipation, and desire for reading

n) An appreciation for the content of books

In brief, the period of preparation for reading is the giving of content to and the sharpening of those functions which have to do with reading. The child should have his physical defects corrected, and should be provided with an attractive, interesting, and understanding school environment wherein he can acquire a background of essential experiences and facility in the use of language.

Doris Waters (32) investigated the pre-reading experience by taking inventory of the types of specific experiences needed for the reading of primers and first readers and by determining the lack of such experiences in her group of

kindergarten children. The wide array of experiences dealt
with in fifty first-grade books was startling. Equally interesting were the experience needs which were lacking on the
part of kindergarten children. Such appraisals of needed
pre-reading experiences make it possible to eliminate much
waste in kindergarten education and to substitute experiences specifically required by a given group.

The preparatory period does not cease with entrance to
first grade. Some pupils will be ready for chart-building
experiences during the first month of school: others may
require a continuation of the preparatory period into the
third or fourth month or beyond, the number of first-grade
failures provides ample evidence that not all children are
ready to read at six years of age. To face reality requires
the postponement of reading until a physical, mental, and
emotional readiness has been acquired.

Reading during the final part of the preparatory period
should be confined to such activities as reading of bulletin-
board and blackboard notices, and the class dictation to the
teacher of stories or experiences. These stories should be
of approximately three to five sentences, dictated by members of the class, and written on the board or chart by the
teacher. Building a reading environment is one of the most
important tasks of the teacher.

Music, science, art, practical arts, and other room activities will serve to broaden experiences and heighten interest.
They should be caused to function as a definite part of the
school program and at no time as busy work. The situation
must be learner-centered embracing interested children, an
enthusiastic teacher, and informed parents.

2. **The period of initial instruction.** Since individual
differences have been increased through the preparatory

period, not all children will be ready to participate in the chart-building activities. Although the children have been previously grouped, the teacher may expect to re-group for this transitional period between the preparatory period and the work with the pre-primer.

Of recent date, much discussion has taken place regarding the value of experience type reading. Most recent manuals for basal readers either advocate or comment on the desirability of such procedures. The typical suggestion is the development of the brief content of the first charts from an excursion taken by the class. However, this is only one way to secure chart content from common experience of the class. Frequently, the class has enjoyed a story read or told by the teacher. The most attractive room is one to which the children have made personal contributions in the form of rocks, shells, pets, practical-arts projects, antiques, pictures, toys, games, and kindred items. All these provide interesting material which may be discussed by the class and later dictated to the teacher in the form of simple stories for the preparation of a chart. The general characteristics of a desirable chart are:

a) Stories based on class interests and experiences

b) Short one-line simple sentences. If the line is broken, it should be done only between phrases

c) Maximum of five or six simple sentences for beginners. (Avoid too many sentences in beginning lessons)

d) Vocabulary directed by teacher so as to prepare children for the vocabulary of pre-primers. (Avoid too many new words in each lesson.)

e) Writing, preferably manuscript, done on blackboard or large sized chart-paper, oak-tag, or white wrapping paper.

f) Lettering or printing done in large letters with wide lines and liberal spacing between the words and between the lines

g) Placed on level with the children's eyes

The chief advantages of the use of charts are:

a) Left-to-right eye progression can be established under controlled conditions. Too frequently teachers take for granted such simple reading informations and skills. In addition to this, some children experience confusions regarding the left-to-right eye movements

b) The large size type read at distance of four to ten feet does not require the degree of visual acuity or eye coordination that reading small size type at ten inches requires

c) Symbols are immediately associated with meaning because the group has thought out the content and the teacher has lettered or printed it for them. For the same reason, the material possesses added interest for the learner

d) Correct oral reading habits, such as pronunciation, can be achieved with the attention and help of the group

e) Silent reading habits, such as reading without lip movement, can be fostered with the aid of the group

f) A common center of attention is afforded the group

g) Children are provided with an opportunity to learn from each other

h) Experience charts are of interest to children because they have helped to build them

The materials of the initial period of reading instruction usually include charts, blackboard reading, word and phrase games, and workbook exercises. This is called the pre-book stage of reading. Most modern reading series include pre-pared charts and seat work which precedes the pre-primer. The chief purpose of such materials is to introduce the class to the characters and vocabulary of the pre-primer. Much of the seat work is overdone and of little educative value. In many situations it would be far better to substitute in-dustrial arts, science, and art activities for many of the seat-work activities because poor habits are acquired unless the work is carefully supervised. Furthermore, most pri-mary rooms are completely lacking in these additional activities which are essential for children at that age.

Gray (19:174) challenges the teacher by stating: "One of the most common errors in classroom activities today is the practice of permitting children to fritter away intellec-tual energy while reading. There is need in every grade of discovering worthwhile purposes for reading, of develop-ing keen interest in reading activities whether for study or recreation, of stimulating the pupil to think actively while reading, of providing opportunities for the use of the infor-mation secured, of setting high ideals of achievement, and of holding pupils definitely responsible for satisfactory results."

Most of the manuals which accompany a good series of readers include a wealth of suggestions for utilizing the experiences and interests of children. Many successful teachers prefer to prepare charts and other material for the pre-book stage of reading. Usually the charts are prepared in duplicate. The second chart is cut into sentence strips and used in activities which involve the matching of the sentence strips with the sentences on the first chart. Later these strips are cut into phrase cards, and finally into word cards. Probably the best advice to a teacher is to suggest a careful study of the manual which accompanies the series of basal readers.

The pre-primers should not be given to the children until they have exhibited their readiness for that type of reading. If the children have not been interested and have not mastered the reading processes involved in the pre-book level of reading, they should not be confused further by initiating them into the pre-primers. Unless the child is near sighted, there are probably few, if any visual defects, which might contribute to difficulty in reading properly made charts. Hence, a teacher can contribute to future difficulties in reading by forcing a child into materials of increasing difficulty for which he is not ready. If a child cannot make visual discriminations between word forms printed in large size type, he cannot be expected to succeed with the pre-primer materials which are printed in sixteen- or eighteen-point type (approximately one-fourth of an inch high).

The chief danger is the dropping of chart work too soon. In a well planned language program, chart work, or class dictated compositions, will be used through the third grade at least. Many successful remedial teachers have used experiences dictated by children as the chief reading materials. If this is a desirable procedure for remedial reading cases, then it would be wise for first-grade teachers to accept this cue.

Not all children of a given first grade can be expected to complete the work of the pre-book stage at the same time, hence the necessity for grouping. Pupils should not be promoted from one level to another on the basis of the number of weeks planned for those activities. Readiness for the pre-primer stage of reading is modified by all the complexity of factors and events which contribute to reading readiness.

Desirable standards of achievement for the pre-book level of reading are:

a) A genuine interest and curiosity for the content of books, signs, etc.

b) An attitude of reading for meaning

c) Ability to make visual discriminations between word forms

d) Ability to use context clues or recognize words in the context

e) Rhythmical left-to-right reading habits

f) Ability to recognize words used in the first pre-primer. (This usually includes a vocabulary of seventy or more sight words)

g) Good habits of enunciation and articulation

h) Fair degree of accuracy in sentence comprehension

3. Initial stage of book reading. The presentation of the pre-primer to each group as they have completed the pre-book stage should be an anticipated occasion. Assuming the pupils are really ready for the pre-primer, the teacher from now on should concern herself with another aspect of reading readiness; namely, attitudes. The children can be prepared emotionally for a given story by discussing the illustrations and tying in their previous experiences. The pre-primer will probably require more motivation than any of the other books in the series because the content is limited by the narrow vocabulary.

The chief emphasis during this period should be on enjoyment and meaning. Extended and tedious drill on word recognition has no place in the program at this period. If this is found necessary for some cases, the pupils involved should be transferred to a group still concerned with pre-book reading experiences. Reading deficiencies are quite sure to result when an attempt is made to force the pupil to progress too rapidly. Here is the time when the teacher can prevent reading difficulties by maintaining interests in reading activities within the grasp of the child.

Reading ability is more easily acquired through the reading of interesting materials. In short, one learns to read by reading. Reading is taught universally at a great cost because most six- and seven-year-old children probably have few needs which require satisfaction through reading. Therefore, even the easiest of reading materials require considerable artificial motivation. The problem then is to secure a suitable quantity of reading material printed in large size type and written with well controlled vocabulary and sentence structure. Since pre-primers more nearly meet these requirements, it is suggested that the use of a number of pre-primers from other series of readers is desirable. Although the vocabularies are noted for their disparity, there is sufficient overlapping to make their use desirable. Care should be exercised to select pre-primers which have relatively similar vocabularies. Not only should a number of pre-primers be used during the initial book reading period but they should also be on the library table for use throughout the primary grades. The average pre-primer costs less than twenty cents.

The chief reason for using a number of pre-primers is the enrichment of the reading program for the fast group and the supplying of needed repetitions for the slower groups. All pupils stand to profit from the reading of easy and well constructed materials. Briefly, children should not be introduced to difficult primer material until they have established efficient and rhythmical left-to-right reading habits on the pre-primer level. The basis for the introduction of the primer should not be memorization of the pre-primer. Children who evidence reversal tendencies should be carefully supervised so that they will not practice confusions. These children should have been identified previously either by formal readiness tests or during the pre-book stage of reading. Other aspects of this problem are discussed in Chapters IV, XIII, and XIV.

The initial period of reading instruction is usually rounded out by the completion of activities connected with the reading of primers and first readers. Before the introduction of the first reader, the child should have a reading vocabulary of about two hundred words. Desirable supplementary materials can be found in other series of readers, science books, and number stories. Not all children can be expected to complete the work of the initial reading period by the end of the first year of instruction. This will be true because many immature children will report for first-grade reading. In addition, varying learning rates will not permit equal achievement by all first-grade children. On the other hand, many children will evidence second-, third-, and possibly fourth-grade reading ability for certain skills, information, and attitudes. The second-grade teacher will find it necessary to begin instruction where each group of children is, rather than accepting the whole class as being ready for the period of "rapid progress in fundamental attitudes, habits, and skills." In short, the school calendar does not control the learning rates and the level of achievement.

Desirable levels of achievement at the end of the first or initial instruction are:

a) Ability to recognize 600 to 700 words in context, probably using context clues, picture clues, general configuration, and visual analysis. (See Chapter XI.)

b) Increasing interest in independent reading

c) Ability to read orally first-grade material with reasonable accuracy and rhythm, i. e., phrasing

d) Ability to read silently with a minimum of lip movement

e) Ability in recognition and interpretation of punctuation

f) Well established habits in left-to-right progression for tenses, phrases, words, and word elements

g) Ability to follow directions

h) Ability to reproduce the general thought of the content read

i) Ability to use table of contents and to find pages

j) Ability to identify each letter of the alphabet in isolation

4. Period of rapid progress in fundamental attitudes, habits, and skills. This period usually includes the work of the second and third grades. Since some children will not have arrived at a desirable group standard and others will be capable of the independent reading of more difficult material, there will be added reasons for grouping the children within the room on the basis of their needs and interests. This will be achieved with less effort than before because the children will be more nearly independent in their ability to plan, initiate, and execute the activities. By the end of the second grade, the pupil who has made average progress in reading should be able to recognize in context at least one thousand words. The number of words which can be recognized and the rate of comprehension will depend in no small degree upon amount of supplementary material provided. The work will consist largely of audience-type reading, specialized training in silent reading, continuation of training in word-recognition skills, and use of books and the library. (All the way through the program provision should be made for individual variations in level of achievement.) At no grade level can all the children be expected to profit by typical instructional materials prepared for the grade. Children just do not learn according to any author's preconceived idea. In most modern teachers' manuals this philosophy is carefully stated. Teachers should be of necessity somewhat statistically minded. Reading materials are usually prepared for that group which clusters around the central tendency. Unfortunately, the central tendency when considered in isolation from the measures of dispersion or deviation from the norm does not adequately describe the needs of those who deviate above or below. Each child must be provided with activities at his level of achievement; otherwise the slow learners will be confused and the fast group will be penalized. If a modern series of readers is used, the pupils at the end of the third grade will have acquired a reading vocabulary ranging from about 1,600 to 2,700 words. To this will be added specialized vocabularies acquired in other school activities such as science and social science. The present tendency is to discontinue the use of a basal series of readers beyond the second or third grade. Concurrent with this policy, is that of substituting art, music, and industrial-art activities for the formal arithmetic work of the first, second, and possibly the third grade. As stated previously, the philosophy of the past has been that of "learning to read" in the pri-

mary grades. Along with this, pupils were forced into
tedious and wasteful formal drill on arithmetic processes
which were not significant to them at that age. Automation
rather than understanding was the goal. Research workers
have brought forth enough evidence to turn the tide of
thinking to child development rather than drilling on skills
which lack significance at the primary level. When the
reading-to-learn philosophy becomes operative in the
schools, pupils who are generally mature enough to profit
by instruction will acquire proficiency in specific reading
skills through the materials of the content subjects.

   5. The period of wide reading. This period of wide
reading to establish fundamental attitudes, skills and information is usually assigned to Grades IV to VI. Unfortunately not all children who are products of the typical
reading program really are prepared for what that program
embraces. On the other hand, a modern program of instruction will provide for fairly wide reading after the
pupils have been initiated into the first reader. Boys appear
to have more difficulty with reading than girls; therefore,
they should be provided with reading materials in science,
industrial arts, and kindred activities, which may be close
to their interest. In any event, intermediate-grade teachers
will be confronted with classes which have reading abilities
varying from those who require continued initial instruction
to those who easily read junior high-school books. The
teacher should not be confused by the periods outlined in
the Twenty-fourth Yearbook (20). To some extent, these
periods were described at a time when there was heightened
interest in grade classification of pupils and in tests standardized on the basis of grades rather than of children. In
other words, norms and standards were stressed rather than

deviations. Although there is at present a great need for more reading materials at the primary level, there were significantly fewer materials in 1925 when the Yearbook was published. At that time, the primary teacher had to depend largely upon sets of readers. The picture can be expected to change still more when children are given reading instruction only after a certain level of general readiness has been achieved. In the meantime, the various periods of reading instruction will continue to serve as guide posts for the instruction of children.

Before the completion of the work of the sixth grade, pupils should have mastered the skills required to identify new words (see Chapter XI). Regarding study skills, the pupils should have a knowledge of sources for help and the ability to locate information quickly. This would include the ability to skim and to use index, table of contents, dictionary, library card files, reference materials, keys, tables, and graphs. The pupils should also have the ability to comprehend quickly and to organize what is read and to select and evaluate material needed. Attitudes for the proper care of books and for attacking reading with vigor should be well established.

6. **The period of refinement in reading.** Although the junior and senior high-school period is usually looked upon as a time when the reading habits are extended and refined, reading skills and study habits should not be neglected. A substantial portion of the school population at that period will be retarded in other school activities because of reading deficiencies. In addition to this, there are specific reading skills which should be learned at the secondary-school level. Many of the skills and information learned at the elementary-school level need extension at this time. Adequate

social adjustment to secondary-school requirements demands efficient reading habits. Individual variation in reading ability at that level is beginning to be recognized in good schools. This situation is being met by providing remedial teachers, supervised study periods, differentiated assignments, and additional easy reading materials.

Many students at the secondary level are branded as slow learners because of an unanalyzed reading deficiency. Children with faulty reading habits cannot be as easily identified when there is little occasion for oral reading. Silent reading has been stressed because of its value in life outside the school, of the difficulty of oral reading, and of the tendency toward regimented and highly compartmentalized instruction. Subject matter has held sway over the needs of learners.

Language skills cannot be adequately controlled by the students until every teacher at the secondary level assumes the responsibility for attending to reading, spelling, and oral and written composition. Language is a tool, not a subject. Instruction in these skills cannot be assigned successfully to any one school department or compartment. Certain language skills cannot be effectively practiced in isolation. For example, mathematics teachers have failed to recognize reading skills; it is not the reading teacher who has failed so completely. The teachers of mathematics, social studies, science, and other subjects must accept their responsibilities for providing practice on the language skills peculiar to their fields.

Sets of Readers

Since 1925, there has been a strong tendency to discontinue the use of sets of readers. In the first place, a set of readers for any one grade cannot meet the requirements of the individual members of the class. A second equally valid reason is that of excessive expenditures. Thirty different books covering a variety of topics on different reading levels are more desirable than one set of thirty readers. The present tendency appears to be that of purchasing from two to five readers from each of several sets. In the third place, reading is a key to other school activities and as soon as possible the pupils should be encouraged to do wide reading in accordance with their interests. The purchase of a few copies of each of several sets of readers permits the reading of more material. The additional material might include science, social science, and literary books as well as number stories. Recent trends, therefore, point to the use of sets of basal readers only in the first and second grades. Beyond that period, pupils have access to an increasing quantity of good reading materials.

Workbooks

Since 1925, teachers have been deluged with workbooks and other types of seat work used for many purposes. Such materials have been a great boon to first-grade teachers confronted with large classes. At the first-grade level, workbooks have been used for seat-work activities. Although in many cases, workbooks have been superior substitutes for much of the seat work of the past, they have also been used to provide busy work. Probably one of the biggest mistakes is the use of workbooks for all members of the class.

Grouping or Classification Within the Room

There have been many discussions among educators and psychologists regarding the pros and cons of grouping.

Anyone who admits the existence of learning differences among individuals will readily acknowledge the advantages of grouping within the room. (On entrance to the first grade, children can be grouped upon the basis of their general readiness for reading. Since education increases differences among individuals, there will be even greater necessity for grouping at succeeding grade levels.)

Children vary not only in their level of readiness for reading but also in their rates of learning. Many children have failed to achieve in reading because of regimented instruction. The teacher who attempts to take any given group or class of children through successive steps in regimented reading instruction will usually penalize many of the pupils. Not all children can be expected to have acquired readiness for reading during a preparatory period of a set number of days, which may have been outlined in advance. Some may be ready for the chart-building period at the end of the first two weeks; others may not be ready until the end of the first semester of the first grade. Likewise, it is the very exceptional first-grade class that can be kept together during the pre-primer and later the primer periods. The teacher who does not group within the room fails to admit actuality.

Among a class of third-grade children it is not uncommon to find some who have difficulty with pre-primers and others who enjoy sixth- or seventh-grade books. In short, strictly third-grade reading materials would probably meet the needs of less than one-half of the class. In such a situation, children who, at their best, can struggle only with second-grade materials will be completely submerged with the sentence structure, vocabulary, and concepts of the third grade. Since double promotion for the more rapid and efficient readers and demotion for the slower readers are not adequate solutions, the most reasonable procedure appears to be that of grouping within the room.

Grouping within the classroom makes possible differentiated assignments in terms of individual needs and interests. In a class of thirty pupils, there may be need for as many as from five to ten groups. This fits in well with either an activity plan or formal instruction.

The grouping is usually based on general reading achievements, specific reading needs or interests. The ideal, of course, is to group in terms of specific requirements and interests. The plan can be initiated by classifying the children into three groups: (*a*) those at grade level, (*b*) those below their grade in reading achievement, and (*c*) those above standard. As the teacher develops in her ability to administer the program and as the children grow in their ability to work in small groups, the class can be further subdivided. Within reasonable limits, the individual needs will be cared for to the degree that the number of subdivisions in the class is increased. Individual instruction is in many respects the ideal, but grouping within the classroom is a compromise with the actuality of mass education.

At this point, it should be understood that the group plan may be varied throughout the year. At one time the whole class may be working in small groups. At another time, there may be only two or three groups functioning while the remainder of the class may be doing independent reading. Occasionally, some of the groups may be engaged in preparing a play or dramatization, or in art, science, or industrial-arts activities. The plan is valuable to the degree it is administered in terms of needs.

Grouping can be used for both silent- and oral-reading

activities of the recreatory or study type. At no time is it necessary to have all silent or all oral reading. Since the purpose of grouping is that of meeting individual needs, some groups will require more of one type of reading than will others. The teacher will find it necessary to supervise more closely the work of the slower groups. If this is not done, faulty habits may be practiced and thus the whole plan is defeated. Children should not be permitted to make their class contributions until the leader or chairman and perhaps the teacher agree that satisfactory preparation has been made.

Under the old recitation plan, each child read to the teacher one paragraph from the same book which all the other members read silently. Although such a plan was not without a few good points, the work was usually stilted and poorly motivated. In addition to the undesirable slow pacing of the silent reading of the rest of the class, there was no semblance of an audience-type situation. Worse still, each child in a large class had very little opportunity for any kind of oral reading. In the grouping plan, a group of two or three can take turns reading orally to each other from one book. In a class of thirty, this means that each individual would have about ten times more opportunity for oral or any other type of reading. The work can be motivated by the purpose of the reading, as in life outside of the school. The type of reading done will depend upon whether or not the goal is the review of an interesting book which the class has not read, a debate, a dramatization, the answer to specific questions in relation to a unit of work, or some similar class activity.

The activities for each group may be determined from the discussions of the entire class or of the group concerned.

If a large unit of work in the social studies is being exe-
cuted, there may be a need for class consideration of the
contribution each group is expected to make. In this case,
the teacher may find it necessary to direct the group to
reading material which they can handle. On the other hand,
there should be many occasions where each group will prepare a dramatization, play, debate, book review, or some
other activity as a surprise for the class. Successful administration of the grouping plan will depend upon the
leader selected for each group, the definiteness with which
the work for each group is planned, and the skill with which
the results are appraised. Since this is not a pupil-recite-to-
teacher plan, each leader or chairman should be held responsible by the class for a definite contribution to the
whole class. The audience-type situation should be made
possible. Work within each subdivision or group should be
conducted so that everyone is learning and contributing to
the learning of the others. Many successful teachers frequently arrange to have one advanced pupil in a group of
two or three slower pupils. However, this should be done
in a manner which will penalize neither the strong nor the
weak pupils.

At each grade level various reading skills should be emphasized. The extent to which these skills are covered
depends upon the skill of the teacher in directing the activities of the class. Children can be taught to locate information more readily if they have specific questions to be
answered in which they are vitally interested. Not all the
reading work needs to be done in small groups. Frequently,
the whole class will be interested in verifying group reports
or opinions expressed in the class. The point in question
is that of definitely planned instruction on specific skills.

Investigators in many subject-matter fields have concluded that skills left to incidental learning are not acquired by the class as a whole. This does not mean that the drill on these skills should not be functional, but it does mean that the teacher should so direct the class activities that these skills will be practiced as necessary and incidental tools.

The chief problem of all teachers is that of caring for those with learning difficulties without penalizing the remainder of the group. The success of a grouping plan hinges on the philosophy of the teacher and her administrative officers. Frequently in the past, the problem of individual differences was met by wholesale demotion or double promotions. It is an indictment against the teacher if either policy is adopted. Mere demotion will not help the child learn to read. On the other hand, school activities should not be made difficult for the more advanced group by double promotions. It is a better policy to enrich the experiences of those who learn easily by adding more worthwhile activities in science, social science, art, music, and industrial arts.

Since many states are serviced with traveling libraries, almost every teacher has the opportunity to provide a large number of books for her children. For example, in New York State a rural-school teacher can receive eighty books at one time. Reading materials can be further supplemented by buying parts of sets of reading material for science, social science, and literature instead of complete sets. Hence, the problem of materials is not the major obstacle in such a program.

Some of the major advantages of a grouping-within-the-room program may be summarized as follows:

a) Better adjustment of the curriculum to individual needs
b) Increased interest on the part of the learners

c) More opportunities for development of individual initiative and independence

d) More opportunities for learning to work with groups

e) Possibility of higher individual achievement for specific skills. More material can be covered

f) Creation of more opportunities for the use of reading skills in real situations

g) More opportunities for individual participation

h) Greater possibilities for the development of good listeners as well as good leaders

i) Reading is conceived to be a means to an end

There are several cautions to be observed in group work: First, the assignment should be definite; otherwise, poor habits of work will be acquired. Second, if the work is not characterized by initiative and self control, the children will be taught to misuse their freedom. Third, definite standards of achievement should be maintained by a careful check-up on the work. In so far as possible, this appraisal should be functional rather than formal.

A good school is an evolution; that is, learning conditions are being improved gradually and consistently. The grouping of children in terms of their interests and needs cannot be expected to be achieved in a month. As a rule, children do not accept responsibility that rapidly. It should always be kept in mind that there will be many occasions when economy calls for certain reading activities involving the whole class and for other activities based entirely on individual work. Grouping should be an evolutionary process developed in terms of pupil needs rather than to the exclusion of other plans.

SUMMARY

1. Reading for meaning should be stressed throughout the reading program.
2. Reading is a tool, not a subject.
3. All teachers have the responsibilities of providing practice on the language skills, attitudes, and information.
4. There is need for reviewing the needs of primary pupils.
5. Parents should be contributors to the educational as well as the financial program of the school.
6. Education increases individual differences.
7. At any one level of instruction, learners vary widely in their abilities and interests.
8. Reading deficiencies contribute to general educational retardation.
9. By means of an intelligent and carefully administered program, reading difficulties can be prevented.
10. At each level there is an urgent need for grouping in terms of needs and interests.
11. There is considerable evidence to validate the contention that a mental age of six to six and one-half years is desirable for beginning reading. This, however, should be interpreted in a statistical sense; that is, some children may be ready for a certain program of reading instruction at an *earlier* age and some may not be ready until a *later* age.
12. The readiness profile of a given child may be expected to vary considerably. This means that a composite of objective factors and judgments, rather than any

one element, should be used to determine reading readiness.

13. There is an urgent need for all learners to have access to reading materials that challenge their abilities. Materials may be too easy as well as too difficult.

14. Remedial procedures are required when first- or maintenance-learnings have been inadequate.

15. Systematic instruction is essential to efficient learning.

16. Instruction on specific reading skills, information, and attitudes should be definitely planned for all age levels.

17. At all levels of elementary and secondary education there is a need for all students to have specific instruction on reading and study habits. Since opportunistic instruction is notoriously ineffective, this means that separate periods should be set aside for the work.

REFERENCES

1. Betts, Emmett A., Everett, Mabel, and Rodewald, Frances. "Remedial Reading Based on First-Teaching," *Journal of Exceptional Children* (February, 1936).

2. Bonar, Hugh S. "Ability Grouping in the First Grade," *Elementary School Journal*, XXIX (May, 1929), 703-6.

3. Bonar, Hugh S. "Segregation of 'Ability Groups' and Achievement on the First Grade Level," *Educational Method*, XI (June, 1932), 531-36.

4. Brown, Gincie. "Reading Material for Slower Groups," *Childhood Education*, I (April, 1925), 381.

5. Bruner, Herbert B. "Determining Basic Reading Materials through a Study of Children's Interests and Adult Judg-

ments," *Teachers College Record,* XXX (January, 1929), 285, 309.

6. Bullinger, Elnora. "Unit of Work in II-A Reading," *Childhood Education,* VI (April, 1930), 366.

7. Burks, Jesse D., and Stone, Clarence R. "Relative Effectiveness of Two Different Plans of Training in Silent Reading," *Elementary School Journal,* XXIX (February, 1929), 431-36.

8. Buswell, G. T. *Fundamental Reading Habits: A Study of the Development.* Chicago: University of Chicago Press, 1922.

9. Carter, Homer L. J. "An Attempt to Increase Reading Efficiency," *Educational News Bulletin,* II (June, 1932), 13-19.

10. Caswell, Hollis L. "Non-Promotion in Elementary Schools," Division of Surveys and Field Studies. Nashville, Tennessee: George Peabody College for Teachers, (1933), x-100.

11. Conolly, Ross Earl. "The Effects of Position of Pupils in the Classroom Upon Recognition and Recall of Printed Matter." Unpublished and filed in University of Pittsburgh Library.

12. Coxe, Warren W., and Richard, Edwin B. *Suggestions for Teaching Silent Reading.* University of the State of New York Bulletin No. 850. Albany, New York: University of State of New York Press (April 15, 1916).

13. Crawford, C. C. "Relative Values of Reading and Outlining as Methods of Study," *Educational Method,* VIII (May, 1929), 434-38.

14. Critchley, M. "Some Effects of Reading and Writing in Children." *Journal of State Medicine,* XXV (1927), 217-23.

15. Danforth, Marie Lusk. "Progress in the Selection and Arrangement of Material in Supplementary Readers," *Elementary School Journal,* XXXIII (February, 1933), 427-33.

16. Darby, O. N. "An Experiment in Teaching Oral Reading," *Journal of the National Educational Association,* XXIV (January, 1935), 11-12.

17. Davis, Georgia. "Procedures Effective in Improving Pupils of Poor Reading Ability in Regular Reading Classes," *Elementary School Journal,* XXXI (January, 1931), 336-48.

18. Donnelly, E. E. "A Study of Word Recognition Skills in Grade One." Unpublished and filed in Boston University Education Library, 1932.

19. Gray, William S. "A Study of Ways and Means of Reorganizing and Improving Instruction in Reading," *Journal of Educational Research,* XV (March, 1927), 166-75.

20. Gray, William S. (Chairman). *Report of the National Committee on Reading.* Twenty-fourth Yearbook of the National Society for the Study of Education, Part I. Bloomington, Illinois: Public School Publishing Co., 1925.

21. Horn, Ernest, and McBroom, Maude. *A Survey of the Course of Study in Reading.* University of Iowa Extension Bulletin, No. 99 (February, 1924).

22. Patterson, Samuel W. *Teaching the Child to Read.* New York: Doubleday, Doran & Co., 1930.

23. Pennell, Mary E., and Cusack, Alice. *The Teaching of Reading for Better Living.* Boston: Houghton Mifflin Co., 1935.

24. Pierce, Paul R., and Quinn, Helen J. "A Study of Certain Types of Work Materials in First-Grade Reading," *Elementary School Journal,* XXXIV (April, 1934), 600-06.

25. Shields, James M. "Teaching Reading Through Ability-Grouping," *Journal of Educational Method,* VII (September and October, 1927), 7-10.

26. Smith, Nila Banton. *American Reading Instruction.* New York: Silver, Burdett & Co., 1934.

27. Stone, Clarence R. *Teacher's Guide and Course of Study in Reading.* San José, California: Board of Education, 1935.

28. Stone, Louise L. "How I Teach Beginning Reading," *Progressive Education,* VIII (November, 1931), 564-9.

29. Storm, Grace E., and Smith, Nila B. *Reading Activities in the Primary Grades.* Boston: Ginn & Co., 1930.

30. Tinley, Lucy Williams. *The First Steps in Reading.* Lincoln, Nebraska: University Publishing Co., 1918.

31. Tutt, Clara. "The Pre-Primer Period," *Childhood Education,* IX (January, 1933), 464-67.

32. Waters, Doris. "Pre-Reading Experience," *Education,* LIV (January, 1934), 308-12.

33. Whipple, Guy Montrose. *How to Study Effectively.* Bloomington, Illinois: Public School Publishing Co., 1934.

CHAPTER III

Factors Underlying Reading Difficulties

*The analyses of recent years have proved that
"reading ability" is not a simple unitary process;
it is multiple and complex.*—Courtis (9:170)

Individual Variations

As education increases measurable differences among
individuals, research multiplies and extends the list of
measures and identifiable functions involved in reading.
The psychology and physiology of reading disability is
essentially the study of individual differences in relation to
specific learnings. Students of the problem more or less
agree that a specific disability is a combination of characteristic symptoms which differentiates the difficulty.

Theories in Isolation

The pragmatist who surveys the literature on reading is
quickly and surely convinced that no one theory can be
used to account for all cases of reading difficulty. This is
a truism for three reasons: (1) Reputable workers in the
field have taught children to read by a variety of methods.
(2) The list of factors that appear to be related to disability
is already formidable and is being increased annually. (3)
Educators are becoming increasingly aware of the need for

51

preventive procedures; a large percentage of disabled readers are now believed to be man-made. *Poor teaching, in a larger sense, is the chief cause of retardation in reading.*

Symptoms

Too frequently all professions fall into the error of diagnosing symptoms rather than analyzing causes. This procedure appears to be a significant step in the process of the reorientation of man's thinking. The symptoms of certain reading disabilities have long been recognized, but the causes for the most part have remained unidentified. Symptoms of reading disability are as many and varied as are the causes. In the main, efficient reading habits produce a rapid rate of comprehension. From the study of eye-movement records, it is found that slow readers make more fixation pauses per line, require longer units of time per fixation, and make more regressive movements than do efficient readers.

Photographs of eye movements provide the symptoms of difficulties. The process of getting thought from the printed page is limited by more than mechanical and sensory factors. Many investigators have concluded that good readers excel poor readers in visual perception. Some individuals evidence a reversal tendency for words or letters, or both, reading *saw* for *was, bone* for *done,* etc. Other symptoms of difficulty are dislike for reading, pointing continued past the first grade, lip movement, vocalization, unnecessary head movement, inaccurate oral reading, low-achievement score, wandering attention, frowning, rubbing the eyes, and holding the book at an unusual angle and distance.

Duffy (4) recorded the reading difficulties of eighty-seven third-grade pupils and summarized the percentages as follows:

READING ERRORS AND FAULTY HABITS (THIRD GRADE)*

Error	Percentage
Ignoring punctuation	49
Word insertion and omission	44
Errors on small known words	38
Guesses at words from word form	38
Poor enunciation of grouped words	38
Head movements	34
Inadequate phrasing	34
Sounds elements too slowly	32
Monotonous tone	30
Immediate recognition low score	30
Word by word reading	25
Habitual repetition of words	25
Strained, high-pitched voice	24
Volume too loud or too soft	24
Analysis by single-letter sounds	22
Inaccurate sounding of elements	22
No method of word analysis	21
Unable to synthesize sounds	20
Spells words with inadequate results	17
Poor enunciation of difficult words	16
Guesses at words from partial soundings	14
Will not attempt hard words unless urged	12

*Rearranged from Duffy data.

Causes of Reading Difficulties

In general, readers who exhibit a rapid rate of comprehension have efficient oculomotor, or eye habits, and excel poor readers in purposefulness, discrimination, and association. Many theories, often conflicting, have been advanced to explain lack of reading aptitude and achievement. Few of the explanations when studied in isolation survived experimental appraisal. All of this has bewildered the busy teacher and school administrator who has not had the time to keep pace with the rapid progress of research workers.

The term "correlate" is used in this chapter to suggest relationship rather than cause. There are many correlates because of the varying degrees and types of difficulty encountered in the correction of reading difficulties. Which of the correlates are causes, is in some instances, still a debated question. In one community the writer found an astonishing number of reading cases were characterized by poor two-eyed vision. In another community where the children were admitted at five and one-half years of age to the first grade taught by poorly trained teachers, there was a preponderance of cases characterized by pedagogical difficulties. Hence, for a given school situation the problems will vary widely. Each community will find the need for a careful analysis of its peculiar problems. To the degree that scientific investigations in kindred fields are integrated and interpreted in terms of school problems, there is hope for the one with learning handicaps. Unbiased scientific analyses tend to disclose urgent needs for administrative and instructional precautions.

The remaining chapters of this book are used for discussing the implications of research findings which involve the prevention, analysis, and correction of reading difficulties. The following is a summary or preview of the factors which appear to be pertinent to the problem.

    I.   Maturation (See Chapters IV and VI)
        1. Defective cerebral development (Hinshelwood-1917)
        2. Delayed cerebral development (Pick-1924)

      3. Confusion of cerebral development (Orton-1925)
         a) Hand preference
         b) Eye preference
      4. Physiological and psychological readiness
         a) Maturation level
         b) Rate of maturation
      5. Interpupillary distance
      6. Background of information

II. Vision (See Chapter VIII)
      1. Acuity
      2. Refractive errors (such as farsightedness, near-sightedness, and astigmatism)
      3. Anomalies of binocular co-ordination
         a) Faulty fusion of small images
         b) Convergence or adductive insufficiency or excess
         c) Oculomotor and perception habits
         d) Size and shape of ocular images
      4. Lighting
      5. Imagery (after, idetic and memory)
      6. Span

III. Hearing (See Chapter X)
      1. Acuity
      2. Span
      3. Perception
      4. Blending or fusing sounds into words

IV. Kinesthesia (See Chapter XIV)
      1. Poor eye co-ordination
      2. Inappropriate eye-movement
      3. Speech defects
      4. Spatial orientation
      5. Vocalization and lip-movement

V. Language (See Chapter XI)
   1. Meager vocabulary
   2. Foreign language
   3. Composition ability

VI. Emotional (See Chapter XII)
   1. Dislike for reading
   2. Instability or lack of integration
   3. Poor attention
   4. Lack of motivation of work by the teacher
   5. Conflict with teacher
   6. Parental interference
   7. Self consciousness and timidity; withdrawal
   8. "Reading tenseness" and fear

VII. Sex differences
   1. Boys outnumber girls

VIII. Pedagogical (See Chapters XII and XIII)
   1. Inadequate instructional materials
      a) Lack of variety of materials for each stage of reading
      b) Sequence of reading materials not carefully graded
      c) Vocabulary burden and rate of introduction of new words
      d) Sentence structure and punctuation
      e) Typography unsuitable
      f) Size of type
      g) Space between lines
      h) Leading
   2. Faulty teaching techniques
      a) First teaching inadequate
      b) Too much drill on words out of context

    c) Establish efficient habits of work
    d) Overemphasis on speed
    e) Overemphasis on word analysis
    f) Lack of attention to readiness
    g) Insufficient maintenance drill
    h) Lack of stress on reading for meaning
    i) No provision for remedial drill
    j) Identification of specific difficulties before drilling on next step in the hierarchy
    k) Elimination of interference factors
    l) Inadequate care of individual differences
    m) Multi-sensory approach
    n) Interest and ability
    o) Classification and promotion on basis of aptitude and achievement
    p) Pupil awareness of small achievement increments

IX. Psychological (See Chapters IV, XIII, and XIV)
  1. Adequacy of concepts
  2. Mental age
  3. Rate of association of ideas
  4. Anticipation of meaning
  5. Perception of relationship

X. External (See Chapters XIII and XIV)
  1. Attendance
  2. Frequent changing of schools
  3. Administrative policies
    a) Size of class
    b) Entrance age for first grade
    c) Provision of quantities of supplementary instructional materials
    d) Inadequate standards for promotion
    e) Professional training of teachers
    f) Clinical service

Disorders of Association

In the early literature of the psychology of reading disability, many descriptive terms were evolved. Aphasia is a language disorder by which the individual loses his speech functions. Agraphia is a disorder by which an individual forgets how to write. The term "alexia" refers to a loss of memory for the process of reading, caused by a pathological condition. Congenital alexia is the term used to designate inherited reading disability. Word-blindness is the inability to interpret the printed symbol. Such terms have been bandied about and seized upon all too quickly to account for reading difficulties. The very fact that many so-called word-blind children have been taught to read discounts the emphasis placed upon this condition by early investigators. This situation can be summarized by stating that cases of true word-blindness are very rare if existent.

Many children fail to associate word symbols with meaning because they have been confused by premature or faulty instruction. Before words can assume meaning for the learner, he must be mature in the experience for which the symbols stand. After a sufficient level of maturity has been reached, emphasis should be on reading for meaning.

SUMMARY

1. A reading disability is normally characterized by a constellation of difficulties.

2. The analysis of reading difficulties calls for the study of causes as well as symptoms.

3. The physical and mental processes involved in reading, as well as general achievement, should be appraised.

4. The causal significance of any one correlate depends upon the individual tolerance or capacity to compensate for the difficulty.

5. Correlation is not used to suggest causation.

6. Word-blindness is a descriptive term. An insignificant number of reading cases can be described as word-blind.

REFERENCES

1. Baker, Harry C., and Leland, Bernice, *In Behalf of Non-Readers.* Bloomington, Illinois: Public School Publishing Co., 1934.

2. Betts, Emmett A. "Physiological Approach to the Analysis of Reading Disabilities," *Education Research Bulletin,* (Ohio State University, XIII (September and October, 1934).

3. Betts, Emmett A. "Prevention and Correction of Reading Disabilities," *Elementary English Review,* XII (February, 1935), 25-32.

4. Betts, Emmett A. "Reading Disabilities and their Correction: National Conference on Research in Elementary School English," *Elementary English Review,* XII (March, April, May, June, 1935), 69-73, 106-10, 131-41, 157-65.

5. Betts, Emmett, A. *Bibliography on the Analysis, Prevention and Correction of Reading Difficulties.* Meadville, Pennsylvania: Keystone View Company, 1934.

6. Betts, Emmett A. "Reading Disability Correlates," *Education* LVI (September, 1935), 18-24.

7. Blom, E. C. "Mirror-writing," *Psychological Bulletin,* XXV (1928), 582-94.

8. Bluemel, C. S. *Stammering and Allied Disorders.* New York: Macmillan Co., 1935.

9. Brueckner, Leo J. (Chairman). "Educational Diagnosis," Thirty-fourth Yearbook of the National Society for the Study of Education. Bloomington, Illinois: Public School Publishing Co., 1935.

10. Buswell, G. T. *Fundamental Reading Habits: A Study of their Development,* Chicago: University of Chicago Press, 1922.

11. Courtis, S. A. "The Prediction of Growth," *Journal of Educational Research* (March, 1933).

12. Durrell, Donald D. "Confusions in Learnings," *Education* LII (February, 1932).

13. Gates, Arthur I. *The Psychology of Reading.* New York: Macmillan Company, 1927. (Also revised edition, 1935.)

14. Gates, Arthur I. *The Psychology of Reading and Spelling with Special References to Disability.* Teachers College Contributions to Education, No. 129. New York: Teachers College, Columbia University (1922).

15. Gates, Arthur I. "Viewpoints Underlying the Study of Reading Disabilities," *Elementary English Review,* XII (April, 1925), 85-90.

16. Gates, Arthur I., and Bennett, G. C. *Reversal Tendencies in Reading,* Teachers College Bureau of Publications (1933).

17. Gillingham, Anna, and Stillman, Bessie W. *Remedial Work for Reading, Spelling and Penmanship.* New York: Ethical Culture School, 1934.

18. Gray, Clarence Truman. *Deficiencies in Reading Ability: Their Diagnosis and Remedies,* pp. 365-409. Boston: D. C. Heath & Co., 1922.

19. Gray, William S. (Chairman). *Report of the National Committee on Reading.* Twenty-fourth Yearbook of the National Society for the Study of Education, p. 336. Part I. Bloomington, Illinois: Public School Publishing Co., 1925.

20. Gray, William S. *Summary of Investigations Relating to Reading.* Supplementary Educational Monographs, No. 28. Chicago: Department of Education, University of Chicago, 1925.

21. Gray, William S. "Summary of Reading Investigations (July 1, 1925, to June 30, 1926)," *Elementary School Journal,* XXVII (February and March, 1927), 456-66, 495-510.

22. Gray, William S. "Summary of Reading Investigations (July 1, 1926 to June 30, 1927)," *Elementary School Journal,* XXVIII (February, March, and April, 1928), 443-59, 496-510, 587-602.

23. Gray, William S. "Summary of Reading Investigations (July 1, 1924 to June 30, 1925)," *Elementary School Journal,* XXVI, (February, March, April, May, 1926), 449-59, 507-18, 574-84, 662-73.

24. Gray, William S. "Summary of Reading Investigations (July 1, 1927, to June 30, 1928)," *Elementary School Journal,* XXIX (February and March, 1929), 443-57, 496-509.

25. Gray, William S. "Summary of Reading Investigations (July 1, 1928, to June 30, 1929)," *Elementary School Journal,* XXX (February and March, 1930), 450-66, 496-508.

26. Gray, William S. "Summary of Reading Investigations (July 1, 1929, to June 30, 1930)." *Elementary School Journal,* III (March and April, 1931), 531-46, 592-606.

27. Gray, William S. "Summary of Reading Investigations (July 1, 1930, to June 30, 1931)," *Elementary School Journal,* XXXII (February, March and April, 1932), 447-63, 510-20, 587-94.

28. Gray, William S. "Summary of Reading Investigations (July 1, 1931, to June 30, 1932)," *Journal of Educational Research,* XXVI (February, 1933).

29. Gray, William S. "Summary of Reading Investigations (July 1, 1932, to June 30, 1933)," *Journal of Educational Research,* XXVII (April, 1934), 564-591.

30. Gray, William S. "Summary of Reading Investigations (July 1, 1933, to June 30, 1934)," *Journal of Educational Research,* XXVIII (February, 1935), 401-424.

31. Hildreth, Gertrude. "An Individual Study of Word Recognition," *Elementary School Journal,* XXXV (April, 1935), 606-19.

32. Jastak, Joseph. "Interferences in Reading," *Psychological Bulletin,* XXXI (April, 1934).

33. Lord, Elizabeth, Carmichael, Leonard, and Dearborn, Walter F. *Special Disabilities in Learning to Read and Write,* p. 76. Harvard Monographs in Education, Whole No. 6. Cambridge, Massachusetts: Graduate School of Education, Harvard University, 1925.

34. Monroe, Marion. *Children Who Cannot Read.* Chicago: University of Chicago Press, 1932.

35. Scheidemann, Norman V. "The Congenitally Word-blind Child," *The Psychology of Exceptional Children,* Chap. XIV. Boston: Houghton, Mifflin Co., 1931.

36. Selzer, Charles A. *Lateral Dominance and Visual Fusion.* Harvard Monographs in Education No. 12 (Harvard University Press, 1933).

CHAPTER IV

Relation of Reading to Growth

Why pay a price for strawberries in February when you can have them abundantly in June at moderate cost?—Elizabeth Irwin (18)

Prevention Versus Correction

Maturation is sheer "growing up" plus training. Some people mature; others just grow older. A child is not born with the capacity or ability to read. Capacity for reading comes with the maturing of certain functions. Reading interests and needs, visual perception, background of information and experiences, memory span, and ability to orient new sensations and associate them with the old are a product of general maturation—physical, physiological, and psychological. The direction of this maturation to the end that the child will learn to read is not too simple a problem for the primary teacher. Effective learning can take place only when the total organism is in a state of readiness. In this way learning is a part of the maturation process.

Growth or maturation in the broader sense is the very heart of the concept of reading readiness. Immaturity, both physical and psychological, appears to be a most significant factor contributing to reading difficulties. To require (pedagogically force) a child to read typical first-grade materials before he is ready frequently means trouble ahead. Even when the work is super-motivated, a significant number of children fail to achieve in reading activities at the first-grade level.

It is quite generally agreed that most reading difficulties can be prevented. Our philosophy regarding learning disabilities has been chiefly concerned with correction rather than prevention. Too many school administrators point with pride to the amount and quality of remedial work in their schools when they should be making their staffs and communities aware of the need for precautionary measures. From available researches, it is probably safe to conclude that many reading difficulties may be forestalled by:

1. *Determination of physiological readiness to read and correction of physical defects.* This should be considered at all age levels and is concerned chiefly with visual and hearing handicaps.

2. *Determination of psychological readiness to read.* This is especially significant for the study of first-grade entrants. Attention span; emotional maturity; desire to learn to read; ability to discriminate between letter, word, and phrase forms; rapid association of ideas; freedom from other language handicaps; and a good background of information are essentials.

3. *Determination of hand preference.* Until further evidence is offered, a child should be encouraged to write with the hand with which he exhibits the greatest facility.

4. *Postponement of initial learning-to-read period until the child exhibits a general readiness to read.*

5. *Correction, in as far as possible, of speech defects.*

6. *Providing the proper external and learning conditions.* This includes such factors as adequate lighting and more desirable administrative policies regarding the curriculum and entrance ages.

Reversal Tendencies

Dr. Helen P. Davidson (11) made an experimental appraisal of the extent to which unselected kindergarten and first-grade children made reversal errors. The Stanford Revision of the Binet and specially constructed Form Perception Tests and Word Perception Tests were administered to 50 kindergarten and to 120 first-grade children. The average chronological age of the kindergarten children was five years eight and eight-tenths months; of the first-grade pupils, six years eight and four-tenths months. Ninety-three and nine-tenths per cent of the kindergarten children and 61.6 per cent of the first-grade children selected one or more reversed forms on the test. On the word reversal tests, 82.6 per cent of the kindergarten children and 32.8 per cent of the first-grade children made one or more errors. This is especially significant in that the *first-grade training failed to overcome the reversal tendency.*

Dr. Davidson devised another experiment (4) to determine the extent to which unselected kindergarten and first-grade children confuse *p, b, d, q, e,* and *n.* With both age groups, the investigator found a tendency toward reversal, e. g., *d* for *b* and inversion, e. g., *d* for *q* or *p.* In general, there was a decrease in error with an increase in age. She concluded *"that a mental age of at least seven and one-half years was necessary to avoid making the d-b, q-p, and b-d errors."*

Dr. Lorene Teegarden (32, 33, 34) made a clinical examination of fifty first-grade children in order to study certain aspects of reading readiness. Her conclusions were: (1) Reversal tendency was independent of intelligence. (2) Kindergarten trained children evidenced less tendency to reversals than non-kindergarten trained children. (3) The child who evidences a reversal tendency upon first-grade entrance has less chance to achieve in reading. (4) Tendency to confuse symbols is somewhat typical among six-year-old children and persists in some cases to the seventh year. (5) Within certain limits, the prospective non-reader may be identified.

Jones (21) tested three hundred first-grade pupils in an attempt to identify prospective poor readers. Sixty-three per cent of the pupils evidenced a reversal tendency. Those who showed the least reversal tendency achieved highest in reading.

Dr. Gertrude Hildreth (19) studied the extent and character of reversal errors made by 220 in the primary grades. She found that the number of reversal errors made to be only a fraction of the total errors. Her general conclusion was that the "reversal tendency declined from lower to higher grades."

Phillips (28) analyzed the reversals made by 136 matched pairs of left- and right-handed children. He also found that the tendency to make reversals decreases from grade to grade. Reversals accounted for about 10 per cent of the errors on his reading tests.

Vision and Maturation

A phase of anatomical maturation or growth meriting further research is the increase with age of the distance between the pupils of the eyes. This distance is measured from the center of the pupil of one eye to the center of the other pupil. In a recent study (6), the writer found the greatest increase in inter-pupillary distance to occur during the sixth year (first grade). Undoubtedly this increase is brought about by the growth of the head. This factor, along with many others having to do with the development of the eyes, leads one to suspect that many children are not physically mature for the strain imposed upon the visual apparatus by the reading process. Such factors are not significant when children read at a distance greater than forty inches because the eye is constructed so that distance seeing is accomplished with a minimum of effort.

Young children are normally farsighted. There is some evidence for the belief that many children's eyes are not mature enough for close work, such as reading, until they are past seven years of age. A six-year-old child is probably under a greater strain while reading typical first-grade reading material than a seven- or eight-year-old.

Farsightedness is usually caused by a short or immature eyeball. Various studies have showed that from 45 to 80 per cent of six-year-old children are normally farsighted. There is a gradual decrease in farsightedness as the eye matures so that by the age of nine only about 18 to 20 per cent of the children are farsighted.

In order to experience comfortable two-eyed vision (visual fusion) for small targets at reading distance, the action of the two eyes must be co-ordinated. Wells (38:12) believes that "the full development of the fusion faculty is not attained until the fifth or sixth year with the normal child." Although this statement has not been entirely appraised under experimental conditions, the well-known existence of individual differences would lead one to conclude that at least 25 per cent of the children mature at a later age.

In a recent survey (5) of 194 first-grade entrants, 25 per cent exhibited difficulty in discriminating between common

word forms; 38 per cent were unquestionably farsighted;
14 per cent lacked normal fusion; 38 per cent did not have
the degree of eye co-ordination and the fusional desire that
comes from experience with two-eyed vision to pass an easy
test of depth perception and 10 per cent evidenced eye-
muscle imbalance. All these items probably are related to
reading disabilities, but in some instances they will become
less significant with added age. To require some children
to learn to read typical first-grade materials at six years of
age is to establish undesirable mechanical reading habits.
A more extended discussion of this aspect of the problem
may be found in Chapter VIII.

Double Standards of Promotion

In a study of pupil failures in elementary schools over
a three year period, Cutright and Anderson (10) found
the largest percentage of failures in the first grade. They
conclude that "it is appropriate that teachers and administrators should be interested in an analysis of the causes of
such failures with a view of eliminating those which are
needless."

The investigators called attention to the inconsistency of
the policy of admitting children to the first grade on the
basis of chronological age and promoting to the second
grade on the basis of skill in reading. Two solutions to the
problem were offered: First, admission of children to the
first grade on the basis of their readiness to read; second,
adjustment of the curriculum to the needs and capacities of
the children at each grade level. The writers believed the
latter policy to be more nearly feasible.

Ayres (1) concluded that the rate of non-promotion
varied from 10 to 34 per cent; Bachman (2), Berry (3),

Caswell (8), and Otto (25) have supplied additional evidence for the statement that the percentage of failures in first grade varies from 10 to 40 per cent. Not all educators and certainly few parents are aware of this tragic situation in the first grade.

The evidence is too extensive to be disputable. Only a few school systems, such as Minneapolis (10), admit the data in actual practice. American educators apparently have failed to sensitize their communities to the need for a careful analysis of local conditions. Tests and surveys have been used too long for the planning of remedial programs. Reality dictates the need for preventive measures.

Teachers' Prediction of Reading Achievement

Lee and others (23) studied the use of ratings by kindergarten teachers for the prediction of reading readiness. They found that even the use of a definite scale did not permit prediction of reading readiness as well as a test for that purpose. In addition, they found kindergarten teachers to vary widely in their ability to predict reading success.

Mental Age and Reading Aptitude

(Reading aptitude, or readiness, embraces physical, mental, and emotional maturity.) The fact that a majority of disabled readers are of normal or superior intelligence does not leave the implication that mental maturity is not a prerequisite for learning to read. On the contrary, many investigators of the question have found that a mental age of six to six and one-half years is one essential to reading success. Raybold (29) concluded that a mental age of at least seventy-six months was essential to success in the typical first grade. Monroe (24: 6) found: "The reading defects may occur at any intellectual level from very superior to very inferior, as measured by intelligence tests." Lee, Clark, and Lee (23: 635) prepared a test which according to their data was a better measure of reading readiness than two intelligence tests.

Efficiency of First-Teaching

In the Stanford Revision of the Binet-Simon Test, emotional reactions are not expected until a given age level. The physical-education teacher knows better than to offer opportunities for certain motor learnings until the children of a given class are mature enough to make instruction profitable. The intellectual learnings are closely associated with those of a motor and emotional nature. Here, too, learning cannot take place efficiently if at all, until the learner is physically and mentally ready.

Approximately 75 per cent of the six-year-old children are taught to read typical reading materials, but at what cost? Wagner (37) using certain of the Betts Ready to Read Tests, found approximately 88 per cent of the kindergarten children possessed fairly normal co-ordination of the two eyes. He also found a definite decrease in eye co-ordination with an increase in grade level. At the sixth-grade level only 63 per cent possessed normal eye co-ordination. Wagner may have found one answer to the question "At what cost do we teach immature children to read?" Certainly no reading test can provide the tell-tale evidence.

The efficiency of first-teaching is significant at all grade levels. With desirable first-teaching, prevention is the keynote.

SUMMARY

1. Teaching is the environmental control of maturation. Both physiological development and training contribute to maturation.
2. The best educational treatment for reading difficulties is not to allow faulty habits to be practiced.
3. The concept of reading readiness has been enlarged to include both physiological and psychological readiness for reading.
4. There is need for consistent policies of promotion. Children are almost universally admitted to first grade on a chronological-age basis and promoted to second grade on basis of achievement in reading.
5. There is need for a unified kindergarten-primary program.
6. The reversal tendency is the normal reaction of an immature child to required reading activities.
7. Rhythmical reading habits resulting in rapid rate of comprehension cannot be fostered in situations where defects of maturation and total maturation is not recognized.
8. Some children are not ready to read until the seventh year. Although no one has presented evidence regarding the minimum age at which a significant number of children may economically be permitted to engage in reading, a majority of children are ready to read at a mental age of six and one-half years. *The forcing of immature children into reading by poorly trained teachers may account for the fact that reading is the most disliked subject.*

9. Failure to achieve in reading is, in part, to say that teachers and administrators fail to recognize maturation levels and varying rates of maturation.

10. To force a child to read before he is ready frequently results in practice of undesirable reading habits.

11. There is a need for the investigation of cost to the learner for achievement in reading at six years of age.

12. Prevention rather than correction should be the watchword in public schools.

13. Parent education is a significant part of any program of prevention.

14. Reading is related to growing up.

REFERENCES

1. Ayres, Leonard P. *Laggards in our Schools,* pp. 141-58. New York: Russell Sage Foundation, 1909.

2. Bachman, Frank P. *Problems in Elementary School Administration,* p. 68. Yonkers-on-Hudson, New York: World Book Co., 1915.

3. Berry, Charles S. *Seventy-ninth Annual Report of the State Superintendent of Public Instruction of the State of Michigan,* pp. 70-97. Lansing, Michigan: State Department of Public Instruction, 1915-16.

4. Betts, Emmett A. "Reading Disabilities and their Correction: National Conference of Research in Elementary School English," *Elementary English Review,* XII (March, April, May, and June, 1935), 69-73, 106-110, 131-41, 157-65.

5. Betts, Emmett A. "Is Reading Related to Growth?" *Progressive Education,* XI (December, 1934).

6. Betts, Emmett A. "Physiological Approach to the Analysis of Reading Disabilities," *Educational Research Bulletin* (Ohio State University) XIII (September, and October, 1934).

7. Brooks, Fowler D. "When Shall Reading Be Taught?" *The Applied Psychology of Learning,* Chap. IV. New York: D. Appleton & Co., 1926.

8. Caswell, Hollis L. "Non-Promotion in Elementary Schools," pp. x-100. Field Studies No. 4. Nashville, Tennessee: George Peabody College for Teachers, 1933.

9. Courtis, S. A. "Maturation as a Factor in Diagnosis," Chap. X. Thirty-fourth Yearbook of the National Society for the Study of Education. Bloomington, Illinois: Public School Publishing Co., 1935.

10. Cutright, Prudence, and Anderson, Walter A. "An Experimental Study of Pupil Failures in the First Grade." Educational Bulletin. Minneapolis, Minnesota: Minneapolis Public Schools, 1934.

11. Davidson, Helen P. "A Preliminary Study to Determine the Extent to Which Unselected Young Children Make Reversal Errors," *Journal of Genetic Psychology* (December, 1934).

12. Deputy, Erby Chester. *Predicting First-Grade Reading Achievement:* A Study in Reading Readiness, p. 62. Teachers College Contributions to Education No. 426. New York: Teachers College, Columbia University, 1930.

13. Dewey, John. "The Primary Education Fetish," *Forum,* XXV, 315-28.

14. Eames, Thomas Harrison. "Comparison of Ocular Characteristics of Unselected and Reading Disability Cases," *Journal of Educational Research,* XXV (March, 1932), 211-215.

15. Gates, Arthur I. "Viewpoints Underlying the Study of Reading Disabilities," *Elementary English Review,* XII (April, 1935), 85-90.

16. Hahn, Julia L. "Reading Readiness in the Third Grade," *Childhood Education,* XL (January, 1935), 179-180.

17. Hardy, Marjorie. "Reading a Letter to Parents," *Childhood Education,* VII (March, 1931), 365.

18. Hardy, Marjorie. *Points of View on the Problem of Reading Readiness.* Washington, D. C.: Association for Childhood Education, 1930.

19. Hildreth, Gertrude. "Reversals in Reading and Writing," *Psychological Bulletin,* XXX (1933), 670-71.

20. Hildreth, Gertrude. "The Success of Young Children in Number and Letter Construction," *Child Development,* III (March, 1932), 1-14.

21. Jones, Mary Agnes. "A Study of the Reversal Tendency in Grade One." Unpublished, filed in Atlanta University Library, 1934.

22. Klapper, Paul. *Teaching Children to Read,* pp. 27-32. New York: D. Appleton and Company, 1916.

23. Lee, J. Murray, Clark, Willis W., and Lee, Doris May. "Measuring Reading Readiness," *Elementary School Journal,* XXXIV (May, 1934), 656-66.

24. Monroe, Marion. *Children Who Cannot Read,* pp. xvi-205. Chicago: University of Chicago Press, 1932.

25. Otto, Henry J. "Implications for Administration and Teaching Growing Out of Pupil Failures," *Elementary School Journal,* XXXIII (September, 1932), 25-32.

26. Patrick, G. T. W. "Should Children Under Ten Years Learn to Read and Write?" *Popular Science Monthly,* LIV, 382-391.

27. Percival, Walter P. "A Study of the Causes and Subjects of School Failure," Doctor's dissertation, Teachers College, Columbia University, 1926.

28. Phillips, Albert J. "Relation of Left-Handedness to Reversals in Reading," *Elementary English Review,* XI (April, 1934), 97-98.

29. Raybold, Emma. "Reading Readiness in Children Entering the First Grade," *Third Yearbook of the Psychology and Educational Research Division,* pp. 98-101. School Publication, No. 185, Los Angeles, California: Los Angeles City School District, 1929.

30. Reed, Mary M. *An Investigation of Practices in First Grade Admission and Promotion,* Teachers College Contributions to Education, No. 290. New York: Teachers College, Columbia University, 1927.

31. Sangren, Paul V. "Information Tests for Young Children," *Childhood Education,* VI (October, 1929), 70-77.

32. Teegarden, L. "Clinical Identification of the Prospective Non-Reader," *Journal of Child Development,* III (December, 1932), 346.

33. Teegarden, L. "Tests for Tendency to Reversal in Reading," *Journal of Educational Research,* XXVII (October, 1933), 81-97.

34. Teegarden, L. "Kindergarten and Reading Reversals," *Childhood Education,* IX (November, 1932), 82-83.

35. Todd, T. Wingate. *Growth and Development,* Brush Foundation Publication, No. 19, 1932.

36. Todd, T. Wingate. *Measuring the Growth of Children,* Brush Foundation Publication, No. 18, 1931.

37. Wagner, Guy W. *The Maturation of Certain Visual Functions and their Relationships to Success in Reading and Arithmetic,* Doctor's thesis, State University of Iowa, 1935.

38. Wells, David W. *The Stereoscope in Ophthalmology*. Boston: E. MaHady Company, 1928.

39. Wheat, Harry Grove. "When Shall Reading Begin?" *The Teaching of Reading,* Chap. III. Boston: Ginn & Co., 1923.

40. Wheeler, Raymond Holt, and Perkins, F. Theodore. *Principles of Mental Development*. New York: Thomas Y. Crowell Company, 1932.

CHAPTER V
Analysis of Reading Difficulties

*Reading is merely a term applied to a variety of
ways of reacting to words.*—Gates (11 : 40)

Specific and General Reading Disabilities

The degree of reading difficulty modifies the extent of
the analysis. Since serious reading disabilities are characterized by a constellation of difficulties, the analysis of
many factors should be made. Fortunately, few cases can
be classified as non-readers; hence, the analysis in most
instances is brief.

In general, there are two classifications for reading difficulties. One class is characterized by specific reading difficulty; the other by general reading disability. The first
group may be low in some one or two reading skills; the
latter may evidence confusions or lack of basic and ele-
mental skills, information, and attitudes.

Usually the difficulties of an individual with a specific
reading disability may be adequately analyzed with a good
diagnostic reading test. In this way the specific difficulties
may be identified and remedial measures applied.

The problems of a severely disabled reader require a
more detailed analysis by a trained and understanding
worker. A knowledge of the physiological and psychological processes involved in the reading is essential for the
determination of effective remedial procedures. In addition to this, the diagnostician should be skilled in handling
parents and co-operating with other community agencies.

A Brief View of the Analysis Program

No one correlate can be said to characterize all reading disabilities; likewise, no one pattern can be set up for the analysis of all reading difficulties. The number of formal diagnostic tests has been increased to the degree that the correlates of reading difficulties have been identified.

In the field of methodology, the tendency has been toward informal teaching methods. Undoubtedly, this same tendency is growing in the field of tests and measurements. A teacher thoroughly skilled in the use of formal tests can make the greatest use of informal analysis procedures. Since most public-school workers are burdened with other duties, the use of formal tests still remains the most economical and fruitful procedure.

The analysis of a case of reading disability calls for an inventory of the oral- and silent-reading habits and of certain individual capacities. Data are secured from the following sources:

1. General achievement tests

2. Intelligence tests

3. Reading-readiness tests (for younger children)

4. Tests of specific reading skills and information

5. Tests of sensory capacities (visual and auditory)

6. Tests for appraisal of perceptual abilities and habits

7. Tests for identification of association difficulties

8. Tests of motor functions

9. Appraisal of individual interests

10. Case history and general observations

As part of the total analysis procedure, the testing program should be designed to define, in so far as possible, the specific nature of the difficulties and to determine the starting point or level of reading ability. Not all the data can be secured by objective procedures. The important problems of parent and teacher attitudes, case history, and the individual's interests and aptitudes will be solved, of necessity, by subjective means.

Orientation of the Problem

Cases of reading deficiency are not always strictly pedagogical problems. Too frequently teachers have assumed that typical schoolroom remedial procedures are sufficient for the correction of reading difficulties. In too many cases, pencil and paper tests do not provide sufficient data. The advice of eye-specialists and other health experts should be secured for cases of learning difficulty. In short, the teacher should not assume that all school difficulties can be adequately solved within the four walls of the classroom. The literature contains sufficient evidence for the statement that the teacher should utilize aids which will permit her to discriminate between psycho-educational difficulties and health problems.

Principles and Assumptions for Analysis

The writer bases his analysis procedures on the following assumptions and principles:

1. Most reading disabilities can be prevented.
2. Individual tests are essential for analysis of causes and symptoms of reading difficulties.

3. The teacher should have access to tests and other instruments for the analysis of the problem cases in her room and to remedial materials which parallel the diagnostic procedures.

4. The teacher and principal, working with the health department, should be in a position to discriminate between (health and pedagogical problems.) Too often the teacher accepts a reading case which is one for the physician or eye-specialist. In such a case, the results of recent researches have emphasized the value of attending to the physical defects before giving pedagogical help.

5. Indices to specific maturations and readinesses are as important as tests of general intelligence. Most tests of general intelligence require reading ability; therefore, children with severe reading disabilities have had their academic powers underestimated. (A child should have a mental age of at least six and one-half years before being introduced to the typical reading program.)

6. The testing of the disabled reader's powers and habits of visual sensation and perception at the normal reading distance is essential to the validity of an analysis technique. Every individual has the right to comfortable vision which is essential to sustained reading comfort.

7. The size of the type used in the diagnostic materials should approximate that found in typical reading materials for the grade level in question.

8. The appraisal of the oculomotor and perception habits at reading distance is essential.

9. The testing of the powers and habits of auditory sensation and perception is essential for the study of learning difficulties of poor spellers and beginning readers.

10. Speaking and reading vocabulary, habits of word recognition, general background of information, adequacy of concepts, ability to readily perceive relationships, and rapid association of ideas are prime requisites for reading achievement.

11. The analysis materials should be practicable and as free as possible from controversial issues of a highly theoretical and questionable nature. Therefore, the materials should be simple, easily administered, and quickly interpreted.

12. The analysis procedures should disclose the nature of the remedial procedures needed.

13. Every child would learn to read if it were in his power to do so. Undesirable attitudes are a result of compensations and rationalizations because there is usually enough social pressure to make reading achievement desirable.

14. The learner must be led to establish a feeling of confidence that his teacher will help him learn to read. This will be gained, in part, from some understanding of the nature of his difficulty as revealed by the analysis.

15. No one theory can be used to account for all types and degrees of learning difficulty.

Observations

Formal tests are designed to permit an analysis of the causes as well as the symptoms of reading difficulties. During the administration of the tests, a trained examiner will note many clues to behavior which should be redirected or corrected. These observations added to those of the teacher and the parents are of paramount importance to any analysis program.

Points of observations which appear to be significant diagnostic signs follow on the next page:

I. Educational factors

  A. Oral reading

    1. Ignores punctuation

    2. Word-by-word reading

      a) Incorrect phrasing

      b) Inadequate phrasing

      c) Lack of emphasis on meaning

      d) Points to each word

    3. Inadequate voice control

      a) Strained high-pitched voice

      b) Monotonous tone

      c) Too little or too much volume

      d) Poor enunciation

    4. Tendency to confuse forms

      a) Word reversals

      b) Letter reversals

      c) Begins at right end of line or word

    5. Omits words

    6. Inserts words

    7. Substitutes words

    8. Mispronounces

    9. Repeats words

   10. Low rate of reading

   11. Inadequate word-recognition habits

   12. Speech defect

  B. Silent reading

    1. Lip movement

    2. Low rate of reading

    3. Comprehension difficulty

    4. Inadequate background of experience

C. Word recognition habits
   1. Inadequate sight list of words
   2. Fails to use context clues
   3. Fails to use pictures clues
   4. Fails to note roots, suffixes, and prefixes
   5. Fails to use configuration clues
      a) Similarities
      b) Differences
   6. Inadequate control over initial sounds and endings
   7. Inability to syllabicate and to note familiar words in long words
   8. Fails to make use of simple phonic principles
   9. Lack of ability in use of diacritical marks
   10. Guesses at word
   11. Sounds word elements inaccurately

D. Study habits
   1. Begins work without interest or vigor
   2. Lacks persistence
   3. Wandering attention
   4. Fails to locate information quickly
   5. Inability to summarize or outline material read
   6. Fails to associate material read with previous experiences

E. Spelling habits
   1. Confuses letters and parts of words
      a) Reverses letters
      b) Reverses syllables
      c) Reverses word forms
   2. Evidence of mirror-writing
   3. Overemphasis on phonetics

4. Spells letter by letter
5. Omits or adds letters
6. Oral spelling superior to written spelling or vice versa
7. Inability to pronounce words to be spelled
8. Fails to remember correct spelling
9. Lack of knowledge of meaning
10. Poor motor control in writing

F. Background
   1. Inadequate speaking vocabulary
   2. Lack of facility in use of the English language
   3. Small foundation of information about science, social science, literature, music, and art

II. Physical factors
   A. Under nourishment
   B. Mouth breathing
   C. Lack of rest
   D. Overwork
   E. Eyes ache or burn
   F. Holds book too near, too far, or at an angle
   G. Evidence of blurred or uncomfortable vision
   H. Frowns
   I. Instability
   J. Headaches
   K. Dizziness
   L. Nausea
   M. Residuals from children's diseases
   N. Easily fatigued
   O. Turning in or out of one eye when fatigued
   P. Failure to see blackboard writing
   Q. Inflammatory condition about the eyes

      R. Double vision
      S. Poor posture
      T. Poor hearing

III. Social attitudes
      A. Indifferences versus enthusiasm
      B. Sullen, negativistic versus co-operative, responsive
      C. Prefers to work alone
      D. Day dreams
      E. Resists reading instruction
      F. Dislike for teacher and for school
      G. Reading tenseness and fear of ridicule
      H. Emotional or nervous instability
      I. Lack of home encouragement
      J. Lack of confidence
      K. Lack of persistence
      L. Oversensitiveness
      M. Must be urged to attempt new words
      N. Lack of interest for books
      O. Carelessness

Reading-Readiness Tests

Recent data confirm the writer's belief that a substantial proportion of reading difficulties can be prevented. A good test of reading readiness would, therefore, provide significant information for the analysis of reading difficulties in the early primary grades. Frequently, children are brought to the reading clinic and found to be too immature to profit by typical reading instruction. For these children, certain reading-readiness activities are prescribed in place of formal instruction.

Most reading-readiness batteries are constructed on the basis that individual tests are better measures at that level than group tests. Children in the pre-primary grades have had little or no experience in following directions for pencil and paper work. In addition, the examiner can secure valuable data for the analysis of the difficulty by observing the responses at first hand. Although individual tests require more time than group tests, the additional time is usually well spent.

The ability to make visual discriminations between word forms is conceded to be an essential aspect of readiness. Previous experience with words in sentences or in isolation is not a necessary prerequisite for such tests. In the Betts Ready to Read Tests (Test V-2, Letter Form) and the Van Wagenen Reading Readiness Tests (Test 5, Word Discrimination), the pupil is required to identify the one unlike form from among five-word forms of which one is different. Stone and Grover in their Classification Test for Beginners in Reading classify pupils on the ability to match word forms and to note similarities and differences in word pairs. In both the Betts Ready to Read Tests and Lee-Clark Reading Readiness Tests, the pupil is also required to match capital and small letter forms. A child who lacks the ability to visually discriminate between word and letter forms is either immature or possesses a visual disability. The visual defects of the preschool child can be detected by the Visual Sensation and Perception Tests of the Betts Ready to Read Battery. (See Chapter VIII.)

Memory span is also an important element contributing to reading aptitude. Such tests are provided in the Betts Ready to Read and the Van Wagenen Reading Readiness batteries. Reading instructions should be postponed for children who make low scores on such tests. If the child is forced into the typical reading situation where failure is sure to characterize the venture, only unhealthy attitudes and poor reading habits will result.

General information is to a great extent a determiner of the learner's interest in reading materials. In lists of legitimate reading-readiness activities and in present approaches to reading at any grade level, various types of experiences are emphasized. The Sangren Information Tests and the Van Wagenen Reading Readiness Tests (Test I, range of information) provide very good formal tests of this aspect of reading readiness. Furthermore, low scores on such tests provide clues to the type of learning needed by the child before initiation into the learning-to-read process.

It is not conceivable that words in the reading material can assume meaning for the young learner when they are not within his speaking vocabulary. The provision of opportunities for the extension of the child's vocabulary during the preparatory period is one of the primary obligations of the teacher. Vocabulary is indirectly measured by means of certain reading-readiness tests. The Van Wagenen tests include a special individual test of vocabulary and the Metropolitan Readiness Tests embrace a group test of this ability.

The greater the number of measures of a given function the more reliable are the results. Test data on the various functions contributing to reading aptitude should be supplemented by teacher observations and judgment. Not all the attributes of reading are measured by reading-readiness tests. For example, desire to read, ability to follow directions, and kindred factors observed by teacher should be added to the criteria for determination of readiness for the typical first-grade reading program.

In general, the factors contributing to reading difficulty can be classified as psycho-educational and physical. Hence, the study of readiness for reading should not be limited to the psychological and educational factors only. It is for this reason that the Visual Sensation and Perception Tests of the Betts Ready to Read Battery were constructed. These tests are discussed in Chapter VIII.

The analysis of reading difficulties at the first-grade level by means of readiness or aptitude tests constitute a significant part of the diagnostic program. It is readily agreed that the chief function of such tests is to permit the grouping of first-grade entrants so that difficulties may be prevented. Since it is usually wise to postpone further formal reading instruction for first-grade children in trouble, such tests are indispensable. From them are taken the clues for the development of the program of school activities.

The following measures have merit for the determination of readiness and for the analysis of reading difficulties in the early primary grades:

1. Betts, Emmett A., *Betts Ready to Read Tests* (Individual Tests), Keystone View Company; Meadville, Pennsylvania, 1934.

    A. Visual Readiness

        (V-1, a & b) Letter forms
        (V-2) Word forms
        (V-3) Phonetic elements

    B. Auditory Readiness

        (A-1) Auditory span
        (A-2) Auditory fusion
        (A-3) Auditory perception
        (A-4) Auditory acuity

C. Visual Sensation and Perception
  1. Introductory slide
  2. Distance fusion
  3. Visual efficiency
     a) two-eyed
     b) left eye
     c) right eye
  4. Vertical imbalance
  5. Co-ordination level
  6. Lateral imbalance
  7. Reading distance fusion
  8. Sharpness of image

2. Hildreth, Gertrude, and Griffiths, Nellie L., *Metropolitan Readiness Tests* (Group Tests), World Book Company, 1933.

Test 1. Perception: Similarities
Test 2. Perception: Copying
Test 3. Vocabulary
Test 4. Sentences
Test 5. Numbers
Test 6. Information
Test 7. Drawing a Man

3. Lee, J: Murray, and Clark, Willis W., *Reading Readiness Tests,* Southern California Book Depository, Ltd., 1931.

Test 1. Matching (capital letters)
Test 2. Matching (small letters)
Test 3. Cross Out (capital letters of various sizes)
Test 4. Cross Out (words)

4. Monroe, Marion, *Monroe Aptitude Tests,* Houghton, Mifflin Company, 1935.

    A. Group Tests

        Visual Test 1. Memory of Orientation of Forms
        Visual Test 2. Oculomotor Control and Attention
        Visual Test 3. Memory
        Motor Test 1. Speed
        Motor Test 2. Steadiness
        Auditory Test 1. Word Discrimination
        Auditory Test 2. Sound Blending
        Language Test 1. Vocabulary

    B. Individual Tests

        Auditory Test 3. Auditory Memory
        Articulation Test 1. Reproduction
        Articulation Test 2. Speed
        Language Test 2. Classification
        Language Test 3. Sentence Length
        Motor Test 3. Writing Name
        Handedness
        Eyedness
        Footedness

5. Sangren, Paul V., *Sangren Information Tests for Young Children,* World Book Company.

    Nature Study
    Numbers
    Vocabulary
    Social and Civic Information
    Household Knowledge
    Language and Literature

6. Stone, Clarence R., and Grover, C. C., *Classification Test for Beginners in Reading,* Webster Publishing Company, 1933.

   Part 1. Word Matching
   Part 2. Noting similarities and differences in word pairs

7. Van Wagenen, M. J., *Reading Readiness Tests* (Forms A & B), Educational Test Bureau, 1932.

   Range of Information
   Perception of Relations
   Vocabulary (opposites)
   Memory Span for Ideas
   Word Discrimination
   Word Learning

General Achievement Tests

General achievement test-batteries are valuable for the identification of children presenting specific learning disabilities as well as for the measurement of educational achievement. In brief, pupil strengths and weaknesses in various subject-matter fields are quickly revealed.

Retardation in reading will lower significantly the scores in most content subjects. This may be caused by the general attitude of the learner toward school as well as the reading difficulty. In the special subject-matter fields, teachers have been prone to let the reading skills involved go by default. Recently more consideration has been given to reading skills involved in music, arithmetic, social studies, and science. Many of the scores on the various subject-matter tests of achievement batteries can be raised by drill on pertinent reading skills. Reading is the key which unlocks the information. It does not necessarily follow that to raise the score by improvement in reading increases the learner's mastery over the information, but such skills permit him to acquire the information with less conscious effort. Hence, the statement that there is no subject matter of reading is valid.

A learner with typical reading difficulties can be expected to achieve in arithmetic computation and fall far below his grade level on the tests where reading is required. Spelling and literature scores are also generally low. In this respect, the educational profile of disabled readers is frequently very erratic.

The following achievement test-batteries provide valuable data especially from Grade IV and up:

1. Allen, Bixler, Conner, Graham, and Hildreth, *Metropolitan Achievement Tests,* World Book Company, 1933.

    Tests (Grades I–VIII inclusive)

    Primary Tests
    　Word Recognition
    　Phrase Recognition
    　Word Meaning
    　Numbers
    Advanced Tests
    　Spelling
    　Reading.
    　Vocabulary
    　Arithmetic Fundamentals and Problems
    　English
    　Spelling
    　History
    　Geography

2. Gates, Arthur I., Mort, P. R., Symonds, P. M., *The Modern School Achievement Tests,* Bureau of Publications, Teachers College, Columbia University, 1931.

Tests (Grades IV–VIII inclusive)

Reading Comprehension
Arithmetic Computation
Arithmetic Reasoning
Spelling
Health Knowledge
Language Usage
History and Civics
Geography
Science

3. Kelly, T. L., Ruch, G. M., and Terman, L. M., *The New Stanford Achievement Tests,* World Book Company, 1929.

Primary Examination

Paragraph Meaning
Word Meaning
Dictation (spelling)
Arithmetic Reasoning
Arithmetic Computation

Advanced Examination

Paragraph Meaning
Word Meaning
Dictation Exercises (spelling)
Language Usage
Literature   •
History and Civics
Geography
Physiology and Hygiene
Arithmetic Reasoning
Arithmetic Computation

4. Tiegs, E. W., Clark, W. W., *Progressive Achievement Tests,* Southern California School Book Depository, 1933.

Reading Vocabulary   Arithmetic Reasoning
Reading Comprehension   Arithmetic Fundamentals
          Language

5. Van Wagenen, Branon, Breuckner, Jordan, Cutright, Kelly, Anderson, Dvorak, *Unit Scales Attainment,* Educational Test Bureau, Inc., 1932.

Reading   Arithmetic Problems
Geography   Arithmetic Fundamental
Literature   Operations
Elementary Science   Spelling
American History   English—Capitalization
          English—Usage

Tests for Analysis of Reading Achievement

Tests over the various skills involved in reading are especially valuable for the analysis of a specific reading difficulty. As defined previously, a learner with a specific reading difficulty is one who is low in only one or two reading skills. Tests for the analysis of such difficulties are constructed to appraise the learning of specific reading skills.

One of the most important contributions of an analysis program is the determination of the reading level attained by the learner. Frequently, fifth-grade boys scoring second grade in reading achievement are struggling with third- or fourth-grade reading materials. It is extremely important to begin at the learner's level. There should be no apologies for beginning at once with materials within the grasp of the learner. Ability and interest cannot be challenged when the task is not within the reach of the learner. Individuals with reading difficulties cannot be expected to establish rhythmical habits of reading for meaning when the vocabulary burden, sentence structure, size of type and kindred items cause reading to be halting and laborious.

In addition to tests over the general reading skills, it is frequently necessary to analyze the subskills contributing to the hierarchy. For example a child may score low on a word-recognition test because he has no system of word analysis. Another may fail to achieve in sentence or paragraph reading because of poor phrasing or word-by-word reading. Still another may fail on tests requiring sustained reading because of visual difficulty. In brief, individuals with extreme reading difficulties may require a more thorough analysis than that obtained by the administration of silent-reading tests.

The following reading tests are valuable for the determination of reading level, for grouping, and for the identification of difficulties with respect to general reading ability.

1. Gates, Arthur I., *Gates Silent Reading Tests,* Bureau of Publications, Teachers College, Columbia University, New York City.

    Primary Tests (two forms)
        Type 1. Word Recognition
        Type 2. Sentence Reading
        Type 3. Paragraph Reading

    Grades III–VIII Tests (two forms)
        Type A. Reading to appreciate the general significance of a paragraph
        Type B. Reading to predict the outcome of given events
        Type C. Reading to understand precise directions
        Type D. Reading to note details

2. Greene, Harry A., and Kelly, Victor H., *Iowa Silent Reading Tests,* World Book Co., 1932.

    Elementary Examination (two forms)

      Test 1. Paragraph Comprehension
               a) Science
               b) History
      Test 2. Word Meaning
               a) General Vocabulary
               b) Subject-Matter Vocabulary
      Test 3. Selection of Central Idea of Paragraph
      Test 4. Sentence Meaning
      Test 5. Location of Information
               a) Alphabetizing
               b) Use of Index
      Test 6. Rate of Silent Reading

3. Sangren, Paul V., and Wilson, May C., *Instructional Tests in Reading* (Forms A & B), Public School Publishing Co.

Test	Grades
Word Recognition	I and II
Phrase Recognition	I and II
Recognition of Meaning of Words .	I to IV
Word Comparison	I and II
Association of Sentence with Illustration	I
Following Directions	I to III
Noting Details	I to IV
Understanding Sentences	I to IV
Anticipating Meanings	I and II
Using Judgment	I and II
Organization of Ideas	I and IV
Selecting the Central Thought . . .	III
Using Effectively Table of Contents and Word Lists	IV
Using Study Outlines	IV

4. Sangren, Paul V., and Woody, Clifford, *Sangren-Woody Reading Tests,* World Book Company, 1927.

    Part I. Word Meaning
        II. Rate
       III. Fact Material
       IV. Total Meaning
        V. Central Thought
      VI. Following Directions
     VII. Organization

Word-Recognition Tests

A check on the ability to recognize words in isolation is a severe but good test of word recognition. This ability can be appraised in a number of ways. One of the most valid procedures is to check on the words used in the basal set of readers. A list of such words is usually printed in the back of the book or in the teachers' manual. The list of words should be duplicated so that both the teacher and the pupil have a copy. The pupil is asked to pronounce the words as the teacher checks the ones miscalled. After the identification of the unknown words, the task for the learner is defined. Remedial procedures are described in Chapter XI.

Formal tests of this ability include the following:

1. Betts, Emmett A., *Betts Ready to Read Tests* "Oculomotor and Perception Habits," Keystone View Co., 1934.

2. Manwiller, Charles E., *Manwiller Word Recognition Test,* World Book Company, 1934.

3. Oglesby, Eliza F., *Detroit Word Recognition Test,* World Book Company.

Comprehension Tests

The following comprehension tests are designed to test the individual level or power comprehension in a situation where speed of reading is at a minimum:

1. Chapman, J. C., and Holzinger, Karl. *Unspeeded Reading Comprehension Tests* (Grades V to VIII, Forms A & B), Educational Test Bureau, 1924.

2. Gates, Arthur I. *Reading: Level of Comprehension and Reading: Speed and Accuracy,* Bureau of Publications, Teachers College, Columbia University, 1931.

Oral Reading Tests

Oral reading tests, either formal or informal from standard readers, provide needed evidence. An experienced examiner can note use of context clues and deficiencies in word analysis as well as tendencies to reverse forms, to repeat, to omit, and to substitute. Not infrequently, children can arrive at the meaning of a silent reading selection and still evidence extremely faulty oral reading.

Selections from readers not used in class will meet average needs. The following standardized oral reading tests are used by many remedial teachers.

1. Gray, William S. *Gray Standardized Oral Reading Check Tests,* Public School Publishing Co.

    Set   I.   Grades I–II
    Set II.   Grades II–IV
    Set III.   Grades IV–VII
    Set IV.   Grades VI–VIII

2. Gray, William S. *Gray Standardized Oral Reading Paragraph Test* (Grades I–VIII), Public School Publishing Co.

Tests for Analysis of Extreme Reading Disability

Four batteries of tests (individual rather than group tests) for the analysis of extreme reading disability have been used to the satisfaction of the writer:

A. Betts, Emmett A., *Betts Ready to Read Tests,* Keystone View Company, 1934.

The case study record blank includes sections for the recording of medical, reading, spelling, arithmetic, and mental test data. Provision is made in the last section for the recording of observations by the teacher. The Betts Ready to Read Tests are described in the manual which is included in the Appendix of this book. In addition to this, a battery of tests has been constructed to measure:

1. Visual Readiness
2. Auditory Readiness
3. Visual Sensation and Perception (See Chapter VIII)
4. Oculomotor and Perception (See Chapter VIII)
5. Hand and Eye Preference (See Chapter VI)

B. Durrell, Donald D. *Procedure for the Analysis of Reading Difficulties,* Grades I–VI, Houghton, Mifflin Co., 1936.

"The object of the procedure is to provide a standard method of observing the difficulties and faulty habits of children who are retarded in reading. These difficulties are best observed in materials of known levels of reading difficulty. Norms are provided in tests of rate and comprehension in oral and silent reading, and for quick recognition of words, word analysis, and rate of handwriting. More important is the check for observation of difficulties during each of the several tests. These check lists are unified in a single master list from which the remedial program is designed. Each item in the master list is followed by a page reference to a remedial manual which shows the type of exercises which have been found helpful in correcting the error.

"The first test consists of eight paragraphs graded in difficulty which the child is to read orally. Oral questions follow each paragraph. The child reads up the scale of paragraphs until he gets beyond his depth. Time norms are provided in each paragraph. The child's faulty habits are recorded on a check list. In this list is included such items as attack on words, phrase reading, voice and enunciation, regard for punctuation, and comprehension.

"The second test is also an oral reading test, constructed exactly like the first, except that the recall is checked by having the child first tell the story unaided by questions, and checking the remaining memories by oral questions. The check list accompanying this test includes adequacy and clarity of recall, eye movements, head movements, posture, and other general reading habits. It also provides for a check on eye-voice span.

"The third section is a silent reading test which consists of eight paragraphs of a mechanical difficulty exactly equal to those in the preceding tests. The recall is checked by the unaided oral recall method. The check list contains items dealing with recall, attention to content, eye movements, lip movements, and comparison of silent and oral reading habits. In grade three and above, the child's oral recall is compared with his written recall on paragraphs of the same level of difficulty.

"The next section deals with quick recognition of words and ability in word analysis. A list of words is presented in a tachistoscope and the child's score is indicative of his ability to recognize words without analysis. The same list of words is presented outside the tachistoscope and the child is given all of the time he needs to pronounce the words. A comparison of his score on these two tests tell whether the remedial program should stress word recognition or analytic methods.

"Tests are included for eye and hand dominance, speed of handwriting from copy, enunciation from oral stimulus, and spelling. A form for recording results of sensory examinations, and for pertinent school and home data is provided.

"The test was planned in co-operation with mature teachers of remedial classes. It includes only those things which have been found to be helpful in guiding a remedial program. It is not particularly helpful for the study of the difficulties of a child who has a sight vocabulary of fewer than sixty words, nor does it include the study skills of the middle grades. Since it is to be accompanied by a group test, no items are included which may be satisfactorily tested on a group test basis. The group test for primary grades includes tests of vocabulary, sentence comprehension, attention to word form, ability in auditory analysis of words heard, as well as general achievement tests. The middle-grade test includes, in addition to these, tests which measure the flexibility of reading and interpretation and association of ideas while reading."

C. Gates, Arthur I. *Diagnostic Reading Tests,* Bureau of Publications, Teachers College, Columbia University, 1935.

Two record forms are used in the administration of the tests. *The Record Booklet for Reading Diagnosis,* is used by the examiner and the *Booklet of Diagnostic Tests* is

given to the pupil. Ample space is provided for the recording of data from the entire battery of tests used for the
analysis of several cases of reading disability. The raw
score, age or grade score, and rating on each test is recorded. Gates (11 : 205) suggests that verbal tests (tests
involving reading) of intelligence are not satisfactory for
the analysis of reading disabilities. For an individual test
of intelligence the Stanford Revision of the Binet is recommended; for a group test such a test as Pintner's Non-
Language Test is suggested.

Space is provided for the recording of data secured from
the Gates Silent Reading Tests. There is also a section for
other silent reading tests. Gray's Oral Reading Test is used
as a part of the battery.

The Gates Diagnostic Tests include:

I. Gates Oral Context

    1. Omissions, words
    2. Additions, words
    3. Repetitions
    4. Mispronunciations
    5. Full reversals
    6. Reversal of parts
    7. Wrong order (5 and 6)
    8. Wrong beginning
    9. Wrong middle
    10. Wrong ending
    11. Wrong several parts

II. Word Pronunciation
    1. Gates Graded Words

III. Perceptual Orientation—Gates Isolated Words
    1. Percentage of Reversals

IV. Perceptual Orientation—Gates Word Recognition
   1. Visual Presentation

   a) Reversals   d) Configuration
   b) Part reversals   e) Wrong ending
   c) Wrong beginning   f) Wrong orientation

V. Visual Perception Techniques
   1. Phonogram Combinations
   2. Initial Vowel Syllables
   3. Initial Consonant Syllables
   4. Vowel-Consonant Phonograms
   5. Vowel Phonograms
   6. Consonant Phonograms
   7. Consonant Vowel Phonograms
   8. Blending
   9. Name Capital Letters
      a) Speed
      b) Errors
   10. Name Lower Case Letters
      a) Speed
      b) Errors

VI. Auditory Perception Techniques
   1. Blend Letter Sounds
   2. Give Letters for Sound
   3. Give Words
      a) Beginning Sounds
      b) Ending Sounds

VII. Auditory Discrimination
   1. Repeat Nonsense Words
   2. Distinguish Words

VIII. Visual Perception
 1. Same-different Figures
 2. Same-different Numbers
 3. Selections of Figures

 IX. Spelling and Writing
  1. Write or Spell Words
  2. Write Spelled Words
  3. Write Letters

  X. Associative Learning
   1. Visual-Visual   3. Auditory-Visual
   2. Visual-Visual   4. Auditory-Visual

 XI. Memory Span
  1. Digits   3. Nonsense Syllables
  2. Letters   4. Familiar Words

D. Monroe, Marion. *Diagnostic Reading Examination,* C. H.
 Stoelting Co., Chicago, 1932.

 I. Analytic Reading Tests
  1. Alphabet repeating
  2. Iota word test
  3. *b, d, p, q, u, n* test
  4. Recognition of orientation
  5. Mirror-reading
  6. Mirror-writing test
  7. Number reversal test
  8. Word discrimination test
  9. Sounding test
  10. Handedness tests
  11. Spelling
   a) Oral   *b*) Written

Intelligence Tests

During the past decade intelligence tests have increased in value because their limitations are better understood. Many investigators have recorded the fact that individuals with reading difficulties do not perform as expected on many of the group tests of intelligence. A large percentage of disabled readers have been found to possess normal or superior intelligence when measured by means of a non-verbal test.

Durrell (9) made a study of the "Influence of Reading Ability on Intelligence Measures." His general conclusions were: "The I. Q's from the group studied appear to vary to a significant degree with the reading accomplishment of the group examined. Since school success depends to a large extent on reading ability, the presence of reading items in a test will not necessarily invalidate it as a measure for the prediction of school success if the reading accomplishment of the child is relatively constant. Yet, it is true that the presence of this large factor of reading in intelligence tests will allow many children to be classed as dull who are really normal or bright but who have poor reading ability. It follows that the group intelligence test involving a great number of reading items should not be used as a basis for intelligence or accomplishment quotients. It appears to be a reading test incorrectly labeled."

For a child of low intelligence, formal reading instruction should be postponed until he has attained a mental age of at least six and one-half years. Such an individual will progress more slowly and require more repetition. The greatest mistake is usually made by initiating the slow learning child into typical first-grade reading activities before he has the mental maturity. Although it appears that many factors other than intelligence contribute to reading aptitude, it is well established that mental maturity is one essential element in the situation.

The following tests have proved to be satisfactory in the Betts' Clinic:

1. Kuhlmann, F., and Anderson, Rose G., *Kuhlmann-Anderson Intelligence Tests* (Grades I to Maturity), Educational Test Bureau, 1933.

2. Pintner, Rudolph. *Non-Language Primary Mental Test* (for kindergarten, and Grades I and II), Bureau of Publication, Teachers College, Columbia University.

3. Terman, Lewis M. *Stanford Revision of the Binet-Simon Intelligence Tests* (Individual Tests), Houghton, Mifflin Company, 1920.

Association Tests

Traxler (21) made a study at the seventh-grade level of the relationship between rate of reading and the rate with which pupils associate ideas with words. He concluded: "Speed of association bears a sufficiently close reaction to rate of reading that the rate with which pupils associate ideas should be considered by the teacher of reading in diagnosing abnormal rates of reading."

Van Wagenen included a test of "Perception of Relationships" in his battery of reading readiness tests. Gates made use of various types of association tests in his diagnostic reading tests. Some qualified investigators seriously question the value of available association tests for the analysis of reading difficulties. Although such tests may provide valuable evidence for the trained psychologist, their value in the typical public-school situation is doubtful.

Tests of Laterality

The evidence regarding the effect of causing a left-handed child to write with his right hand is inconclusive. Likewise, available data neither prove nor disprove the content on that left-eyed and left-handed or left-eyed and right-handed children evidence greater difficulty than right-sided individuals in reading from left-to-right. Tests of hand-preference are administered as a part of the writer's procedure on the assumption that an individual will have fewer handicaps if permitted to use his preferred hand in unimanual activities. These problems are discussed in Chapter VI.

Eye-Movement Records

The value of eye-movement records in a typical public-school situation has been questioned by qualified investigators. Serious cases of reading deficiency are studied because they have not achieved in reading. It has been demonstrated in many research centers that retarded readers make many fixation pauses (or stops) and regressive movements per line. Eye-movement records provide only symptoms or signs of inefficient and unrhythmical reading habits. This phase of the problem is discussed more fully in Chapter VII.

Health

Often it has been repeated that philosophically one never arrives at the cause of a given difficulty. Regardless of the truth of this statement, a number of possible causes of reading difficulty have been revealed so that distinctions can be made between symptoms and causes. Enough evidence has been reported in the literature to substantiate the contention that individuals experiencing learning difficulties should have a thorough health examination. Specialists and other health experts should be secured for cases of learning difficulty. Too frequently, the typical school medical examination falls short of providing crucial data in such cases. Educators, to a great degree, are responsible for this because few school situations are administered so that the educational implications of medical data are given practical interpretation. There cannot be adequate use of such data where the health and education departments are divorced from each other by strict compartmentilization. A great need exists for the training of school doctors in the educational implications of their findings. Likewise, a similar need exists for the training of teachers so that they can intelligently co-operate with the health department.

The health department can usually supply some information on the following items:

1. Defective vision
2. Defective hearing
3. Infected or obstructive tonsils
4. Obstructive adenoids
5. Glandular disturbances
6. Toxic conditions
7. Anatomical or functional anomalies of the organs of speech
8. Defective teeth
9. Malnutrition
10. Brain injuries
11. History of previous illness

From the point of view of reading deficiencies, the weakest points in the typical school health examination are the tests of vision and hearing. The visual tests are usually inadequate because the co-ordinate functioning of the two eyes at reading distance is not appraised. The whisper and low voice tests of hearing do not provide sufficient information for the diagnosis of difficulties in phonetics and music.

Pupil Interests

Appeal to pupil interests is not an idle comment. Before remedial procedures based on learner interests can become a reality, it is necessary to arrive at the peculiar interests and aptitudes of the children. In the writer's clinic success has been achieved, in part, by beginning with interests in industrial arts, music, science, or social-science activities. From these individual projects, the child is interested in school and finally in reading to learn more about the activity. One of the biggest problems for the remedial teacher is that of changing the attitude of the child who is in difficulty. Because of the social pressure in any community, most children at seven or eight years of age would enjoy reading if it were in their power to do so. In order to rationalize the situation many poor attitudes are acquired.

Case History

The history of the case will frequently bring to light certain information which will prove to be helpful for planning the course of action. Pupils who have been irregular in attendance may have gaps in their previous school experience which need to be analyzed and corrected. Irregularity of attendance may also be due to poor home co-operation or illness which has educational implications.

In securing information from the parents, the teacher is in a strategic position to mold intelligent parent attitudes toward the difficulties of the child. It is not uncommon to find parents in the supposedly best of homes using corporal punishment because of low grades or school failures. In other situations, the parents may blame the teacher for the difficulty. Here, again, attitude is one key to the situation. Co-operation with the home is essential to the success of the school program. Several items regarding school history and home conditions merit consideration:

1. School history
   a) Age at entrance to first grade
   b) Extent of pre-first grade training
   c) First awareness of the difficulty on the part of the teacher
   d) Number of grades repeated
   e) Attitude of parents
   f) Regularity of attendance
   g) Frequency of transfer from one school to another
   h) Record of illness
   i) Achievement in other school subjects
   j) Attitude toward teacher and school
   k) Special school interests and aptitudes

2. Home data
   a) Occupation of parents
   b) Nationality
   c) Language spoken in the home
   d) Social-economic condition of home
   e) Reading difficulties of parents or siblings
   f) Parents' attitude toward school
   g) Parents' attitude toward difficulty of child

Who Shall Examine?

The individual who is responsible for the remedial work should make the examination. Of course, the health data shall be secured from the school doctor or nurse. With the exception of the Stanford Revision of Binet-Simon Intelligence Tests, all of the above mentioned tests can be given by a well-trained elementary-school teacher. Many school systems now employ remedial teachers whose functions are to aid in the determination of reading readiness and in the analysis and correction of learning deficiencies. In such situations, the required tests are made available in each building.

In addition to the training of the examiner, one of the most important qualifications of a remedial teacher is the right attitude. In the hands of a teacher who lacks enthusiasm and confidence in the learner's ability, methods become only cold mechanical devices. A teacher who would challenge the interests of a boy who has experienced failure in learning must supermotivate the reading by approaches through his particular interests.

Through the analysis, the learner, as well as the teacher, should come to a better understanding of the obstacles to success. Although automation in the mechanics of reading is the goal, the burden is lighter if the pupil is given some insight into the job to be done. This, of course, should not be imposed. Co-operation is essential to the success of the undertaking.

SUMMARY

1. Serious reading difficulties are usually caused by a complex and peculiar combination of circumstances.

2. An individual characterized by a specific reading difficulty is one who needs his attention and efforts directed to the learning of one or a few specific skills and information such as location of information, word meaning, or comprehension techniques.

3. A general reading disability is a retardation caused by a deficiency in the basic and elementary skills, information, and attitudes.

4. The remedial teacher should secure information regarding the learner's physical readiness or fitness for sustained reading.

5. Reading readiness tests are valuable for analysis of difficulties at the primary level.

6. General achievement tests are used to determine the extent of learning difficulties.

7. A verbal intelligence test (involving reading) should not be used for the determination of the mental age of a disabled reader; however, such a test would provide data for comparison with non-verbal intelligence test scores.

8. An analysis of achievement for certain reading skills afford a desirable basis for the grouping of children within the classroom. Frequently, it is unnecessary to proceed further with the analysis.

9. An appraisal of the disabled reader's system of word analysis is essential at all elementary-grade levels.

10. The diagnostic procedure should indicate whether or not there is a comprehension or mechanical difficulty.

11. The grade level at which the individual readily acquires rhythmical reading habits should be determined. One prerequisite for successful teaching is to begin where the learner is.

12. The periods used for the analysis of the reading difficulty should be informative and a pleasant experience for the subject. Motivation is just as essential
for testing as it is for remedial work.

13. The analysis should reveal the interests and aptitudes
of the learner. It is through these interests and
aptitudes that the remedial instruction can be effectively given.

14. The analysis should begin rather than stop with the
symptomatic behavior.

15. The examiner may expect to find a complex of difficulties (emotional, physical, and pedagogical) charac-
terizing the disability, any one of which might be
normally tolerated by the individual.

16. The analysis of the difficulties should be continued
throughout the remedial teaching period.

17. No one reading disability correlate should be used to
account for all types of reading difficulty.

18. No extensive analysis is required for most cases of
retardation in reading. In many instances, the classroom teacher can use a series of reading books to
discover the approximate reading level and the deficient word-recognition skills and information of the
learner. She is also in a position to understand the
child's special interests and aptitudes.

REFERENCES

1. Baker, Harry J. *Characteristic Differences in Bright and
Dull Pupils.* Bloomington, Illinois: Public School Publishing Co., 1927.

2. Betts, Emmett A. "A Physiological Approach to the Analysis of Reading Disabilities," *Educational Research Bulletin* (Ohio State University), XIII (September, 1934).

3. Betts, Emmett A. "Prevention and Correction of Reading Disabilities," *Elementary English Review,* XII (February, 1935), 25-32.

4. Betts, Emmett A. "Reading Disabilities and Their Correction, Annual Research Bulletin of National Conference on Research in Elementary School English," *Elementary English Review,* XII (March, April, May, June, 1935), 69-73, 106-10, 131-41, 157-65.

5. Betts, Emmett A. "Teacher Analysis of Reading Disabilities," *Elementary English Review,* XI (April, 1934) 99-102.

6. Betts, Emmett A., Everett, Mable, and Rodewald, Frances. "Remedial Reading Based on First-Teaching," *Journal of Exceptional Children* (February, 1936).

7. Courtis, S. A. "Analysis of Reading Ability," *Journal of Educational Research,* IV (November, 1921), 287-93.

8. Dearborn, Frances F. "A Study of Erroneous Word Concepts in Reading," *Elementary English Review,* VI (January, 1929), 3-6, 23.

9. Durrell, Donald D. "The Influence of Reading Ability on Intelligence Measures," *Journal of Educational Psychology,* XXIV (September, 1933), 412-17.

10. Farley, Eugene S., Frey, Albin J., and Garland, Gertrude, "Factors Related to the Grade Progress of Pupils," *Elementary School Journal,* XXXIV (November, 1933), 186-93.

11. Gates, Arthur I. *The Improvement of Reading,* New York: Macmillan Company, 1935.

12. Gates, Arthur I. "Viewpoints Underlying the Study of Reading Disabilities," *Elementary English Review,* XII (April, 1935), 85-90.

13. Gray, Clarence Truman. *Deficiencies in Reading Ability: Their Diagnosis and Remedies,* pp. 365-409. Boston: D. C. Heath & Co., 1922.

14. Gillingham, Anna and Stillman, Bessie W. "Remedial Work for Reading, Spelling and Penmanship." New York: Ethical Culture School, 1934.

15. Mitzefield, Lucy L. "A Diagnosis of Study Habits Used in Reading," *Detroit Educational Bulletin,* XVI (November, December, 1932), 4-7. Detroit, Michigan: Board of Education.

16. Monroe, Marion. *Children Who Cannot Read,* pp. xvi-205. Chicago: University of Chicago Press, 1932.

17. Mort, Paul, and Gates, Arthur I. *The Acceptable Uses of Achievement Tests,* Teachers College Bureau of Publications, 1932.

18. Robinson, Francis P. "The Tachistoscope as a Measure of Reading," *American Journal of Psychology,* XLVI (January, 1934), 132-41.

19. Smith, Nila Banton. "Matching Ability as a Factor in First Grade Reading," *Journal of Educational Psychology,* XIX (November, 1928), 560-71.

20. Tinker, Miles A. "Diagnostic and Remedial Reading," *Elementary School Journal,* XXXIII (December, 1932), 293-307.

21. Traxler, Arthur E. "The Relation Between Rate of Reading and Speed of Association," *Journal of Educational Psychology,* XXV (May, 1934), 357-65.

CHAPTER VI
Hand and Eye Preferences

There are in the literature several broad hints at a psychological theory of motor left-sidedness.
—Joseph Jastak (18:259).

Preview

Hand and eye preference, sometimes referred to as handedness and eyedness, is an intriguing problem for teachers, psychologists, and physiologists. The educational implications are many and varied, especially on the preschool and primary levels. In this chapter, it is the intention of the writer to present a brief sketch of research findings and to indicate how they may be translated into school practice.

Handedness Types

It is a well established fact that most individuals are either right-handed or left-handed. The right-handed are usually referred to as "dextrads"; left-handed individuals as "sinistrads." Where no clear-cut manual pattern exists, the term "ambidextrous" is applied. Some individuals appear to be equally facile with either hand. A "dextro-sinistrad" is one with left-hand preference who has been caused to use his right hand for such activities as writing.

Undoubtedly, many cases of so-called ambidexterity, or mixed handedness, are caused by training of the right hand at home and in school when the left hand is preferred. It has been the writer's experience that in schools where both

116

the parents and teachers have been aware of the need for permitting the child to use the preferred hand, there are more left-handed children. Parson (35) points out the fact that children are not changed from right to left hand except in case of injury; therefore, we do encounter variation in test results for the determination of hand preference.

It is interesting to note the probable origin of the terms "sinistrad" and "dextrad" which are used in the literature on handedness. Jordan (15) writes: "Left-handedness is commonly associated with abnormality, physical and mental defect, ill omen, and things accounted 'sinister.' The universal feeling of the more favorable nature of right-handedness has crystallized the word dexterity."

Man is a bilateral being, the two halves of the body being antitropic. He is characterized by reversed symmetry; that is, the body functions asymmetrically in that a right-handed individual may be capable of mirrored or reversed movements with the left hand.

Theories of Hand Preference

Many ingenious theories have been advanced to account for hand preference. Parson (35) summarized the principal theories. By and large, the discussions are resolved to two points; namely, is hand preference congenital (inborn) or acquired (a habit)? Some professionally respected investigators believe that left-handedness is inherited in terms of the Mendelian law. Others maintain that a visceral displacement toward the right side of the body is a cause of right-handedness. A few authorities contend that hand dominance results from an uneven blood supply to the cerebral hemispheres. In early investigations, the possibility of greater blood pressure in the right subclavian artery appeared to merit consideration. The literature of the subject is frequently punctuated with assertations that right-handedness depends on left-brain dominance. Many have thought that hand preference is coincident with ocular dominance or eye preference. Lastly, there is the group that believes hand preference is a socially acquired habit.

The educational significance of hand preference is dependent upon the validity of the above contentions. True it is that the controversy is not settled, because many of the proposals have not stood the acid test applied by the scientific investigator.

Is Handedness Related to Growing Up?

From available data, we are led to believe that hand preference may be, to a degree, related to maturity or growth. Watson (43:263) emphatically states: "In early infancy there is certainly no preferential use." His findings were deduced from having worked with twenty babies ranging in ages from 120 to 160 days. Updegraff (42) found that handedness, determined by tests and observations, was established before the second year of life. Studying children of two to six years of age, she found no apparent age differences.

Incidence of Left-Hand Preference

Conclusions regarding the incidence of left-handedness vary with the age of the population studied and the testing devices used. Various investigators conclude that from 2 to 40 per cent of the population are left-handed. Students of the problem find a bimodal distribution; that is, at one end of the handedness scale a large number are found to be right-handed; at the other end of the scale

there are many left-handed persons, while a small group
appears to be ambidextrous. Parsons (35) indicated that
his findings of 29.3 per cent, representing the left-handed
population, was in accordance with the Mendelian principle
where right-handedness is the dominant and left-handedness the recessive characteristic. Haefner (16), studying
1,144 cases, found that approximately 88 per cent were
right-handed, 6 per cent left-handed, 5 per cent mixed-
handed, and less than 1 per cent doubtful. His figures
showed a slightly greater incidence of left-handedness
among girls.

The data of various investigators are summarized in the
following table:

INCIDENCE OF LEFT-HANDEDNESS

Investigator	Percentage
Baldwin and Hyrtle	2.00
Ballard	4.00
Barleleben	32.80
Beeley . . . . (14% ambidextrous)	40.00
Gordon	7.30
Gould	6.00
Haefner	6.18
Hinks	33.00
Jones	4.00
Jordan	25.00
Lombroso	4.00
Mead	6.00
Parson	29.30
Pyle and Dronum	7.00
Ramaley	16.66
Selzer . . . . . *(estimate) 10.00 to 12.00
Smith	5.00
Woo and Pearson (6.59% ambidextrous)	28.79

Hand Preference and School Achievement

Using the Stanford Achievement Test, Haefner (16) found a greater variability in performance in the left-handed group, but no reliable differences between the school achievement of the left-handed and the right-handed group.

Handedness and Social Adjustment

Regarding social adjustment, Haefner (16) concluded: "As measured by a somewhat crude instrument, the left-handed group seemed slightly better adjusted to the school situation than was the right-handed group." Left-handed and right-handed groups of children differ very little with respect to types of things that arouse emotion or worry. Since Haefner found so few left-handed (6.18 per cent) children in the population studied, this may account for the slight variation in favor of the left-handed group. Perhaps children in the right-handed group had been changed from the left to the right hand.

Handedness and Language Disabilities

Handedness as a part of the scheme of lateral dominance is a much confused issue. Many controversies are being waged on the relation of hand preference to language disabilities. On two issues the problem seems to be fairly clear-cut; namely, where the cases studied have been definitely right- or left-handed. The borderline cases of apparent mixed dominance are in need of further intensive study. No one has succeeded in clearly defining the problem.

It is interesting to note, in passing, that the data and the interpretation of the data are modified by the type of cases studied and the background of the investigators. Some theories are postulated on the basis of pathological cases by neurologists and physiologists. Educational and psychological research workers, not having the background of the other investigators, have concerned themselves with the functional aspects of the problem and its relation to schoolroom practices. Hence, it is difficult to integrate the mosaic of findings.

Mirror-writing is apparently more common among left-handed individuals than among the right-handed. Some authorities find that mirror-writing is normally resorted to by the dextro-sinistrad (a left-handed person who has been trained to write with his right hand). The relation of left-handedness to language disabilities, such as mirror-writing, speech defects, reading disabilities, and spelling handicaps, has been debated by a number of investigators. Teachers are concerned with the problem because it has a direct bearing upon the analysis procedure and remedial work for such cases.

Woody and Phillips investigated "The Effect of Handedness on Reversals in Reading" (44). No child was included in the investigation if there was evidence of having been changed from the left to the right hand. They reported finding a preponderance of boys who were left-handed and no significant differences between the types of reading responses made by left-handed and right-handed pupils.

Tests for Determination of Hand Preference

Few, if any, tests for handedness permit clear-cut discriminations between handedness types. Regardless of the cause or causes of hand preference, environmental influ-

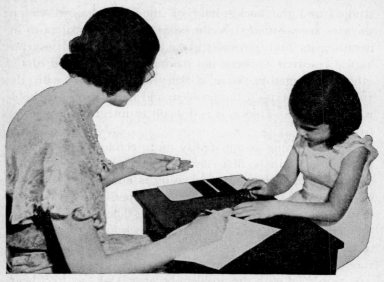

Testing for Hand Preference

ences undoubtedly play a rôle of paramount importance in
determining hand preference for certain acts.

For the determination of hand preference certain criteria
may be safely set up as follows:

1. A battery of several tests should be used. No one test
   is a test of handedness or of general laterality.
2. Tests should be used which will not elicit behavior
   peculiar to one sex.
3. Observations should be taken from both guided and
   unguided activities.
4. In general, both unimanual and bimanual activities
   should be used in the final judgment.
5. The subject should not be informed regarding the
   purpose of the observations and tests.

6. For unimanual tests such as tapping, a number of pretest trials should be given. This is done to acquaint the person about to be examined with the testing techniques. All such trials should not be counted in the final data.

7. For unimanual tests, a handedness ratio should be established by dividing the right-hand scores by the left-hand scores. This procedure adds to the convenience of test comparisons.

The following unimanual activities have proved to be adequate for inclusion in a battery of tests:

1. **Tapping.** The tapping test may be accomplished with an electric recorder, a mechanical recorder, or a pencil and paper. Several readings are usually taken, alternating between hands. The writer has found this type of test more nearly discriminative for the elementary-school child. For this test, the rhythm exhibited by each hand should be noted. Frequently, after several tests, the individual will exhibit more fatigue in the non-preferred hand.

2. **Handwriting.** An index to hand preference may be had by recording the time required to write the individual's name with one hand, then with the other. Other variations of this test are making of "O's," "X's," or vertical lines on a ruled paper or blackboard. The number of such marks made in twenty seconds will permit a handedness ratio to be established.

3. **Throwing.** Many variations of this procedure have been used successfully. The hand used for throw-

ing a ball should be determined. In the school-room, the subject can be asked to stand about fifteen feet from a waste basket and toss a ball or an eraser into it.

4. **Using scissors.** Unless the subject exhibits equal facility with both hands, he usually will be able to use the scissors successfully with one hand only.

5. **Strength of grip.** Strength of grip is usually de-termined by a small, simple instrument called a dynamometer. After one or two preliminary trials, the subject is asked to grip as firmly as possible. Usually after four trials, the hand exhibiting the greater strength of grip is recorded as the pre-ferred one.

Among many other tests of hand preference are: pick-ing up objects, hammering nails, sawing, spinning a top, and the like. The classroom teacher would probably do well to rely heavily upon the handwriting test. Kinder-garten children and first-grade entrants can be interested easily into making X's on the blackboard. After all, the teacher is concerned only with the problem of determining which hand the child should use for writing, painting, and the like.

Bimanual tests of handedness are frequently used. Test-ing devices include any activities where the subject is required to use both hands. Sweeping, raking, shoveling, batting, and the like are frequently used. Ojemann (27) suggests that the hand farthest away from the "business end" of the shovel or broom is the preferred hand; that is, one who places his left hand nearest the shovel and shovels to the left side is right-handed.

Eye Preference

A dominate or leading eye is found in practically all cases. Some individuals are right-eyed, others, left-eyed. Miles (25) found a majority of right-handed individuals to be right-eyed and left-handed to be divided about equally between right- and left-eyed dominance.

Test of Eye Preference

Several tests of the eye preference have been developed. The Miles A-B-C Test (25) deserves special mention because it is easily administered by the untrained worker. The subject is requested to view certain prepared charts "Through a paper funnel or V-scope that is made of folded white cardboard formed in such a manner that it must be pressed open between the two hands if the subject is to see through the aperture." (25 : 117.) The chief advantage of this test is that the subject is unaware of the eye used for viewing the test card. The examiner sees the dominate eye which is used for viewing the card.

Testing for Eye Preference

Other tests of eye preference can be administered easily. A simple procedure is to have the child look through a mailing tube. The eye used is the dominant or preferred eye.

The peep-hole test is also a good one. A one-half inch hole is cut in an 8½x11 inch sheet of paper. The subject is requested to hold the paper with both hands at an arm's length and to look at the examiner through the hole. The eye used for sighting is the preferred one.

Educational Implications

A study of the references cited at the end of this chapter shows that there is no scientific evidence to prove or disprove the hypothesis that left-eyedness and right-handedness or any other combination of eyedness and handedness contributes to confusions in the language functions. Likewise, changing an individual for writing and eating purposes from the left hand to the right hand probably does not result in a language disability. The writer believes, however, that a child should not be forced to use the nonpreferred hand for unimanual activities such as writing. The added emotional burden is not worth the cost. In the meantime, the public-school worker should await further research findings and look elsewhere for the difficulty.

SUMMARY

1. Although this is a right-handed world, the left-handed individual probably has no greater learning difficulties than the right-handed.
2. Mixed hand-eye preference or left-eyedness and left-handedness are not clearly associated with language difficulties.
3. A left-handed child should not be forced to use his right hand in unimanual activities.
4. Hand and eye preference can be determined by the classroom teacher, using home-made devices.

REFERENCES

1. Anderson, Irving, and Crosland, H. R. *The Effects of Combinations of Handedness and Eyedness on Letter-Position, "Range of Attention" Scores.* University of Oregon Publication, IV (March, 1934).

2. Anderson, Irving, and Crosland, H. R. *The Effects of Eye-Dominance on "Range of Attention" Scores.* University of Oregon Publication, Vol. IV, No. 4.

3. Anderson, Irving, and Crosland, H. R. *The Effects of Handedness on "Range of Attention" Scores,* University of Oregon Publication, X (January, 1934).

4. Blom, E. C. "Mirror-Writing," *Psychological Bulletin,* XXV (1928), 582-94.

5. Carmichael, Leonard, and Cashman, Helen. "A Study of Mirror-Writing in Relation to Handedness and Perceptual and Motor Habits," *Journal of General Psychology,* VI (1932), 296-329.

6. Clark, J. E. *The Relation of Reading Disability to Left-Handedness and Speech Defects in Other Members of the Family,* Smith College Studies in Social Work (1933), 66-79.

7. Crider, Blake, "The Lack of Cerebral Dominance as a Cause of Reading Disabilities," *Childhood Education,* X (February, 1934), 238.

8. Cuff, N. B. "Study of Eyedness and Handedness," *Journal of Experimental Psychology,* XIV (April, 1931), 557-59.

9. Cutright, Prudence, and Anderson, Walter. "An Experimental Study of Pupils in the First Grade," Bulletin, Curriculum Department, Minneapolis Public Schools, 1934.

10. Gahagan, Lawrence. "Visual Dominance-Acuity Relationships," *Journal of General Psychology,* IX (July, 1933), 455-59.

11. Gast, Ira M. "A Study of Handedness," *Journal of Educational Sociology,* II, 487-91.

12. Gates, A. I., and Bennett, C. C. *Reversal Tendencies in Reading: Causes, Diagnosis, Prevention and Correction,* p. 33. Teachers College, Bureau Publications, 1933, Columbia University.

13. Giesecke, Minnie. "Problems of Hand Preference," *Childhood Education,* IX (December, 1932), 124-28.

14. Gillingham, Anna, and Stillman, Bessie W. *Remedial Work for Reading, Spelling and Penmanship.* New York: Ethical Culture School, 1934.

15. Jordon, H. "Left-Handedness and Mirror Writing," *Brain,* 43 (1920), 530.

16. Haefner, Ralph. *The Educational Significance of Left-Handedness,* Teachers College Contributions to Education, No. 360. New York: Teachers College, Columbia University, 1929.

17. Hincks, Elizabeth M. *Disability in Reading and Its Relation to Personality,* p. 92. Harvard Monographs in Education, No. 7. Cambridge, Massachusetts: Harvard University Press, 1926.

18. Jastak, Joseph. "Interferences in Reading," *Psychological Bulletin,* XXXI (April, 1934).

19. Jones, W. F. *Study of Handedness,* University of Southern California, 1918.

20. Jones, W. F. *A Study of Handedness,* University of South Dakota, XVII (1918).

21. Kirk, Samuel A. *Hemispheric Cerebral Dominance and Hemispheric Equipotentiality,* Comparative Psychology Monographs, Vol. II, No. 5, Serial No. 55. Baltimore: Johns Hopkins Press.

22. Koch, Helen Lois, *A Study of the Nature, Measurement, and Determination of Hand Preference,* Genetic Psy-

chology Monographs, Vol. XIII, No. 2 (February, 1933).

23. Kraskin, Lewis H. "A Study of the Factors Entering Into the Determination of Handedness," *American Journal of Optometry*, XII (February and March, 1935).

24. Lewis, A. R., and Meyers, C. R. *Speech Defects and Lateral Dominance*, Ontario Hospital Publications, II (September, 1933).

25. Miles, W. R. "Ocular Dominance in Human Adults," *Journal of General Psychology*, III (1930), 412-30.

26. Ojemann, R. H. "Studies in Handedness: I. A Technique for Testing Unimanual Handedness," *Journal of Educational Psychology*, XXI (August, 1930), 597-611.

27. Ojemann, R. H. "Studies in Handedness: II. Testing Bimanual Handedness," *Journal of Educational Psychology*, XXI (September, 1930), 695-702.

28. Ojemann, R. H. "Studies in Handedness: III. Relation of Handedness to Speech," *Journal of Educational Psychology*, XXII (February, 1931), 120-26.

29. Orton, S. T. "A Physiological Theory of Reading Disability and Stuttering in Children," *New England Journal of Medicine* (November, 1928), 199, 1046-52.

30. Orton, S. T., and Travis, L. "Recurrence of Stuttering Following Shift from Normal to Mirror Writing," *Archives of Neurology and Psychiatry*, XXI (February, 1929).

31. Orton, S. T. "Special Disability in Spelling," *Bulletin Neurology Institute*, I (1931), 159-92.

32. Orton, S. T., and Gillingham, A. "Special Disability in Writing," *Bulletin Neurology Institute*, III (1933), 1-32.

33. Orton, S. T. "The Three Levels of Cortical Elaboration in Relation to Certain Psychiatric Symptoms," *American Journal of Psychiatry* (1928-1929), 8, 11, 647-59.

34. Orton, S. T. "Training the Left Handed," *Hygeia,* V (September, 1927), 451-54.

35. Parson, B. S. *Left-Handedness,* New York: Macmillan Company, 1924.

36. Peters, Clarence A. "A Study of Facility in Mirror Reading," Master's Thesis, School of Speech, University of Iowa, 1934.

37. Scheidman, N. U. "A Simple Test for Ocular Dominance," *Journal of Genetic Psychology,* III (1930), 412-30.

38. Selzer, Charles A. *Lateral Dominance and Visual Fusion,* p. 119. Harvard Monographs in Education, No. 12 (Harvard University Press, 1933).

39. Spencer, Peter L., Kennedy, Helen, and Dart, Carrol. *A Study of Lateral Dominance and of Visual Fusion in Relation to Reading Ability,* American Association for the Advancement of Science, Sec. Q, Berkeley, California (June, 1934).

40. Updergraff, Ruth. "The Correspondence between Handedness and Eyedness in Young Children," *Journal of Genetic Psychology,* XL (1933), 42, 490-92.

41. Updergraff, Ruth. "Ocular Dominance in Young Children," *Journal of Experimental Psychology,* XV (1932), 758-66.

42. Updergraff, Ruth. "Preferential Handedness in Young Children," *Journal of Experimental Education,"* I (1932), 134-39.

43. Watson, John B. *Psychology from the Standpoint of a Behaviorist,* Philadelphia: J. B. Lippincott Co., 1924.

44. Woody, Clifford, and Phillips, Albert J. "The Effects of Handedness on Reversals in Reading," *Journal of Educational Research,* XXVII (May, 1934), p. 651-62.

CHAPTER VII
Eye-Movements

Inefficient eye-movements and narrow span of apprehension always accompany defective reading habits.—Miles Tinker.

Eye-Movements During Reading

About 1878 Javal, observing the eyes during reading by reflection from a mirror, made the important discovery that eyes do not sweep across the line in an uninterrupted movement. He found instead that during the reading process the eyes make *saccadic* or discontinuous movements. Since this early discovery there has been increased interest in the measurement, function, and nature of eye-movements.

Reading is largely a set of mechanical and perceptual habits. Teachers of beginners should not take for granted that the child knows how the mechanical reading process is achieved, but instead should give the learner the information and be constantly alert for word and sentence situations in which such habits are stressed and practiced. Gates and Bennett (7) suggest that the teacher demonstrate left-to-right progression. Practice makes perfect only that which is practiced. If a child is permitted to practice attacking a word in the middle or from right-to-left, he is making perfect the wrong habits. When this is carried out over a period of time, the learner exhibits many confusions during reading, consequently becoming a slow reader or giving up entirely.

The chief causes of inappropriate eye-movements are visual inefficiency, lack of adequate first-teaching, continued practice on materials with difficult vocabulary, too meager stock of sight words, inadequate system of word analysis, and using reading materials difficult to comprehend. The writer's attitude is that eye span, appropriate eye-movements, and the ability to anticipate meaning may be "stepped up" by creating the proper mind set or attitude and by correcting visual defects, but that it is also important to build background and give the child practice in relating the new impressions to that background.

Fixation Frequency

The number of stops or pauses the eyes make per line is referred to as fixation frequency. Approximately 5 to 6 per cent of the reading time is consumed by eye-movements. Poor readers make more fixations per line than good readers. The nature and difficulty of the material being read modifies the number of fixations per line. Systematic left-to-right eye-movements are characteristic of good readers. Failure to attack words from left-to-right may result in such errors as reading *saw* for *was* and *on* for *no*. The number of fixations per line decreases with each succeeding grade level as illustrated in the table on the opposite page.

The length of time required for the eye to fix on a given part of the line in reading is called fixation pause duration. It is commonly believed that there are no visual impressions during eye-movements. Tinker (14) found that pauses or perception time (sum of pause durations) account for about 94 per cent of the reading time. The total reading time is equal to fixation duration plus time spent in eye-movement.

Median Number of Fixations per Line*

Fixation Pauses

Grade	Oral Reading	Silent Reading
I B	16.0	18.6
I A	14.5	15.5
II	12.0	10.7
III	10.4	8.9
IV	10.3	7.3
V	8.7	6.9
VI	8.9	7.3
VII	8.7	6.8
College	8.4	5.9

*Arranged from Buswell's data (2:26, 37).

The time required for perception is modified by the difficulty of the reading material, familiarity with content, legibility of the print, and visual efficiency. Miles and Segal (9) found that third-grade pupils make an average of 3.8 fixations per line. Buswell (2) using other reading materials and a different technique found third-grade children making a median of 8.9 fixations per line. Erdman and Dodge (14) concluded that the first fixation pause was always within the line and the last always before the end of the line. Huey (8: 19) found that the number of fixation pauses was increased in proportion to the distance the page was held from the eye.

Span of Recognition

The amount recognized at each fixation pause is called the span of recognition. This span is greater in silent reading than in oral. Schmidt reported in the *Third Yearbook of the Department of Superintendence* that elementary pupils perceive a range of .86 to 1.62 words per fixation pause during oral reading and 1.04 to 2.44 during silent reading. In general the more mature the reader the greater is the recognition span. As the number of fixations decrease, the span of recognition increases.

Regressive Eye-Movements

The right to left return of one or both eyes during reading is referred to as a regressive movement. Poor readers make more regressive eye-movements than do good readers. Studies by several investigators show that readers who make a large number of regressive movements also have many fixation pauses per line. Regressive movements are necessary when a word or phrase is reviewed for identification purposes.

The number of regressive movements decrease with an increase in grade level as shown in the following table. This may be another factor contributing to the reversal tendency exhibited by young pupils.

MEDIAN NUMBER OF REGRESSIVE MOVEMENTS PER
LINE IN SILENT READING*

Grade	Average Number of Regressive Movements
I B	5.1
I A	4.0
II	2.3
III	1.8
IV	1.4
V	1.3
VI	1.6
College	0.5

*Rearranged from Buswell's data (2:34).

Return Sweeps

A return sweep is the movement of the eyes from the end of one line to the beginning of a succeeding line. Definite training should be given the beginner in achieving this task. The return sweep usually requires a slightly longer period of time than a fixation pause.

Methods of Measuring Eye-Movements

Eye-movements have been measured by direct observation, mechanical recording apparatus, and by photographing devices. The first is used by teachers and clinical workers. The second method was used only during the pioneer period of the early 1900's. Many advances have been made since the pioneer period. Many clinics are now equipped with a portable apparatus for eye-movement photography.

1. Direct observation. Javal first observed eye-movements reflected from a mirror. At present the most practical means of observing eye-movement is the Miles Peep-Hole Method (10). This is achieved by cutting a small hole about three-sixteenths of an inch in diameter between the lines in the center of the page to be read and posting the reading materials on cardboard. The observer holds the material at normal reading distance from the reader's eyes and looks through the hole while the subject reads. By this means the observer can determine number of fixation pauses and regressive movements made by the eyes during the actual reading process. Direct observation methods are of use only for estimating the number of fixation pauses. Pause duration, speed of eye-movements, and regressive movements cannot be reliably determined by observational methods.

2. Mechanical apparatus. Huey (8) was the first to measure the speed as well as the number of eye-movements in reading by attaching the recording apparatus directly to the eye. Such procedures have not found popular favor with investigators for they interfere with eye-movements and may cause permanent damage to the eye.

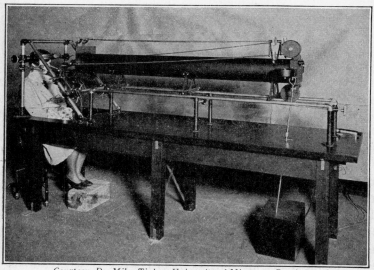

Courtesy, Dr. Miles Tinker, University of Minnesota Psychology Laboratory
The Eye-Movement Camera

3. The photographic method. W. F. Dearborn, Judd, Buswell, Dodge, C. T. Gray, Miles, and others have developed various approaches to the photographic method of recording eye-movements. Since then Dr. Miles Tinker (1) and his associates at the University of Minnesota have made a generous contribution to this field. The photographing of eye-movements consists in recording on a moving film a beam of light reflected from the cornea of the eye during reading.

The Ophthalm-O-Graph developed by J. Y. Taylor of the Educational Laboratories, Brownwood, Texas, and distributed by American Optical Company, is a compact and very practical instrument for the photographing of eye-movements. In addition to its simplicity of operation, the chief advantage of this instrument is that corneal reflections from both eyes are photographed on the same film. By means of such devices the examiner can secure an index to the co-ordinate functioning of the two eyes as well as a record of fixation-pause duration, fixation frequency, regressive movements, and return sweeps.

The Development of Efficient Eye-Movements

Faulty eye-movements are symptoms of reading difficulty. Conversely, rhythmical eye-movements usually characterize good readers. Regressive eye-movements are made when the word or phrase is reviewed. The development of precise and rapid habits of perceiving and interpreting the groups of words read as well as the acquisition of left-to-right reading skills is necessary in order to reduce the number of regressive movements per line.

Too often teachers take for granted left-to-right reading habits of beginners. The chart-building period affords the best opportunities for the explanation and practice of such skills. With the attention of the entire group centered upon the chart, left-to-right eye-movements for sentences, phrases, and words can be practiced. These left-to-right techniques are basic to the subsequent reading instruction. On succeeding levels of instruction, emphasis on the initial sounds of words will reinforce the previous learnings.

When writing, and incidentally spelling, is introduced another kinaesthetic element is added, which further aids in establishing automatic left-to-right progression. An analysis of the above statements shows how auditory, visual, and kinaesthetic imageries are caused to reinforce one another in order to establish a given skill. The learner establishes a visual "feeling" for the left-to-right movements by following the pointer across the chart. This is further established by listening to the sequence of sounds when the material is read orally. The kinaesthetic imagery is built up by oral reading (vocal cords) and by moving the pointer from left-to-right beneath each sentence. Additional kinaesthetic imagery is built when writing is introduced.

Feeling for the spatial orientation of words is apparently not present in children who evidence certain types of immaturity. In Chapter IV the scientific data on this point were reviewed. From these data, it appears that some children tend to reverse letter and word forms until they reach the age of seven and one-half years. The implication is that reading should be postponed until the spatial orientation of letters and words have significance for the learner. In other words the learner should evidence some feeling for isolated letters and for the sequence of letters in a given word. If this is not done, great care should be exercised to prevent practice on saying "saw" for "was" and the like. Obviously, if a young learner is permitted to continue his struggle without close supervision, confusion will result. Practice makes perfect that which is practiced. For example, continued practice in reading by the young learner before he has a sense of orientation for word forms will make perfect the miscalling of words unless special atten-

tion is given to word perception skills. Reading for meaning thus becomes impossible.

The writer is inclined to believe that initial reading instruction should be postponed for some children until they
have a general maturity of about seven years. For children
identified by means of a reading-readiness test as a prospective non-reader, the initial period of reading instruction
should be further delayed. Another key factor in avoiding
confusion in the visual perception of word and phrase forms
is that of meaning. A child who can be caused to feel a real
need for reading to learn is probably much more mature
than the average six-year-old. In any event, a reading program based on reading for meaning will embrace a system
of word recognition where context clues are heavily emphasized. Hence, reading attitude is complementary with reading for meaning.

Confusions resulting in reversals and other twistings of
word forms account for about 10 per cent of the difficulties in reading. In the past, teachers have been misled by
the deluge of professional articles on mirror reading and
reversal tendencies. Some of the most serious reading disabilities are in no way characterized by reversal tendencies.
The number of fixation pauses (or stops) per line is probably modified by both peripheral (sensory defects and the
like) and central (perception, association and the like)
factors. There is some meager evidence that in a few cases
faulty eye co-ordination and visual defects (which can be
corrected by an eye-specialist) may be one factor contributing to excessive number and duration of fixation pauses.
It is well established that the number and duration of fixation pauses is conditioned by the difficulty of the reading
material. The factors contributing to the difficulty are

cared for simultaneously with maturation, both physical and mental.

Apprehension of successive words, or anticipation of meaning, is an important factor in systematic eye-movements. The reader's attitude or mental set during reading as well as familiarity with the context contributes to rapid perception evidenced by few fixation pauses of short duration. Tinker (16) believes there is little real reason "for concluding that the faulty eye-movements cause reading disability, or that training eye-movements improves reading efficiency." He points out that typical procedures for "pacing" eye-movements are not limited to eye-movements alone. When pacing is resorted to, there is usually an emphasis on increasing speed and comprehension which influences mind set or attitude. Another significant factor is that individual instruction usually produces desirable results. In short, direct attempts of such nature are legitimate procedures for increasing reading efficiency regardless of the theoretical considerations of what is actually happening.

The Metron-O-Scope developed by J. Y. Taylor for the American Optical Company is a device intended to aid in the establishment of rhythmical left-to-right reading habits. The possibilities of the machine are many. The apparatus is a box-like affair in which rolls similar to those used in a player piano are inserted. Words, phrases, stories, and arithmetic combinations are printed in each roll. One line at a time can be seen through the aperature of the case containing the roll. In the manual which accompanies the machine the inventor states: "A triple shutter arrangement directs the vision across the line in three rhythmical steps or fixations. That is, words appear in groups of two or three, then disappear. There can be no regression, for the

words once presented, go out of sight." Instruments such
as the Metron-O-Scope are frequently called "pacing" devices. The implication is that by a direct mechanical pacing
of the eye-movements rhythmical and efficient reading
habits will be established. Although the value of such instruments is not questioned, the typical explanation of
what is actually happening needs scientific appraisal. Three

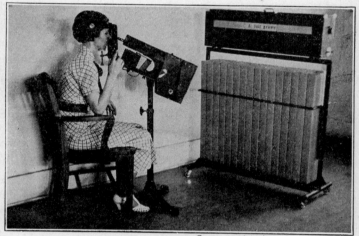

Courtesy, American Optical Company

The Metron-O-Scope and the Ophthalm-O-Graph

situations are created: (1) The individual is given practice
in reading materials printed in large size type. (2) Habits
of rapid perception are established. The reader soon learns
that regressive eye-movements take time and that the initial
perception must be accurate as well as rapid. (3) The work
is well motivated, the goal being to get the meaning of the
phrase during the short exposure period. In certain situations, these three items alone probably are sufficient to bring

about improvement in reading ability which is reflected in more efficient eye-movements. The point is that the eye-movements are indirectly improved. The Metron-O-Scope is an effective device for developing rhythmical reading and rapid perception. It should be a part of the equipment of a reading clinic.

SUMMARY

1. An analysis of eye-movement records shows fixation frequency, regressive frequency, pause duration, and total perception time.

2. The eyes make many fixation pauses or stops per line.

3. Fixation pauses are usually long in duration and eye-movements very rapid; and conversely, one who makes many fixations per line usually exhibits longer fixation pauses.

4. Faulty eye-movements are usually regarded as symptoms rather than causes of poor reading.

5. The Miles Peep-hole method is a practical way for the classroom teacher to estimate the number of fixation pauses per line.

6. The character of the eye-movements varies widely with the attitude of the reader and the type of reading material.

7. Immature reading habits may be detected by measuring eye-movements.

8. For normal children eye-movements improve progressively.

9. Poor readers evidence many fixation pauses of long duration and many regressive movements.

10. Eye-movements of good spellers and good readers tend to be systematic.

11. No visual impression enters consciousness during the period of discontinuous eye-movements. Only under certain conditions is vision possible during movement.

12. There appears to be some evidence for the contention that at least the training incidental to the pacing of eye-movements increases reading efficiency.

13. There is no substantial evidence that training eye-movements develops effective motor habits which in turn directly improve reading ability.

14. Increasing the distance the page is held from the eye also causes an increase in the number of fixation pauses per line.

15. Each individual has a natural reading pace which for the same type of material is consistent from one page to another.

REFERENCES

1. Betts, Emmett A. *Bibliography on the Problems Related to the Analysis, Prevention, and Correction of Reading Difficulties,* Meadville, Pennsylvania: Keystone View Co., 1935.

2. Buswell, G. T. *Fundamental Reading Habits: A Study of Their Development.* Supplementary Educational Monographs, No. 21. Chicago: Department of Education, University of Chicago, 1922.

3. Cobb, Percy W., Moss, Frank K. "The Fixational Pause of the Eyes," *Journal of Experimental Psychology,* IX (October, 1926), 359-67.

4. Eurich, Alvin C. "The Growth of Reading Ability as Measured by Photographic Eye-Movements Records." Unpublished independent study, 1932-34.

5. Eurich, Alvin C. "The Reliability and Validity of Photographic Eye-Movements Records," *Journal of Educational Psychology,* XXIV (February, 1933), 118-22.

6. Ewert, Harry. "Eye-Movements During Reading and Recall," *Journal of General Psychology,* VIII (January, 1933), 65-84.

7. Gates, A. I., and Bennett, C. C. *Reversal Tendencies in Reading: Causes, Diagnosis, Prevention, and Correction,* p. 33, Teachers College, Bureau of Publications, 1933.

8. Huey, Edmund B. *The Psychology and Pedagogy of Reading.* New York: Macmillan Co., 1924.

9. Miles, W. R., and Segel, David. "Clinical Observation of Eye-Movements in the Rating of Reading Ability," *Journal of Educational Psychology,* XX (October, 1929), 520-29.

10. Miles, W. R., and Shen, Eugene. "Photographic Recording of Eye-Movements in Reading of Chinese in Vertical and Horizontal Axes: Methods and Preliminary Results," *Journal of Experimental Psychology,* VIII (October, 1925), 344-62.

11. Robinson, Francis P. "An Aid for Improving Reading Rate," *Journal of Educational Research,* XXVII (February, 1934), 453-55.

12. Robinson, Francis P. *The Rôle of Eye Movements in Reading with an Evaluation of Techniques for Their Improvement,* p. 32. University of Iowa Studies in Education, No. 39 (Iowa City, June, 1933).

13. Tinker, Miles A. "Apparatus for Recording Eye-Movements," *American Journal of Psychology,* XLIII (January, 1931), 115-18.

14. Tinker, Miles A. "Eye Movement Duration, Pause Duration and Reading Time," *Psychological Review,* XXXV (September, 1928), 385-97.

15. Tinker, Miles A. "Photographic Measures of Reading Ability," *Journal of Educational Psychology,* XX (March, 1929), 184-91.

16. Tinker, Miles A. "The Rôle of Eye Movements in Diagnostic and Remedial Reading," *School and Society,* XXXIX (February 3, 1934).

17. Tinker, Miles A. "Use and Limitations of Eye-Movement Measures of Reading," *Psychological Review,* XL (July, 1933), 381-87.

18. Vernon, M. D. *The Experimental Study of Reading,* pp. xv-190. Cambridge University Press, 1931.

CHAPTER VIII
The Work of the Eyes

*To understand the nature of the reading process,
it is necessary to have some acquaintance with the
psychological and physiological phenomena of
vision.*—M. D. Vernon (37)

Preview

A study of the work of the eyes in reading includes at
least four interrelated factors: lighting, visual acuity, sharpness of focus, and eye co-ordination. It is a truism to state
that the mechanical process of reading is normally accomplished by means of the eyes, yet in the past this one factor
has apparently been overlooked. In our professional effort
to rationalize the problems presented by retarded readers
we sometimes have lost our sense of direction in a maze of
theories. As a result, teachers have not been aware of the
need for discriminating between physical and pedagogical
problems; remedial teachers frequently have made the erroneous assumption that every child can learn to read through
well-motivated repetitive drill.

Morgan (31) states: "Many a teacher has tried in vain
to teach some child to read, and has even gone so far as to
consider him feebleminded because he has not progressed,
when the real trouble has been that he has not been able to
see clearly the printed page before him." On the other
hand, there is an equal danger that uncritical teachers may
attempt to excuse poor teaching in the light of this or similar factors. It is the purpose of this chapter to orient the

reader relative to this one factor of vision by indicating the purpose, advantages, and limitations of tests now available for use by the teaching profession. A chapter on the work of the eyes in reading has been included in this book for the following reasons: (1) Good vision is essential to comfort during sustained reading effort. (2) Many investigators have concluded that there is a positive relationship between certain types of visual difficulties and reading deficiencies. (3) Most systems for beginning reading stress the ability to make visual discriminations between word forms. Hence, tests of physical readiness for reading should include an appraisal of visual efficiency.

Sensation

The term "sensation" is usually used to denote an experience aroused from outside the central nervous system. Visual sensation is caused by the sensitivity of the eye to light waves. After sensation there is the interpretative process brought about in the central nervous system. This phase of the problem, therefore, resolves itself into the peripheral (outside the nervous system) and the central (within the central nervous system). How much of a reading disability can be caused by a sensory defect and how much of it is a central problem is still a debatable question. It is logical to assume, however, that the analysis of a reading disability should begin at the most accessible point. Such a statement should appear to be reasonably irrefutable.

If a sensory defect is present, the aid of an eye-specialist should be solicited. The teacher should not attempt to substitute for the doctor. From recent studies we can conclude that there is a greater incidence of visual and ocular difficulties among retarded readers than among good readers.

In any one situation, the percentage of retarded readers who evidence visual disabilities varies with the extent to which other factors contribute to the general difficulty. The writer found 90 per cent of the reading clinic cases to have visual difficulties in one city where there were well-trained teachers, an abundance of reading materials, grouping within the room, and a policy of introducing first-rate entrants to reading on the basis of their general readiness for the activity. In another city where conditions were questionable, only 47 per cent of the retarded readers evidenced visual troubles. Investigators who attempt to determine the extent to which faulty vision contributes to reading deficiency are only wasting their time unless they control the other contributing factors. In the meantime, it should be sufficient to state that visual comfort is the right of all children. On this basis of this assumption, the writer uses the Visual Sensation and Perception Slides of the Betts Ready to Read Tests to check all cases whether or not they are wearing glasses.

Interpretation

Reading is essentially an interpretative process. The central nervous system is the master key to the ultimate goal of reading instruction; namely, rapid rate of comprehension. Perception is the mental awareness of sensation. Faultless sensation must precede accurate perception. Sensation alone gives us no knowledge of what is seen or read. It is the combination and association of the present sensation with past sensations which makes the words and phrases of the printed page take on meaning. Hence, rapid rate of association of ideas involving a rich background of experiences is also an essential factor contributing to efficient reading habits. But it is obvious that the appraisal of interpretative functions must be preceded by the intelligent study and elimination of physical and physiological factors which contribute to faulty sensation.

Visual Efficiency

Formerly visual acuity, or keenness of vision, was considered the only index to the efficiency of the visual apparatus, but today it is viewed as only one aspect of it. The requirements for normal visual efficiency are: (1) The *physical* structure of the refracting mechanism, i. e., eyeball, lens, cornea, etc., must be reasonably free from defects. (2) The *physiological* functioning of the receptor must be normal; that is, the retina must be highly sensitive and the neuro-muscular system must co-ordinate the movements of the eyes so that the images are precisely placed on the two retinas. (3) On the *psychological* level, the interpretative mechanism must be accurate, discriminating, and normally free from associational disturbance.

In 1862 Professor H. Snellen of Utrecht offered a practical and scientific method of determining visual efficiency. Since then the Snellen Letter Chart has become the standard method for checking visual acuity in schools. The Snellen Vision Test is a chart on which are several rows of letters. The letters on each succeeding row from top to bottom are reduced in size, thereby requiring a consecutively greater amount of visual acuity in order to read them. The per cent of visual acuity is determined by the number of rows correctly read.

The Snellen Letter Chart and Lowell's Visual Acuity Tests (a modification of the Snellen Chart) have come into common use because all teachers have been able to give the tests. For illiterates, children, and foreigners, the Seitz Test and the McCallie Test for visual acuity are well known.

Tests of visual acuity, such as the Snellen Letter Chart, are usually given under the following conditions: (1) The subject is told to stand on a line twenty feet from the chart. (2) One eye is covered, without pressure on the eyeball, and the subject is told to read aloud the items in each line, from left to right, until he has read the smallest letters that he can see.

Checking the results of Snellen Test Chart against the Visual Sensation and Perception Tests of the Betts Ready to Read unit, the writer has found that only 5 to 40 per cent (varying with the examiner and the school population) of the children are identified who need the help of an eye-specialist. The chief visual factors contributing to school failures are not identified by the Snellen Charts.

An analysis of the limitations of the Snellen Chart Test for the diagnosis of reading difficulty shows: (1) The test does not appraise the efficiency of the eyes at reading distance (ten to sixteen inches). (2) The test does not appraise the co-ordination of the two eyes. Many individuals have normal visual acuity in each eye, but do not have good two-eyed vision. (3) The test provides not even a crude index to the degree of farsightedness. (4) The test is not critical in detecting astigmatism because an individual can with conscious effort force his eyes to read small enough type to pass the test even though his refractive error is such as to make sustained reading difficult and uncomfortable.

Farris (19) studied visual defects as factors influencing achievement in reading and concluded in part: "The fact that achievement in reading is often affected by muscular eye functions is believed to account for the progress in reading achievement frequently found among those pupils of this study with a low visual acuity rating, and argues in favor of the adoption of a more comprehensive standard than the visual acuity rating in appraising the efficiency of the visual function. The superficial eye tests (with the Snellen charts alone) which are at present being given in many of our public schools are inadequate and should be replaced by more thorough and more complete visual tests."

Even with Professor Snellen's contribution of 1862, teachers have been without a means of checking crucial factors contributing to good vision and school success. The Visual Sensation and Perception slides of the Betts Ready to Read Tests were developed with the co-operation of a group of eye-specialists for the purpose of giving the teacher a means of discriminating between the physical and pedagogical aspects of a learning difficulty. Not all children having difficulties in schoolwork can be said to be characterized by visual disabilities; hence, there is a need for a quick and simple analysis of this one phase of the problem. A complete eye examination of all school children would be advisable, but such a program would be costly in time and money. Even if a program were carried out, probably only 20 to 25 per cent of those examined would need correction. Hence 70 to 80 per cent of this effort would be wasted. The Betts Ready to Read Tests enable the teacher or school nurse to identify those needing the examination.

Reading Distance

Notson's (32) study of the distances the book is held from the eye by individuals of various age levels is interesting and should be studied further. His findings are summarized in the table on the following page.

DISTANCES THE BOOK IS HELD AT VARIOUS AGE LEVELS

Grade	Distance in inches
I	8.2
II	9.0
III	9.9
IV	10.4
V	11.0
VI	11.7
VII	12.2
VIII	13.0
University students	13.8

The distance the book is held from the eye is modified by the size of type, sensitivity of retina, binocular co-ordination, and many other factors. Repeatedly telling a child to hold his book at a greater distance and a better angle will not entirely correct the situation. Instead, materials with large size type which meet his level of physiological readiness to read should be provided. Notson's data are, therefore, significant from the standpoint of what the child is ready visually to read.

Sharpness of Image

At a distance of twenty feet and beyond, the visual axes of the eye are normally nearly parallel. When attention is directed to an object closer than twenty feet, the eyes automatically converge (turn in so that the image will fall on corresponding points of the retina of each eye) and accommodate (adjust the lens of the eye to keep a sharply focused image on the retina). This total process is called accommodative-convergence. With the exception of a pathological, or diseased, condition of the eye, and refractive error (blurring of the vision caused by improper focus) the visual disabilities contributing to low-reading achievement will usually be the result of faulty accommodation, or convergence. The mechanisms controlling accommodation and convergence usually are well co-ordinated. Normally, as a subject adjusts the focus of his eyes on the page of a book, both eyes automatically turn and point precisely to the word or letter of regard. The two functions of precise focus and pointing are normally conditioned upon each other. Often faulty habits develop, disturbing this finely co-ordinated relationship. The eyes either converge too much or too little as the focus is adjusted correctly, hence they point to different parts of the word thereby causing confusion, or they point precisely and fail to focus sharply. Frequently, the vision is normal when measured with the subject looking at an object at a distance of twenty feet or more, but is found to be deficient in some important respects when measured while the subject is viewing a target at the normal reading distance. The latter situation requires accommodation and convergence.

1. **Farsightedness.** The eyeball of a normal six-year-old child, like other parts of his anatomy, is not fully grown and is too short from cornea to retina. This condition is called farsightedness. As a result, the light rays do not come to a proper focus upon the retina. In near vision (when an object is viewed at a distance of less than twenty feet) the lens in the normal eye, according to accepted theories, is bulged or made convex in order to bring the image into a clear focus. An abnormally farsighted individual places the eye under an extra strain at the reading

distance (ten to sixteen inches). This condition can be corrected by means of a proper lens which decreases the amount of bulging the lens must do in order to focus clearly. All too frequently the child having difficulty with reading will be pronounced normal by the health department because he appears to have better than normal vision. Recent studies show that such children are probably farsighted and should not be required to read until they have "grown out of it" or have had the condition corrected with glasses. If reading is to be mastered without this help, it should be done from the blackboard, charts, or sight-saving materials. To require such a child to read type smaller than the large twenty-four point found in sight-saving books is to do irreparable harm, physically and emotionally.

In a recent survey (7) of 183 first-grade entrants, the writer found eighty to be farsighted in both eyes, one in the right eye, and five in the left eye. This high percentage of farsighted individuals is not alarming. Zoethout (40:9) comments: "It will be recalled that nearly all children are born with slightly hyperopic (farsighted) eyes."

The prevalence of farsightedness among children is widely recognized by doctors. In a recent study (33) of 2,625 unselected children between the ages of one and fifteen years, a great preponderance of farsightedness was reported. Of the children between one and two years of age, 82 per cent were found to be farsighted, 75 per cent at seven and eight years, and 53 per cent at fourteen to fifteen years. Very few, if any, of these cases would have been identified by means of the Snellen Chart Test.

2. **Nearsightedness.** A short eyeball causes farsightedness and a long eyeball causes nearsightedness. Occasionally the eyeball continues to lengthen after the normal

length has been attained, resulting in nearsightedness. All such cases should be in the hands of a competent eye-specialist. If the condition is progressive, blindness may result. Proper lenses are prescribed for correction. Many nearsighted people become known as "book worms" because they are not able to participate in activities requiring good distance vision. Few nearsighted cases, excluding candidates for sight-saving classes, have been brought to the writer's reading clinic. In the writer's study of 183 first-grade entrants, less than 3 per cent were found to be near-sighted. Zoethout (40:90) again remarks: "The causes of myopia are two-fold: a weakness of the tunics (membranes which envelop the organs) of the eye, and excessive near work. That the last is an important factor is seen from the fact that savages are seldom myopic, and that the prevalence of myopia amongst civilized people is in some proportion to the amount of near work. In the lower-school grades, few children are myopic; more are found in the higher grades, and in high schools and colleges it is very common. How near work tends to cause myopia is not clear."

In England, a recent study (33) of 2,625 children between the ages of one and fifteen years, revealed from 2 to 10 per cent free from refractive errors, depending on the age. Myopia (nearsightedness) was rare in children under five years but was found to increase from 2 to 5.5 per cent between the eighth and fifteenth year. Farsightedness decreased with the advance in age.

3. Lack of uniform clearness of image. An unequal curvature of the cornea (transparent portion of the outer covering of the eyeball), or an unequal curvature of the lens creates an *astigmatic* condition. Usually accommodation (adjustment of the lens of the eye) cannot overcome the blurring which results from astigmatism. The only satisfactory correction is the wearing of proper glasses.

The constant effort put forth by the eye in attempting to adjust the lens to an astigmatic condition leads, in severe cases, to ocular fatigue and consequent discomfort and loss of efficiency. Many severe cases of reading disability brought to the writer's attention have been traced to astigmatism as one possible contributing cause.

In the writer's study of 183 first-grade entrants, sixty-seven had astigmatism in both eyes, twenty-five in the right eye, and twelve in the left eye. Zoethout (40:99) comments: "The prevalence of astigmatism may be gathered from the fact that Nordenson on examining 425 people, from seven to twenty years of age, found only forty-two (or 9 per cent) free from this trouble. Of the 363 cases of astigmatism, 85 per cent had the greatest curvature in the vertical, 1.5 per cent in the horizontal, and 13.4 per cent in an oblique meridian. The predominance of the greater curvature in the vertical meridian has been attributed to the flattening of the cornea by the pressure of the eyelids. While in youth the astigmatism is more often with-the-rule (in vertical meridian), in advanced life that against-the-rule (greater curvature in the horizontal direction) is frequently encountered."

Eye Co-ordination

The mechanics of the reading porcess are normally achieved by the co-ordinate action of the two eyes. An individual is said to have good binocular (two-eyed) vision when he can co-ordinate the movements of the two eyes for the seeing of fine detail. The eyes may adequately perform when directed toward a target twenty feet or beyond and fail to meet the requirements for seeing at reading distance (ten to sixteen inches). If we were a one-eyed race, our reading difficulties from the point of vision would probably be fewer. A person using only one eye which has normal visual acuity usually has fewer visual troubles but cannot enjoy true depth perception. An individual with normal visual acuity in both eyes presents a different problem; not only must the dominant eye fix on a word or phrase, but its companion also must fix on the same target simultaneously and with as much precision and speed. In addition to this, he must fuse (unify or combine) the right- and left-eye images into one for normal interpretation. Some reading problems appear to be traceable to a lack of co-ordination between the two eyes and to the probable failure to combine the right-eye and left-eye images for correct interpretation.

The process of blending or unifying the image received by each eye in order to secure single binocular vision is called visual fusion. Normal reading or seeing of fine detail is accomplished by one small part of the retina called the *macula,* the most highly sensitive area of the retina. Both the right and left eyes have macular areas. In order to fuse two images into one, it is necessary for them to fall upon corresponding parts of the retina of each eye; that is both eyes must be pointed precisely toward the object of regard. This is achieved by the desire to fuse and the subsequent reflex action of convergence and accommodation which normally are conditioned upon each other.

Using the fusion slides of the Betts Ready to Read Tests (7), the writer tested 194 first-grade entrants. Thirteen per cent could not fuse the small targets at the distance equivalent of forty inches; 13.7 per cent of the pupils could not co-ordinate their eyes for fusion of the targets at reading distance. Although the co-ordinated action of the two eyes is only one mechanical factor contributing to efficient and rapid reading, fusion difficulties should be corrected by eye-specialists as a part of any prevention and correction. school health program.

Man is probably one of the few animals with the degree of binocular co-ordination and with the necessary eye structure which permits depth perception (stereopsis). Without binocular co-ordination of a high degree, true depth perception is not possible. The value of two-eyed vision for tri-dimensional perception is easily demonstrated by the attempts of a person to thread a needle with one eye closed. Depth perception is brought about by the disparity, or unlikeness, of the image received by each eye viewing the object from different angles. A test of depth perception, therefore, would be a power test or a measure of the. co-ordination level of the two eyes. Although depth perception per se is not required for reading on the usual flat surface, the degree of visual fusion possessed by individuals with the two-eyed vision required to pass this test appears to contribute to the mechanics of rapid reading habits.

Dr. Wells (39) believes that "When the facts are known, it is quite possible that visual tests will not stop with measuring the acuity of each eye and testing the color sense, but that a certain standard of stereopsis (depth perception) will be required." Doctors, the country over, are exhibiting increased interest in checking this important aspect of vision. It is not enough to check only the visual efficiency of each eye; instead, the extent to which two-eyed vision is comfortable should be carefully appraised. Using the

co-ordination level (stereopsis) slides of the Betts Ready to
Read Tests, the writer found only 60 per cent of the first-
grade entrants to possess the degree of eye co-ordination
necessary to pass the test. As stated in Chapter III, Dr.
Wells believes that the power of fusion is largely a product
of maturation. All such evidence leads the writer to suspect
that a significant percentage of six-year-old children should
not be reading the small print found in present first-grade
readers. The reading of large size type with proper spacing
between the words and the lines is good eye-training exercise. To force a child to read small size type is to set up
a mechanical obstacle to the formation of efficient eye
habits.

Size and Shape of Ocular Images

The first research to determine that the size and shape of
the image of one eye differs from that of the other eye
was initiated at Dartmouth Medical School in 1927. Reports of Ames, Ogle, Gliddon, Carlston, and Madigan (1, 2,
3, 14) bearing on this problem have appeared largely in the
publications of the American Medical Association and the
Optometrical Journal. In the past, scientists have been
chiefly concerned with refractive errors (nearsightedness,
farsightedness, and astigmatism) and eye co-ordination.
The third factor now introduced is that of the relative size
and shape of the ocular images of the two eyes.

The following conclusions of the investigators may have
some bearing on the problem of reading difficulties: (1)
Any abnormal difference between the size and shape of the
ocular images in a horizontal direction deranges the apparent position of objects in the visual field. All abnormal
differences in the ocular images constantly make themselves

known through disturbances in visual perceptions. (2) Correction of size differences apparently brought complete relief in about 20 per cent of such cases, partial relief in 60 per cent of the cases, and no relief in 20 per cent.

In 1932, an instrument for measuring differences of size and shape of ocular images (aniseikonia) was designed for the Department of Educational Psychology of the Graduate School at Harvard University. Recently, Dearborn and Comfort (10) made a report, without establishing definite conclusions, of the study of 164 cases. Their investigation is pertinent because 117 of the cases had specific learning disabilities, 78 per cent of whom had a significant amount of size differences. They found, as investigators on other phases of reading disabilities have concluded, that "It is not so much the degree of the defect, as it is the degree of counterpoise of the individual in compensating for the defect, that determines the amount of distress that is caused."

Eye-Muscle Balance

The twelve extrinsic muscles of the eyes, by highly co-ordinated action, rotate the eyeballs and turn the eyes inward or outward. With normal muscle balance, the visual axes of the eyes are parallel or nearly so for distance seeing. Some eyes have a *tendency* to deviate outward, others to deviate inward. The deviation of the eyes inward or outward is called lateral eye-muscle imbalance. The condition in which one of the eyes deviates upward is called vertical imbalance. Such conditions, with exception of strabismus (crossed eyes), are not observable by the unaided eye. Using the lateral imbalance and vertical imbalance slides of the Betts Ready to Read Tests, the writer found among first-grade entrants 11 per cent lateral imbalance and only 2 per cent vertical imbalance. These conditions can be corrected by eye-specialists. In some instances fusion, or eye-training exercises prescribed by the eye-specialist are sufficient for correction; in other cases glasses are needed. Frequently, both exercises and glasses are prescribed.

The amount of eye-muscle imbalance a subject can overcome is an individual matter. Many cases can compensate, through the desire for binocular (two-eyed) vision, for high degrees of imbalance; others experience double vision or suspend the vision in one eye. Obviously, faulty fusion of the images received by each eye would be a significant obstacle to rapid rate of comprehension during the reading process. The reader is referred to the manual, contained in the Appendix of this book, for an extended discussion of the relative value of eye-muscle imbalance tests for the analysis of reading difficulties.

Betts Ready to Read Tests

The complete battery of Betts Ready to Read Tests consists of Visual Readiness Tests, Auditory Readiness Tests, Visual Sensation and Perception Tests, and Oculomotor and Perception Tests. The original battery was made available in 1934. In the 1936 revised edition, certain changes were made in order to insure greater accuracy of response and ease of administration and interpretation. The specialized vocabulary used in the 1934 edition has been discontinued wherever possible. The research data are being reported in magazine articles, and, therefore, are not included in this teacher's book.

The ten Visual Sensation and Perception Slides of the Betts Ready to Read Tests were constructed for use by teachers, doctors, nurses, and clinicians. By following the simple directions in the manual (see Appendix), the teacher can administer the tests in six to twelve minutes. A knowledge of optics is not required to give the tests. Most cases needing the help of an eye-specialist can be identified in one or two minutes, because the first test slide failed provides sufficient evidence of such need. Pre-first grade children require more time to take the tests. As a result of the administration of these tests, children needing the attention of an eye-specialist will be identified.

Leading doctors and educators strongly urge the keeping of a cumulative health record for each child. Doctors are usually willing to send a report of their findings so that they may be filed in the individual pupil folder. If health examinations are to be functional rather than routine and mechanical, this procedure is essential.

The Keystone Ophthalmic Telebinocular is designed for binocular tests of visual functions. With this instrument and the accompanying slides the vision of each eye can be studied while both eyes function simultaneously. These simple tests provide practically the only rational means of measuring the binocular relationship.

The simple construction of this instrument separates the fields of vision and permits the left eye to see only its half of the slide and the right eye to see only its half. Through the process called "fusion" the left-eye and the right-eye images are combined into one. The distance between the eyes of the subject (i. e., the P. D., or inter-pupillary distance) is compensated for by the optical construction of the instrument. This construction of the telebinocular provides an artificial set-up whereby measurements can be made at reading distance equivalents ranging from twelve inches

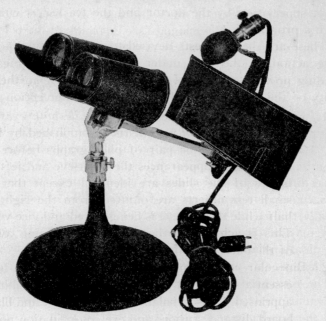

The Keystone Ophthalmic Telebinocular

to infinite (ordinarily infinity is considered twenty feet or beyond). The placing of the slide holder at the distance equivalent marks on the top of the shaft accomplishes this result.

All tests of Visual Sensation and Perception are mounted on standard Keystone Slides and used in the Keystone Ophthalmic Telebinocular. The need for these particular tests was determined by a careful examination of doctors' reports of cases referred to them by the writer's clinic. In all cases where visual handicaps have existed, the doctors have been most co-operative with the school and the home. The constant supervision by the doctor and the teacher is vital to such a program.

These are the first tests devised to appraise the co-ordinate action of the eyes under conditions simulating the reading process. The chief factors contributing to the validity of the tests of Visual Sensation and Perception are:

1. Each eye is tested independently *while both eyes are seeing as habitually.* This is accomplished by having a stereoscopic pair of photographs before the eyes. To all appearances the right-eye and left-eye halves of the slides are identical except that the small test objects are omitted from the right-eye half while the left eye is being tested and vice versa. This is achieved without the subject being aware of the phenomenon.

2. Binocular co-ordination which is suspected as being essential to rapid and efficient reading habits is appraised. Muscle balance, book distance and blackboard distance fusion, and eye co-ordination power are tested.

3. Two-eyed visual efficiency as well as the acuity of each eye is tested.

The basic set of Visual Sensation and Perception Slides included in the Betts Ready to Read battery consists of tests for the following functions:

Test 1 (Slide DB-10) Introductory slide (used to interest children)

Test 2 (Slide DB-4) Distance Fusion (far-point macular fusion)

Test 3a (Slide DB-1) Two-eyed visual efficiency (visual acuity)

Test 3b (Slide DB-2) Left-eye visual efficiency (visual acuity)

Test 3c (Slide DB-3) Right-eye visual efficiency (visual acuity)

Test 4 (Slide DB-8) Vertical imbalance

Test 5 (Slide DB-6) Eye co-ordination level (stereopsis)

Test 6 (Slide DB-9) Lateral imbalance

Test 7 (Slide DB-5) Reading distance fusion

Test 8 (Slide DB-7) Sharpness of image (ametropia)

The question has arisen frequently regarding who shall administer the tests. The answer is that the tests of Visual Sensation and Perception are being used successfully by teachers, nurses, doctors, and psychologists. Who shall be responsible for the administration of the tests should be decided in terms of the local policies of the board of education. In no case should a teacher attempt to make scientific interpretations of the various test results. This is the work of an eye-specialist. The tests were developed for the purpose of co-ordinating the health and education departments of a school system. Doctors and nurses can administer the Visual Sensation and Perception Tests, but health specialists usually cannot interpret the Oculomotor and Perception Slides. If strict departmentalization is desired, the health department should administer the Visual Sensation and Perception Tests and the teacher or psychologist should give the Oculomotor and Perception Tests, the Betts Visual Readiness Test, and Auditory Readiness Tests. In any event, the health department should do the follow-up work on the visual tests. If there is no health department, some member of the education staff should assume the responsibility.

The ten slides for testing the Oculomotor and Perception Habits of the Betts Ready to Read Tests are used also in the Keystone Ophthalmic Telebinocular. The words are graded carefully for use in the first three grades. The slides are of value, however, on higher grade levels, because the common words are often a main source of difficulty. The chief uses of the Oculomotor and Perception tests are:

1. To study the perception habits or word recognition skills.

2. To study movements of both eyes under controlled reading conditions.

3. To study the efficiency of perception of each eye independently while both eyes are seeing as habitually.

4. To determine the specific corrective procedures for this one phase of the problem.

5. To detect the presence of alternating vision or ignoring of the vision in one eye in a situation which requires the use of two eyes.

6. To provide further means for determining whether or not the tendency toward reversals and confusion of words is a central disturbance or a matter of faulty oculomotor control, both of which are amenable to treatment.

Dr. Gray (23) reported a study of reading efficiency of each eye made by Dr. Farwell of the National College of Education, Evanston, Illinois. In one case Dr. Farwell found the left eye read 16 per cent more content in a given time than the right eye, and 9.3 per cent more than both eyes; the left eye read with 27.7 per cent fewer errors than both eyes. Apparently the two eyes of the case studied had

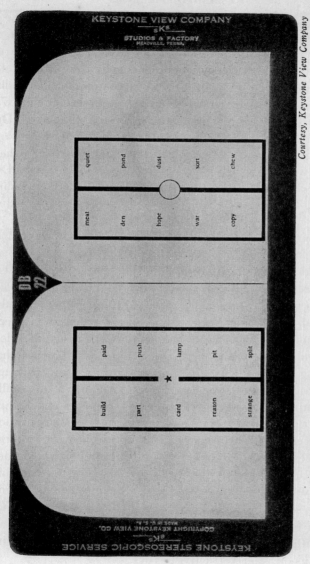

Courtesy, Keystone View Company

This is a sample of the Betts Oculomotor and Perception Tests

not learned to function together to maximum advantage. Such studies as this tend to show the need for more careful appraisal of the efficiency of the two eyes for reading. In Dr. Fendrick's study (20) of children taught by the look-and-say method, 50 per cent of the poor readers and 75 per cent of the good readers had normal vision. Dr. Thomas H. Eames (16, 17, 18) has found that significant differences do exist between good and poor readers when certain two-eyed visual efficiency factors are measured. Dr. C. A. Selzer (34) concluded that there is a relationship between lateral muscle imbalance and certain reading disabilities.

The writer, using the Betts Ready to Read Tests, has found a number of cases who improved their reading, as measured by standardized tests, when certain focusing errors were corrected and good two-eyed vision was established. On higher-grade levels the difference between the good and poor readers, as judged by the criterion of speed and comprehension when tested with the stereoscopic slides, appear to be less pronounced. It is the writer's belief that a reading test requiring one or two hours of concentrated effort would be influenced by ocular fatigue which usually accompanies uncomfortable vision. If comfort and endurance in reading are to be considered, the Visual Sensation and Perception Tests are much more critical in determining differences between good and poor readers on higher-grade levels. But certainly, few feel that one possible reading disability correlate can be used to account for all reading difficulties. Some individuals appear to evidence a higher degree of counterpoise for overcoming eye-muscle imbalance, differences in size and shape of ocular images, faulty visual fusion, and refractive errors.

The earliest and most intensive research in the field of reading had to do with eye-movements. Few books on reading methodology or reading disabilities fail to include chapters on the work of the eyes in reading. Many significant recent investigations in reading, conducted in the fields of optometry, physiological optics, phychology, and education have been related to specific factors in seeing with the two eyes.

Lighting

Lighting is one of the most important external factors in the hygiene of reading. The work of the eyes in reading cannot be fully appraised until the hygienic conditions under which they work are studied. Luckiesh and Moss (28:2) illustrate the advances made by the Illuminating Engineering Society in recommending foot candles of light in the following table:

	1915	1918	1921	1928
Fine manufacturing..	3.5–6	4–8	10–20	12–20
Office or clerical.....		4–8	5–10	8–10
Office, close work....				10–15

Luckiesh and Moss (27) devised an ingenious experiment whereby they were able to measure the muscular tension developed during reading under three different intensities of light (1, 10, and 100 foot candles). They concluded that the amount of nervous muscular tension decreased significantly as the level of illumination was increased. In a recent publication (28) they recommend ten to twenty foot candles for ordinary reading tasks.

Tinker (35 : 670) finds: "The varying effects of intensity increase at different levels of brightness is revealed by a 67.7 per cent increase in acuity from one-tenth to one foot candle, the 43.6 per cent increase from one to five foot candles and the mere 8.2 per cent increase from five to twenty foot candles." He concludes (35 : 672) "intensities considered most comfortable for continuous reading were found to be about six foot candles for large type and about thirteen for medium size type." Ferree and Rand (22 : 9) found that "The room well-lighted by daylight gives the best results for the eye that have as yet been obtained, and we will not go far from wrong in taking it as our pattern for artificial lighting with regard to intensity as well as for color and composition of light and the factors which come under the head of distribution." But they insist that "caution must be urged against the increase of intensity through the introduction of high brilliancies into the field of view or glare on the working surface."

All teachers should be aware of such research findings because it has been the writer's experience that many children in the classrooms are working under one to four foot candles of light. Although a large share of the blame may not be within her control, the teacher should make full use of the control she does have over the situation. Desks should be free from a high gloss which increases glare, and the desks and seats should be adjusted for good posture. Attention should be directed frequently to the position of the curtains, which should be adjusted so that all parts of the room receive a maximum of light without the glare of direct sunlight.

Intensity, direction, quality, diffusion, and distribution of light are the chief factors which have been subjected to scientific study. Luckiesh and Moss (28:20) have found that an increase in quantity of light up to at least twenty foot candles increases speed of vision, speed of reading, visual acuity, and accuracy of vision. Man's eyes were evolved for distance seeing in thousands of foot candles of light (daylight). Heretofore, civilization has demanded much near work under a few foot candles of light with greater eye strain as the result. A minimization of ocular fatigue can be achieved, in part, by better lighting. Ferree and Rand (21:16) point to poor lighting as a contributary cause to nearsightedness, nervous exhaustion, and lowered efficiency.

SUMMARY

1. Teachers should be thoroughly familiar with the health aspects of reading.

2. Teachers should have some understanding of the concept of two-eyed vision.

3. Sensory defects require the attention of eye-specialists.

4. A teacher should have access to tests which will enable her to discriminate between pedagogical and health problems.

5. There is a greater incidence of visual defects among poor readers than among good readers.

6. Accurate perception cannot be preceded by faulty sensation.

7. The Snellen Chart Test and other similar tests are not adequate for testing the visual efficiency of children with learning disabilities.

8. Refractive errors (farsightedness, nearsightedness, and astigmatism), visual acuity, and binocular co-ordina-

tion, and differences in size and shape of ocular images are important factors in seeing.

9. Fifteen to twenty-five foot candles of light, with the least possible amount of glare, are minimum lighting standards for close work by children.

REFERENCES

1. Ames, A., Ogle, K., Gliddon, G. H. "Size and Shape of Ocular Images, Methods of Determination and Physiologic Significance," *Archives of Ophthalmology,* VII (April, 1932), 576-97.

2. Ames, A., Ogle, K. N., Gliddon, G. H. *The Importance of the Relative Size and Shape of Ocular Images in Vision.* Boston, Massachusetts: Annals of the Distinguished Service Foundation of Optometry, 1932.

3. Ames, A., and Ogle, Kenneth H. "Size and Shape of Ocular Images, III Visual Sensitivity to Differences in the Relative Size of the Ocular Images of the Two Eyes," *Archives of Ophthalmology,* VII (June, 1932), 904-24.

4. Atkinson, Thomas G. *Ocular Muscles and Fusion.* Chicago: Professional Press, Inc., 1933.

5. Betts, Emmett A. *Bibliography on the Problems Related to the Analysis, Prevention, and Correction of Reading Difficulties.* Meadville, Pennsylvania: Keystone View Company, 1935.

6. Betts, Emmett A. "Is Reading Related to Growth?" *Progressive Education,* XI (December, 1934).

7. Betts, Emmett A. "A Physiological Approach to the Analysis of Reading Disabilities," *Educational Research Bulletin* (Ohio State University), XIII (September, and October, 1934).

8. Betts, Emmett A. "Prevention and Correction of Reading Disabilities," *Elementary English Review,* XII (February, 1935), 25-32.

9. Betts, Emmett A. "Reading Disability Correlates," *Education,* LVI (September, 1935), 18-24.

10. Betts, Emmett A. "Reading Disabilities and Their Correction: National Conference on Research in Elementary English," *Elementary English Review,* XII (March, April, May, June, 1935), 69-73, 106-10, 131-41, 157-65.

11. Betts, Emmett A. "Teacher Analysis of Reading Disabilities," *Elementary English Review,* XI (April, 1934), 99-102.

12. Betts, Emmett A. *A Manual of Directions for Betts Ready to Read Tests.* Meadville, Pennsylvania: Keystone View Company, 1934.

13. Betts, E. A. Everett, Mabel, and Rodewald, Frances. "Remedial Reading Based on First-Teaching, *Journal of Exceptional Children* (February, 1936).

14. Carleton, Elmer H., and Madigan, Leo. F. "Size and Shape of Ocular Images, II Clinical Significance," *Archives of Ophthalmology,* VII (May, 1932), 720-38.

15. Eames, T. H. "Improvement in Reading Following the Correction of Eye Defects of Non-Readers," *American Journal of Ophthalmology,* XVII (April, 1934), 324-25.

16. Eames, T. H. "Physiologic Exophoria in Relation to Age," *Archives of Ophthalmology,* IX (January, 1934).

17. Eames, T. H. "Low Fusion Convergence as a Factor in Reading Disability," *American Journal of Ophthalmology,* XVII (August, 1934).

18. Eames, T. H., and Peabody, Robert Winthrop. "A Non-Reader Reads," *Journal of Educational Research,* XXVIII (February, 1935), 450-55.

19. Farris, L. P. "Visual Defects as Factors Influencing Achievement in Reading," *Junior High School Clearing House,* IX (December, 1934), 226-28.

20. Fendrick, Paul. "A Study of the Visual Characteristics of Poor Readers," Doctor's thesis, Teachers College, Columbia University, 1935.

21. Ferree, C. E., and Rand, Gertrude. "Lighting and the Hygiene of the Eye," *Archives of Ophthalmology,* II (July, 1929), 1-26.

22. Ferree, C. E., and Rand, Gertrude. "Size of Objects in Relation to their Visibility and to the Rating of Vision," *Archives of Opthalmology,* IV (July, 1930), 37-72.

23. Gray, William S. "Problems of Reading Disabilities Requiring Scientific Study," *Elementary English Review,* XII (April, 1935), 96-100.

24. Guibor, George P. (M.D.) "Some Possibilities of Orthoptic Training," *Archives of Ophthalmology,* II (March, 1934).

25. Kempf, Grover, Jarinen, Bernard, and Collins, Selwyn. *A Special Study of the Vision of School Children,* Reprint No. 1235 from the Public Health Reports, United States Health Service. Washington: Government Printing Office, 1929.

26. Luckiesh, M., and Moss, Frank. "A Correlation between Illumination Intensity and Nervous Muscular Tension Resulting from Visual Effort," *Journal of Experimental Psychology,* XVI (1933), 540.

27. Luckiesh, M., and Moss, Frank. *Lighting Plus Vision Equals Seeing.* Lighting Research Laboratory. Cleveland, Ohio: General Electric Company, 1930.

28. Luckiesh, M., and Moss, Frank. *The New Science of Lighting.* Lighting Research Laboratory, Nela Park, Cleveland, Ohio, 1934.

29. Luckiesh, M., and Moss, Frank. *The New Science of Seeing,* Lighting Research Laboratory, Nela Park, Cleveland, Ohio, 1929.

30. Luckiesh, M., and Moss, Frank. "Size of Pupil as a Possible Index of Ocular Fatigue," *American Journal of Ophthalmology,* XVI (1933), 393.

31. Morgan, John J. B. "Disorders of Sensation," *The Psychology of Abnormal People,* chap. ii. New York: Longmans, Green and Company, 1928.

32. Notson, E. B. "Reading Distance and Some of Its Implications," *School and Society,* XXV (March 19, 1927), 353-54.

33. *Report of Committee of Inquiry into Problems Connected with Defective Vision in School Children.* London, England: His Majesty's Stationary Office, 1931.

34. Selzer, Charles A. *Lateral Dominance and Visual Fusion,* Harvard Monographs in Education, No. 12 (Harvard University Press, 1933).

35. Tinker, Miles A. "Illumination and the Hygiene of Reading," *Journal of Educational Psychology,* XXV (1934), 669-80.

36. Verhoeff, F. H. "A New Theory of Binocular Vision," *Archives of Opthalmology,* XIII (February, 1935), 151-75.

37. Vernon, M. D. *The Experimental Study of Reading.* New York: Cambridge University Press, 1931.

38. Wallin, J. E. Wallace. "Keenness of Sensibility," *Clinical and Abnormal Psychology,* chap. xi. Boston: Houghton, Mifflin Co., 1927.

39. Wells, David W. (M.D.) *The Stereoscope in Ophthalmology.* Boston: E. F. Mahady Company, 1928.

40. Zoethout, W. D. *Psychological Optics.* Chicago: The Professional Press, 1927.

CHAPTER IX

The Mechanics of Reading Materials

If we assume for the moment that young children read smaller type as rapidly and as accurately as they read larger type, it remains to prove that the use of smaller type does not result in more eyestrain or fatigue in reading.—W. S. Gray (9:199)

Preview

The typography and mechanical makeup of reading materials are being viewed with increasing interest by the teaching profession and by the book publishers. During the last ten years publishers have showed their interest by subsidizing educational-research projects in this field. Although there is at present little conclusive evidence to guide them, publishers have succeeded in developing reading materials which are probably more nearly hygienically correct and certainly more attractive than formerly.

Teachers have been made aware of the need for materials which minimize optic fatigue and decrease perception time. The typographical standards of materials for disabled readers have not been sufficiently studied, but it is the writer's opinion that corrective materials should be printed in a large size type with suitable leading between the lines and spacing between words. It appears reasonable to assume that every mechanical obstacle should be reduced to a minimum. However, many cases which encounter reversal or other perception difficulties when reading ordinary print will also experience similar trouble with the larger sized type.

Standards relating to the type page involve size of type, legibility, length of line, margins, indentions, and length and proportion of page. In addition to these, the mechanics and content of the illustrations are especially significant for reading materials in the primary grades.

Type Face and Legibility

Indexes to the ease of seeing of words are obtained by measures of speed and accuracy of reading and the distance from the eyes that letters and words can be read accurately. The physiological cost to the reader has not been experimentally controlled. Patterson and Tinker (24) found that type faces in common use are equally legible.

Investigators indicate that the following mechanical factors appear to be significant to legibility of isolated letter forms: (a) size of letter form; (b) simplicity of outline; (c) thickness of the vertical lines of the letter; (d) area of white space within the letter; (e) position of the letter in the word; (f) shape, size, and general legibility of adjacent letters; (g) color contrast or brightness difference between print and paper; (h) distinguishing features of the upper portions of the letters; (i) distance between lines; (j) number of letters per inch; (k) angle at which the book is held.

Several investigators have studied the relative legibility of letters and figures. The letters a, t, i, z, o, e, s, and c have been found to be least legible. It is interesting to note that four of these letters are vowels. Such studies probably do not offer valid evidence to account for very many of the errors made by disabled readers in contextual reading where the letters are not read in isolation. As noted above, the mechanical factors contributing to legibility are interrelated and many. Furthermore, most disabled readers exhibit the same confusion tendencies when the materials offer a possible minimum of typographical difficulty. However, such data are significant in that they may account for confusion of individual letters.

The matter of legibility has other educational implications for the primary teacher. Turner (26) and others have shown that manuscript writing has a significant margin of superiority over cursive writing from the point of view of quality, speed, and legibility. The writer advocates the use of materials prepared in manuscript form for both retarded readers and primary children. The use of manuscript writing removes one more mechanical factor from reading and writing situations.

Size of Type

Other things being equal, size of type is an important factor in determining legibility. As the size of type decreases, fatigue increases and the relative legibility is lowered.

The printer's unit of measurement is the "point," which is approximately one seventy-second of an inch. Type is measured by the vertical size or height of the metal on which the type face is cast. Hence, twenty-four point type means that the capital letters are twenty-four seventy-seconds of an inch high. This system of measurement came into general use about 1878. Previously, each type size was known by a distinguishing name. But the sizes to which these names referred lacked uniformity among different type founders, and this confusion led to the adoption of the point system.

For the most part, the results of investigations in the size of type are confusing in their details. No one investigator has successfully controlled the multitude of variables which characterize the situation. Chief among these variables are optic fatigue, speed of seeing, perception time, leading, spacing, length of line, and previous training in the reading of materials printed according to traditional typographical specifications.

Blackhurst (2) concluded, in terms of rate and accuracy, that eighteen-point type is the smallest size that should be read in the first four grades. Twenty-four point type was found to be most adequate for first-grade materials and to present no inherent difficulties in the second grade.

In a later investigation Buckingham (4) studied the cost and readability of Monotype No. 8 type in twelve, fourteen, and eighteen point and Venetian in twenty-four point type. On the basis of speed, comprehension, and cost, he found, for first-grade children, twelve-point type to be the most adequate, *with very little difference among the other three sizes*. The data for second-grade children led the investigator to similar conclusions.

Tinker (14: 101) summarized the limitations of Buckingham's investigations as follows: "Buckingham's results are of no value either to the printer or to the educator for the following reasons: (1) the selections employed were not satisfactorily equated for difficulty according to the sequence in which they were to be read; (2) no account was taken of sampling errors which are apt to be large in short samples of reading performance; and (3) no measure of dispersion of scores or significance of differences between averages is given. Considering both the uncontrolled nature of the experiment and the method of presenting results one cannot be sure that even the largest differences obtained are significant. Indeed, it is questionable to assume that variations in typographical arrangement within rather wide limits produces constant differences in reading performance at any age level at which reading habits have not become stable."

In 1896, Griffing and Franz found that fatigue increases rapidly as the size of type decreases. In addition, their experiments showed that the legibility of the large size type was less controlled by illumination intensity.

The writer has found that some retarded readers can read material printed in twenty-four point type twenty words per minute faster than they can read the same material printed in fourteen-point type. Until further evidence is presented, it is probably hygienically correct to insist on larger size type in primary-reading materials. Using stereoscopic slides the writer has found that some children can fuse twenty-four point targets when they fail on smaller ones. If the factor of fatigue were controlled, there would probably be a preponderance of evidence in favor of twenty-four point type for first-grade readers. The question has probably been one of expense of publication rather than of hygiene for the learner. This factor of size of type is now being studied by the writer using a physiological approach to the problem. As yet, not even tentative conclusions are available.

Approximately 96 per cent of the reading time is spent on fixation pauses. If an increase in reading rate is desired, the gain must be made largely by decreasing perception time. A part of this gain can be achieved by drill on word-recognition skills, and the like; the remainder of the gain can be made by providing materials which offer a minimum of mechanical difficulties. Since a substantial percentage of retarded readers have visual difficulties, it is reasonable to assume that many of them can profit from reading materials printed in type large enough so that there will be little reason to question its adequacy. In addition, there is an increasing amount of evidence to the effect that the average six-year-old child may be visually too immature for eighteen point and sixteen point type. The use of materials printed in twenty-four, or even thirty-two point type can be justified from another point of view; namely, the effect on eye-movements. During the first few grades the organization of eye-movements for reading purposes is in the formative stage, not being achieved until about the fourth or fifth grade. Hence, the matter of type being too large, within reasonable limits, for retarded readers or for primary children can be questioned largely from the point of view of cost of publication, rather than the frustration of the establishment of desirable eye-movements. Sight-saving materials are printed in twenty-four and thirty-two point type. The writer has used with satisfactory results this type of material for retarded readers and for primary children having difficulty; and therefore its use is recommended.

Length of Line

To a degree, the length of line depends upon the size of type used. There probably is no great discrepancy between "what should be" and "what is" used for materials in the primary grades because length of line is not significant for appropriate eye-movements or on the basis of social utility. On higher grade levels the matter of social utility causes the length of line to be an important issue. There is little evidence on this point for normal learners and no data, to the writer's knowledge, concerning the retarded reader. In the main, it is quite likely that habit has considerable to do with speed of reading for any given line length.

Blackhurst (2) concluded that with eighteen to twenty-four point type "the most desirable length of line for the first four grades lies around one hundred millimeters (approximately four inches)."

Investigating the typography of first-grade books, Buckingham (5) made no statements regarding length of line because he believed there was actually little difference when size of type was held constant. The British Association for Advancement of Science (3) recommended a 100 millimeter line for children eight years and under and a 93 millimeter line for children over eight. Dearborn (9:194) states that a line from 75 to 85 millimeters is advantageous (approximately three to three and one-half inches).

Javal (10:409) found a line shorter than 90 millimeters to be desirable because a longer line requires too much a-symmetrical accommodation, or adjustment of the eyes required in moving them from the beginning to the end of the line. Here, again, this argument cannot be taken too seriously for materials on the lower-grade levels because large size type can be used to minimize optic fatigue, and head-movement as well as eye-movements are used. Another argument advanced against the use of long lines is the greater amount of attention required for the return sweep from the end of one line to the beginning of the next. From the above evidence, it is safe to conclude that the line should not exceed four inches for primary materials. Moreover there is still a great need for research on the optimum length of line for each size of type for each age level.

Leading

The term "leading" refers to the vertical space between lines, paragraphs, and the like. Leading is usually measured in points. The amount of leading varies with the size of type, type face, and the lateral spacing between words. Shaw (12) recommended 4.5 millimeters for the first grade, 4.0 millimeters for second and third grade, and 3.6 millimeters for fourth grade. Blackhurst's (2) findings for first and second grade were inconclusive. Bently (9:197) found 2.5 millimeters of leading suitable for twelve-point type to produce the most rapid reading. Huey (10:409) pleads for a larger size of type and a maximum of 2.5 millimeters of leading.

In summary, the spacing between the lines (leading) is a factor meriting consideration, especially in the primary grades. Most first-grade teachers find it necessary for children to use oak-tag markers or guides in order to identify the line being read. It would, therefore, appear desirable to increase the leading to a point where the majority of first-grade children could read without crutches such as guides or markers. This same principle applies to the reading materials for retarded readers at higher grade levels. Materials prepared on the typewriter should be double or triple spaced.

Spacing

By "spacing" is meant lateral spacing between words, sentences, or columns, and paragraph indentions. Huey (10:407), after summarizing the research, concluded: "The space within the letters between the vertical strokes should not be less than 0.3 millimeter, according to most investigators. There is probably little to be gained by increasing the distance between the letters beyond that which is usual in the better printed books of the time."

Margins

There are no scientific data to validate any contentions regarding the regularity of margins (white space around the printed page). In 1921, Blackhurst (2) summarized the tendencies and found the trend to make both margins irregular. The chief argument for irregular margins on the right side of the page is that words should be printed in thought units. Dearborn argues for regularity of margins because it makes possible a regularity of eye-movements.

No one knows, therefore, what is scientifically desirable. In the absence of sufficient evidence it is probably safe to conclude, on the basis of social utility and aesthetic appearance, that the margins should be regular. In addition, it would be more nearly hygienically correct to set the type near the outside of the page in order to eliminate the necessity of reading on the curved surface caused by printing the material too close to the bound edge of the page.

Paragraph Indention

Should paragraphs be indicated by a hanging line or an indented line? Only arguments, not data, can be advanced. The use of the hanging line is advocated to reduce the number of broken sentences in lower grade materials. There are no data from which to conclude that the use of the margin for the beginning of a paragraph facilitates reading for beginners or adults. Likewise, the indention of the first line of a paragraph is probably no advantage over the hanging line. The indented line has one advantage in that it approximates adult materials and written composition standards, and thus would be serviceable in building desirable habits in writing and later reading. In view of this, the writer advocates the indention of paragraphs.

Illustrations

Illustrations in all types of instructional materials, from readers to arithmetic texts, have captivated the attention of educators and publishers to the end that a high degree of excellence has been attained. The elementary-school child of the future will undoubtedly have still more attractive materials.

Smith (13 : 202-203) summarizes recent trends as follows: "The mechanical makeup of readers has reached a high degree of excellence. Their most striking feature is the beautiful, bright-colored pictures which one finds so generously distributed through their pages. Primers and first readers often devote 40 per cent of their space to full-page pictures, excellently drawn, truly portraying their accompanying content, and often appearing in vivid, three-color combinations. There is a strong note of realism in all the pictures of the new readers. Even the characters in fanciful stories are usually portrayed as real people and real animals, without artificial dress or action. The readers for the grades above the first now contain more pictures. The illustrations in the new second and third readers are colored, but less brilliantly than in the primers and first readers. The pictures in the fourth, fifth, and sixth readers are generally in black and white, although some recent series have used color in the illustrations of their intermediate readers."

Highly artistic drawings in color with freedom of design

and placement on the page are probably ideal where they can be afforded. But by and large, the colored illustrations in many primary readers are poor art specimens. If it is important for children to be exposed to good art, well-drawn black and white illustrations should be preferable to inferior color drawings. Recently there appears to be an increased interest in attractive black and white illustrations which meet both high standards of art and the requirements of the content.

Apparently the chief requirements are that the illustrations should unite with the context both mechanically and meaningfully. No doubt, the next desirable departure will be the avoidance of the boxed-in effect of present illustrations. Until this is done illustrations cannot be effectively and mechanically combined with the context. Tradition has dictated the placing of illustrations in a box at the top of the page. There are no significant data concerning the effect of placement of pictures on the attention of the reader. Since children are probably the least concerned with adult traditions, children's artists can be quite free to experiment, with cost of printing as the primary limiting factor.

Remedial materials are greatly in need of illustrations which are interpretative and interesting. Undoubtedly, a well-illustrated book properly used would contribute greatly to the super-motivation needed by disabled readers.

Paper

The paper used in printing is an important factor. Chief requirements are a maximum of legibility and a minimum of glare. Legibility is achieved by: (1) The contrast between black print and white paper. Investigators have found higher accuracy of apprehension to accompany greater luminosity between symbol and background. (2) The print of one side should not show through unduly to the other side. (3) The printing on one side should not cause the reverse side to be uneven. Glare is produced when the paper is too glossy. Materials for sight-saving classes are printed on paper dull in finish. In this case what is good for the sick is probably good for the well.

SUMMARY

1. Desirable typography should produce a minimum of optic fatigue and permit rapid reading.

2. Any one typographical factor is significant only when considered in terms of all such interrelated factors.

3. On the primary-grade level, the chief consideration should be clear, large size type.

4. During the period when the child is learning to read, the development of appropriate eye-movements cannot be achieved to any great extent by mechanical arrangements. Furthermore, the primary consideration at this level should be legibility with a minimum of optic fatigue.

5. Paragraph indention is desirable from the point of view of building serviceable habits.

6. Highly artistic drawings in color with freedom of design and placement on the page are probably ideal when they can be afforded. Good black and white illustrations are probably more desirable than inferior colored illustrations.

7. There is little scientific justification for the determination of standards for the mechanics of reading materials.

REFERENCES

1. Bentley, Madison. "Leading and Legibility," *Critical and Experimental Studies in Psychology from the University of Illinois*. Psychological Review Monograph Supplements, Vol. XXX, No. 3. Princeton, New Jersey: Psychological Review Co., 1921.

2. Blackhurst, James Herbert. *Investigations in the Hygiene of Reading*, p. 63. Baltimore: Warwick and York, Inc., 1927.

3. British Association for Advancement of Science, 1913. "Report on Influence of Textbooks upon Eyesight," Report of 83rd Meeting of Association. London: John Murry, 1914.

4. Buckingham, B. R. "New Data on the Typography of Textbooks," *The Textbook in American Education,* pp. 93-125. Thirtieth Yearbook of the National Society for the Study of Education, Part II. Bloomington, Illinois: Public School Publishing Co., 1931.

5. Buckingham, B. R. "The Typography of First-Grade Textbooks." Unpublished, on file in Dr. Buckingham's office, 15 Ashburton Pl., Boston, Massachusetts.

6. Cosgrave, G. P. "The Relative Legibility of Horizontal Segments of Words." Doctor's dissertation, filed in University of Toronto Library, 1928.

7. Gates, Arthur I. "What Do We Know about Optimum Lengths of Lines in Reading?" *Journal of Educational Research,* XXIII (January, 1931), 1-7.

8. Gilliland, A. R. "The Effect on Reading of Changes in the Size of Type," *Elementary School Journal,* XXIV (October, 1923), 138-46.

9. Gray, William S. "Hygienic Requirements of Printed Materials," pp. 191-203. *Summary of Investigations Relat-*

ing to Reading. Chicago: University of Chicago Press, 1925.

10. Huey, Edmund B. *The Psychology and Pedagogy of Reading.* New York: Macmillan Co., 1924.

11. Rothlein, Barbara E. "The Relative Legibility of Different Faces of Printing Types," *American Journal of Psychology,* XXIII (January, 1912), 1-36.

12. Shaw, E. R. *School Hygiene,* pp. 170-79. New York: Macmillan Co., 1901.

13. Smith, Nila Banton. *American Reading Instruction,* Silver, Burdett and Company, 1934.

14. Tinker, Miles A. "Experimental Study of Reading," *Psychological Bulletin,* XXXI (February, 1934), 98-110.

15. Tinker, M. A., and Paterson, D. G. "Influence of Type Form on Speed of Reading," *Journal of Applied Psychology* (August, 1928 and April, 1929), 359-68.

16. Tinker, Miles A. "Legibility and Eye Movement in Reading," *Psychological Bulletin,* XXIV (November, 1927), 621-39.

17. Tinker, Miles A. "Physiological Psychology of Reading," *Psychological Bulletin,* XXVIII (February, 1931), 81-98.

18. Tinker, Miles A., and Paterson, Donald G. "Reductions in Size of Newspaper Print," *Journal of Applied Psychology,* XVI (October, 1932), 525-31.

19. Tinker, Miles A. "The Relative Legibility of Black Print and White Print," *Journal of Applied Psychology,* XV (June, 1931), 248-51.

20. Tinker, Miles A., and Patterson, Donald G. "Simultaneous Variation of Type Size and Line Length," "Studies of Typographical Factors Influencing Speed of Reading, V," *Journal of Applied Psychology,* XV (February, 1931), 72-78.

21. Tinker, Miles A. "Size of Type," *Journal of Applied Psychology,* XIII (1929), 120-30.

22. Tinker, Miles A. "Spacing between Lines or Leading," *Journal of Applied Psychology,* XVI (1932), 388-97.

23. Tinker, Miles A., and Patterson, Donald G. "Studies of Typographical Factors Influencing Speed of Reading: Length of Line," *Journal of Applied Psychology,* XIII (June, 1929), 205-19.

24. Tinker, Miles A. "Styles of Type Faces," *Journal of Applied Psychology* (January, 1933).

25. Tinker, Miles A. "Type Form," *Journal of Applied Psychology,* XII (1928), 359-68.

26. Turner, O. G. "The Comparative Legibility and Speed of Manuscript and Cursive Writing," *Elementary School Journal,* XXX (June, 1930), 780-86.

27. Wheeler, H. E. "Suggestions for Research on the Typography of School Textbooks," *Elementary School Journal,* XXIX (September, 1928), 27-31.

28. Whipple, Guy Montrose. "Needed Investigations in the Field of the Textbook," *Elementary School Journal,* XXXV (April, 1935).

CHAPTER X
Hearing

That serious defects of hearing tend to produce school retardations has been fully demonstrated.
—Terman (14: 224)

Defective Hearing

Normal hearing and vision as significant factors contributing to success in the mastery of the language arts frequently have been overlooked in the average classroom. Many investigators have demonstrated the value of seating children with learning disabilities in the front of the classroom. It is not uncommon to find children of normal or superior intelligence with serious visual or auditory handicaps which interfere with learning.

Scientific studies have multiplied the number of identifiable variations among individuals. Regarding hearing, Terman (14: 223) concluded "that from 10 to 20 per cent of school children do not hear normally and that learning of from 2 to 5 per cent is very seriously impaired. Sex and age differences are very slight, practically non-existent."

Deafness

Inherited deafness is called congenital deafness. Deafness may also result from other causes such as accident and disease. The deaf are usually taught either by manual or by oral methods. By the manual method the learner is taught a manual alphabet and a system of sign language.

The oral method consists of teaching lip reading and communication by speech.

Auditory Acuity

Auditory acuity is the term used to designate keenness or power of hearing. The whisper and low voice tests of auditory acuity can be administered by the health department or the classroom teacher. While it is not an accurate test of hearing, it is of chief value for the identification of cases needing medical attention. The procedure for giving the test is very simple. The subject is requested to stand at a distance of twenty feet from the examiner. The subject should turn his back to the examiner and close the ear not being tested by pressing on the tragus with the fore-finger. The examiner then gives a series of numbers, such as six, eight, four, seven, and ten, requesting the subject to repeat each number given. The writer prefers that the numbers should be repeated in a low voice rather than in a whisper. In order to minimize the amount of memory span required, a response is requested after the oral presentation of each number. The room in which the tests are given should be as quiet as possible. Suggestions regarding the measurement of auditory factors are included in the manual for the Betts Ready to Read Tests. In larger school systems and in research laboratories, instruments, called audio-frequency oscillators and audiometers, are used for the study of hearing.

Audio-Frequency Range

The range of vibrations usually heard by normal individuals lies somewhere between twenty per second and twenty thousand per second. Some children appear to have a very narrow auditory frequency range; that is, they cannot hear low- and high-frequency sounds. A child will experience difficulty in fusing sounds into words if he cannot perceive them. The sounds of *f, v, s,* and *t* are characterized by high frequencies. The writer has had cases in his clinic who apparently said *wich* and spelled *w-i-c-h* because they did not hear *which*. The examiner should not be content, therefore, in determining auditory acuity for any one sound frequency.

Auditory Span

Recent researches have led us to believe that the tendency to confuse and reverse letters and words decreases with an increase in the age of the child. One index to the maturation level of the learner can be secured by the administration of a memory-span test. The typical memory-span test is devised to determine the maximum number of related or unrelated elements which the subject can reproduce after a single presentation. When the items to be reproduced are presented orally by the examiner, the test of memory span is frequently referred to as an auditory memory or auditory-span test.

The Betts Ready to Read Tests and the Van Wagenen Reading Readiness Tests make use of similar techiques for the measurement of auditory span. In each instance, the child is given sentences of increasing difficulty which he is requested to say just as the examiner has given them. The Stanford Revision of the Binet-Simon Tests of intelligence is an excellent illustration of the use of digits for measuring memory span. In his Diagnostic Reading Tests Gates uses both nonsense syllables and digits for the determination of auditory-memory span.

Auditory Perception

Auditory perception may be defined roughly as mental awareness of sounds. Before associating a sound with a previously learned sound or the visual form, the learner must be able to perceive, or hear, the sound. The Auditory Perception Test, a part of the Betts Ready to Read battery, is useful for the analysis of auditory perception difficulties. Such a test is sometimes called an echolalia test. The subject repeats the sounds spoken by the examiner. Test XI 1, Repeating Nonsense Words of the Gates Diagnostic Test is valuable for the study of auditory perception ability.

Auditory Fusion

Auditory fusion, or blending, tests are constructed to secure an index to an individual's ability to fuse sounds into words. The words included in such tests are broken down into isolated sounds which are usually given at the rate of one per second, the subject giving the word which the sounds make. The Betts Ready to Read Test, Gates Diagnostic Reading Tests, and Monroe Diagnostic Tests embrace tests of this ability.

Auditory Discrimination

The ability to visually discriminate between word forms is essential to reading success; otherwise, confusions, such as *horse* for *house,* may result. Only to a slightly lesser degree, the ability to make auditory discriminations between word sounds is important for success with certain types of beginning reading programs. Undoubtedly, such auditory abilities contribute in a large measure to spelling achievement. Hincks (12:87) gave Seashore's Test of the sense of pitch to fourteen cases of extreme reading disability and found ten of them below average.

The Gates Test XI 2, Distinguishing Words, consists of fourteen pairs of words, some of which are alike and some are different. Each pair of words is presented orally to the subject who is requested to tell whether the words are the same or different.

Cutright and Anderson (5) found the poor groups of readers to possess less than average ability to hear differences between similar words. Dr. Bond's findings (1) substantiate this conclusion.

Auditory Training

One of the most significant researches reported in this field is that of Dr. Guy Bond (1) in "A Study of Auditory and Speech Characteristics of Poor Readers." Dr. Bond, by means of the "matched controls" technique, compared the influence which auditory and speech factors had upon reading achievement when second- and third-grade pupils were taught by an oral-phonetic or by a look-and-say method of instruction. In general, he concluded that auditory abilities were significant determiners of success in schools using an oral-phonetic system of reading instruction. Such investigators succeed in sensitizing teachers and school administrators to the need for grouping and for building the primary reading program in terms of individual differences.

In brief there are three general classes of first-grade entrants. One group cannot profit by extended phonetic training because they are confused by the sounds they cannot perceive. If this group were given auditory training, they might be led into learning confusions. An exaggerated analogy would be that of attempting to teach a color-blind individual to discriminate between red and green. A second group will learn to read "in spite of the system" and hence should not be burdened with any great amount of formal work on the auditory analysis of words. The third group will need auditory training because they require the auditory reinforcement of their visual and motor learnings. In other words, the last group can profit by seeing, learning, and writing words.

The development of auditory readiness is an essential part of a reading-readiness program. Such a program should include: (*a*) attention to good speech habits; (*b*) development of rhyming sense; (*c*) knowledge that words consist of sounds; (*d*) recognition of words by sounds; (*e*) listening to the good speaking voice of the teacher which children unconsciously imitate; (*f*) practice with phrases enjoyed by children; (*g*) imitation of sounds; and (*h*) whispered directions.

In the past there have been many heated discussions over two methods of teaching phonics. In the final-blend method, sometimes referred to as the traditional method, the vowel is blended with the succeeding consonant, as *b-at* and *c-at*. In the initial-blend method, sometimes called the natural method, the vowel is blended with preceding consonant as *ba-t* and *ca-t*. There is no scientific evidence to show the superiority of one method over the other.

Cordts (2) found considerable variation in the frequency with which words contained consonants occurring before or after the vowel. This coupled with the fact that many successful teachers have not found it advisable to teach either the initial- or final-blend method exclusively has led to the use of a combination of the two methods.

A fourth method, the non-separation or word method, has been developed on the belief that there should be little or no emphasis on separate letters or sounds. One of the greatest dangers in the use of any phonic method is the distortion of the consonant sounds. It is not uncommon to find a child confused by the teacher's sounding *cat* as though it were spelled *cuh-at*. One of the chief errors in study of phonics is the emphasis on the auditory aspect. In the final analysis, phonics is largely a matter of visual analysis. An extended discussion of word analysis is included in Chapter XI.

SUMMARY

1. Poor auditory acuity is a handicap in certain types of beginning reading programs.
2. The ability to fuse or blend sounds into words contributes to achievement in certain types of programs for beginning reading.
3. Auditory span (memory span measured by giving an auditory stimulus) is a significant factor in reading achievement.
4. Beginning systems of reading should be modified in terms of the capacities of the learners. Children with auditory handicaps should be taught to learn to read by methods wherein oral-phonetic type of instruction is not emphasized.
5. Hearing deficiencies are learning handicaps.
6. Some type of phonic training is essential to a complete system of word analysis.

REFERENCES

1. Bond, Guy L. "A Study of Auditory and Speech Character-
    istics of Poor Readers." Doctor's thesis, Columbia Uni-
    versity, 1935.

2. Cordts, Anna Dorothea. "An Analysis and Classification of
    the Sounds of English Words in a Primary Reading
    Vocabulary," Unpublished Doctor's thesis, Department
    of Education, University of Iowa, 1925.

3. Cordts, Anna Dorothea. "Facts for Teachers of Phonics,"
    Elementary English Review, III (April, 1926), 116-21,
    125.

4. Currier, Lillian Beatrice, and Duguid, Olive C. "Phonics
    or No Phonics?" *Elementary School Journal,* XVII (De-
    cember, 1916), 286-87.

5. Cutright, Prudence, and Anderson, Walter. "An Experi-
    mental Study of Pupils in the First Grade," *Curriculum
    Department Bulletin* (Minneapolis Public Schools), 1934.

6. Dauner, W. M. Jr. "The Effect of Auditory Pacing on
    Regular Speed and Comprehension," *Psychological Bul-
    letin,* XXXI (October, 1934).

7. Dewey, Godfrey. *Relative Frequency of English Speech
    Sounds,* xii-148. Cambridge, Massachusetts: Harvard
    University Press, 1923.

8. Dimmick, .C. C. "The Auditory Memory after Image,"
    American Journal of Psychology (1923), 34, 1.

9. Durrell, Donald D. "Confusions in Learning," *Education,*
    V (February, 1932), 330-33.

10. Fletcher, H. *Speech and Hearing.* New York: D. Van
    Nostrand Co., 1929.

11. Gates, Arthur I. "An Experimental Study of Teaching the
    Deaf to Read," *Volta Review,* XXVIII (June, 1926),
    295-98.

12. Hincks, Elizabeth M. "Disability in Reading and Its Relation to Personality," p. 92. Harvard Monographs in Education, No. 7. Cambridge, Massachusetts: Harvard University Press, 1926.

13. Saunders, Margaret Jane. "The Short Auditory Span Disability," *Childhood Education,* VIII (October, 1931), 59-65.

14. Terman, Lewis M. *The Hygiene of the School Child.* Boston: Houghton, Mifflin Co., 1914.

15. Thompson, Helen. *An Experimental Study of the Beginning Reading of Deaf Mutes,* Teachers College, Bureau of Publications. New York: Columbia University, 1927.

16. West, Robert. "Speech and Hearing," *Volta Review,* XXXVII (October, 1935), 573-626.

CHAPTER XI
The Vocabulary Burden

*In order to provide the careful development of
sight vocabulary and the constant practice required
for successful corrective work in reading, a narrow
vocabulary of well chosen words is necessary."*
—Donald D. Durrell (10)

Vocabulary Studies

During the past fifteen years, considerable emphasis has
been placed on vocabulary burden of reading materials.
There probably has been as much scientific interest in this
phase of reading as any other one phase. Despite the
number of investigations in this field, there is a great
vocabulary disparity among reading and spelling books at
any one grade level. In one study (22), 472 different
words were found to be used in fourteen pre-primers. If
modern theories regarding reading are to be put into practice without confusing the learner, there is a need for a
greater overlapping of vocabularies used in primary reading materials or a need for each publisher to expand the
offerings and to control the vocabulary in literary, science,
and social-science materials, especially for the primary
grades.

McClusky (26) made a quantitative analysis of the difficulty of reading materials at the college level. His chief
conclusion was: "Analysis of the passages indicates that
the easy material is characterized by the short simple sentence structure and easy familiar vocabulary; while the

difficult material is characterized by a technical, unfamiliar
vocabulary and a complex sentence structure. All the types
of material contain about the same number of ideas per
hundred words."

In spite of the fact that there have been a great number
of worthwhile vocabulary investigations, there is a great
need for further research on both speaking vocabulary and
the learning difficulties peculiar to given words. In 1929,
the writer (1) constructed an electric apparatus for the
recording of oral-language activities. By the use of the
apparatus a study was made of the accuracy of the records
of various types of reporters. It was found that the reporters unintentionally edited their records and therefore
the reports had little scientific accuracy. The results are
summarized in the table given below:

SUMMARY OF DATA FOR THE FIVE TECHNIQUES USED BY COURT REPORTERS

Technique	Per cent* accurately recorded	Per cent† accurately recorded
Electric recording	99.7	99.7
Court reporters	80.4	84.9
Shorthand reporters	53.3	82.9
Longhand reporters	32.0	83.9
Phoneticians	14.9	87.6

*Based on Electric Recording.
†Based on Reporters' Records.

Students of the problem have concerned themselves with
speaking, reading, or writing vocabularies. A knowledge
of the speaking vocabularies of preschool and primary
children is necessary for the preparation of reading materials for beginners. Both vocabulary and interests are

closely related. Teachers who plan to build charts based
on children's interests should acquaint themselves with the
vocabulary of the reading materials used as well as the
most frequently occurring words in the speaking vocabulary of children at a given age level. One of the objects of
reading instruction is the building of a reading vocabulary.
Readiness for a given story is developed, in part, by preparing the children for the new words in the story.

The Child Study Committee of the International Kindergarten Union (2) compiled a list of 2,500 words used by
children before entering the first grade. Since this list
provides a good index to the speaking vocabulary, it is
especially valuable for the construction of pre-primers and
other beginning reading material.

Gross (22) reported 238 words used four or more times
in ten pre-primers. Of this number seventeen were the
names of characters, such as Dick and Jane. The total
vocabulary of the ten pre-primers was 393 words. Only
four words (*a, and, I,* and *the*) were found to be common
to all ten pre-primers.

Wheeler and Howell (40) compared the vocabularies of
ten primers and ten first readers with the Gates Reading
Vocabulary for the Primary Grades (1926 edition). They
reported that 26 per cent of the words in the readers did
not appear in the first five hundred of the Gates list.

Stone (35) reported a list of 1,276 new words appearing
in three or more of sixteen readers commonly used in the
second grade. Only sixty-seven of the new words at the
second-grade level were common to ten or more of the
readers. He pointed out the utter lack of standardization
of vocabulary and the need for the pupil to have skill in
recognizing new words.

Horn's (24) *Basic Writing Vocabulary* comprising 10,000 words most commonly used in writing is the monumental work among vocabulary studies. This research report has been used largely as a basis for the construction of spelling books since its publication in 1926. The vocabulary of children's letters written in life outside the school was studied by Fitzgerald (14). Two thousand one hundred and six words occurring eight or more times were reported for the fourth-, fifth-, and sixth-grade level. Two thousand of the words were used in all three grades.

Thorndike's *A Teacher's Word Book of the Twenty Thousand Words Found Most Frequently and Widely in General Reading for Children and Young People* (39), published in 1931, is an extension of his *Teacher's Word Book* (38), published in 1921, containing 10,000 words. The Thorndike report on reading vocabulary and the Horn report (24) on writing vocabulary are the two most extensive studies in this field.

The Gates *Reading Vocabulary* (17) of 1,811 words for the primary grades is a report of a composite study based on speaking and reading vocabularies. The vocabularies of most recent primary books are checked against the Gates list. Primary teachers, especially, should familiarize themselves with this list.

Faucett and Maki (11) prepared a list of words "to provide teachers and the students with a means of distinguishing *indispensable, essential,* and *useful* words from *special* words in the English language." This compilation was based on the Thorndike (38) and Horn (24) lists.

The Durrell list (10) of 656 words is based on the Fawcett, Maki, and Fitzgerald reports. He maintains: "The list for corrective reading should contain only words which have a high frequency in both adult and child usage. The standard word lists are not satisfactory for the purpose. Gates' *Reading Vocabulary for Primary Grades* is too long and contains a great many childish words which appear so infrequently in adult literature that the learning is uneconomical. Ogden's *Basic English* is well chosen and is about the right length, but it contains a large proportion of words not used by children. It seems desirable not to complicate the beginning corrective work by including words not in the child's speaking vocabulary."

C. G. Shambaugh and Olive L Shambaugh (31) submitted to elementary-school children a list of four hundred stimulus words "representing all phases of the experience and the environment of the elementary-school child." From this study a core vocabulary for elementary-school pupils was derived. This study is a departure from the other mechanically derived lists.

Word Recognition

Systems of beginning reading in which phonics or any other one method for the teaching of word recognition are emphasized have been relegated to the dusty collections of the past. Scientifically minded investigators contributing to a better understanding of the nature of reading difficulties have caused educators to reappraise their thinking in this respect. Gates (17:242) emphasized the importance of "versatility of word attack"; Smith (32:501) calls attention to the need for use of a "variety of cues and clues"; others recite in like manner by calling for a *system of word analysis.*

Smith (33) investigated the systems of attacking new words made by children who had been given no training

in word analysis. She found them making the greatest use
of context and picture clues. The analyzing and synthesiz-
ing of compound words and the analyzing of a known word
to get a smaller unknown word within were also resorted to
by a great many cases. The sounding of syllables and
letters and the spelling of words were used by "repeaters"
in the class who had received phonetic training. The investigator concluded that too much emphasis had been
placed on learning the sounds of word elements.

Word mastery involves the analysis of word forms and
acquiring knowledge of word meanings. Overemphasis on
word analysis usually results in word calling or word-by-
word reading. On the other hand, overemphasis on reading for meaning may result in guessing. In order to phrase
properly and to secure maximum comprehension, the
learner should have enough skill in word analysis to make
for rapid visual discrimination and sufficient mastery over
the reading vocabulary and the concepts involved for quick
understanding. In short, word recognition is more than
mechanics, it is also a problem in meanings.

For beginners, word recognition is usually taught by
means of sight-list techniques. Mere formal instruction
calls for the association of meaning with isolated lists of
words. Informal instruction involves the use of a more
nearly functional procedure; that is, reading is emphasized
as a meaningful process which is basic to other activities.

Not all children in a given class will require extended
systematic instruction in word recognition, hence the need
for grouping. It is the duty of each teacher to aid children
with their learning difficulties and to enrich and extend the
experiences of those who are accurate and independent in
their reading. This can be achieved by providing an abund-

ance of interesting supplementary reading materials for the advanced groups, leaving more time to help the slower groups.

1. Recognition by general configuration. From the point of view of contrast between the black print and the white background, word forms offer various recognition clues such as variation in length and the number and location of ascenders, such as *b, d,* and *l,* and descenders, such as *p, q,* and *j.* It has been reported frequently that children remember the words *elephant, breakfast, Honolulu, bicycle,* or *chocolate* more easily than a short word such as *me, this, these,* or *there.* The longer words differ more in pattern or total configuration than the short ones. An additional explanation may be that there are more meanings or experiences associated with words such as *elephant* or *chocolate.* Attention to configuration clues is an aid in discriminating between common reading errors such as *kitten* for *cat.* Although the use of configuration clues should be encouraged, it should not be overemphasized.

Among the most commonly used words are *than, their, them, then, there, these, they,* and *this.* Word-recognition skills other than the use of configuration clues are essential if confusion on these words is to be avoided. Furthermore, many other commonly used words which are used in the construction of first-grade reading materials cause similar difficulties unless care is taken to introduce them gradually.

2. The use of context clues. The attitude of reading for meaning should be encouraged from the time of the child's first contact with printed symbols. Readiness, or mind set, is essential in all learning, and the development of the use of context clues is no exception. In the primary

grades, readiness for a given story can be developed by
discussing the illustrations and the pupil's experiences related to the story. After an anticipation for the story has
been developed, the pupils should be permitted to exercise
their curiosity by reading the story. If the new words have
been presented in advance and the material is within the
grasp of the group, the pupils should be encouraged to
attempt new words or unrecognized old words in new context by "guessing" the meaning. If necessary the correct-
ness of the response can be checked by applying word recognition techniques. A response can be appraised also by
checking the meaning with the rest of the context.

One of the most important factors contributing to word
recognition is that of word meanings. Reading becomes
possible to the extent that meanings are associated with the
symbol or word form. A rapid rate of association of ideas
which contributes to fluent and easy reading is not possible
until the child has first formed many associations with
words and groups of words. Exercises designed to cause
the pupil to anticipate meanings can be easily constructed
by the teacher. The completion type of exercise can be
used in the early stages of reading. For example: the color
of grass is .... The multiple-choice exercises can
be used for similar purposes. For example: The color of
grass is (1) queer (2) gray (3) green (4) greet. The
extent to which the skills on this type of exercises carry
over into reading needs experimental appraisal. A skillful
teacher probably can teach the child to anticipate meanings
more economically during oral reading.

3. The use of picture clues. Courtis and Smith prepared the *Picture-Story Reading Lessons,* published by the
World Book Company in 1927. This was the first attempt

to make systematic use of a pictured dictionary as a means of self-help in word recognition. The Gates and Huber Dictionary for use with their *Peter and Peggy* book, published by the Macmillan Company in 1931, is another excellent example of how pictures may be used to build meanings for word recognition. There is an almost universal use made of picture clues in reading systems for beginners.

Children who require additional help with word-recognition skills can profit by making their own pictured dictionary. It is also advisable during the chart-building period to permit children to prepare illustrations for each chart which provide clues to the content. In addition to being a good device for extending and enriching word meanings, it is also one way to correlate art with reading.

No one type of word-recognition skill should be practiced to the exclusion of all others. Illustrations should be regarded as part of the context. Picture clues can be used from two angles; namely, the interpretation of illustrated stories and the illustration of context by the pupil. Before reading a story the group should discuss the illustrations, the teacher guiding the discussion so that it will contribute to the context.

4. Visual analysis. By and large, ability in word recognition involves meaningful association, visual analysis, and auditory analysis. The child's first encounter with word symbols should be from the standpoint of meaning. Before the child has had occasion to read, he has established some feeling for language through hearing and meaning. To this association with language is added visual discrimination between word forms. Most of the techniques described in this chapter have to do with visual discrimination.

Reading is done with the eyes and therefore is largely a visual proposition. Visual discrimination between word forms involves noting the general configuration or word pattern, word details, word elements, and similarities and differences. Skills are learned by repetition and not by talking about them. Some children require very little training in word recognition; others require extended practice of diverse types. All the practice should be directed by the teacher so that the pupil acquires a system of word recognition. Matching exercises and the like in meaningful situations are generally believed to be a necessary part of a program of reading. This matter of visual discrimination between word forms is further discussed in the next section.

5. Phonics. Phonetics is the science of speech sounds. Phonics is the term usually used to designate the application of phonetics to the teaching of reading. The terms are used synonymously by reading authorities. Noah Webster included the study of phonetic elements in his famous blue-black speller (*American Spelling Book*) published in 1790. Around 1840 phonetic and word methods for teaching beginners were substituted for the A B C method and emphasized with the appearance of the McGuffey readers. The Beacon and other readers, published about 1912 and based on extreme phonetic methods, continued to dominate classroom procedures until recently. Most manuals which accompany modern readers for first and second grades contain suggestions for systematic instruction in phonics. Although the pendulum has swung from extreme phonetic systems to no phonetic instruction, most writers believe that some phonetic skills should be a part of the child's equipment for independent recognition of new words.

Regarding instruction in phonics, many significant questions arise. (1) Should phonic instruction be included in a reading program? (2) What type of phonic program is most effective? (3) What preparatory activities should precede phonic instruction? (4) When should phonics be introduced? (5) How should phonic instruction be given? (6) What are the limitations of phonic instruction? There are some scientific data on each of these questions, but there is an urgent need for further research. In brief, it may be said that a modified program of phonics in terms of individual needs is advocated as a part of systematic instruction in word recognition.

a) *Why phonic instruction?* Gray and Liek (21:20) advise "First, the recognition of word elements and their sounds is only a subordinate clue to the recognition of a word, and second, the ultimate aim is not to acquire proficiency in the recognition of isolated elements, but to enable the reader to grasp the meaning of a selection quickly and accurately. Therefore, isolated drills on word elements are inadvisable, except in very unusual cases."

Gates (18:61) expresses his opinion as follows: "Investigation has shown, first, that a conventional course in phonetics is rarely, if ever, indispensable to learning to read. The fact that children do learn to read without any phonetic training and that children who are deaf-mutes learn to read without any experience whatsoever with word-sounds is evidence of this fact. On the other hand, it must be said that phonetic training is often helpful. Some of the pupils who are given no phonetic training reveal weaknesses in working out recognition and pronunciation of words and an extreme dependence upon context clues, which a familiarity with word-form and word-sound clues would remedy.

It is possible that many children who have not acquired in the primary grades some degree of what we may call phonetic skills would have benefited by this training."

White and Hanthorn (41 : 39) suggest: "Children differ in their need for phonic training. Some children learn to read with little or no phonic training, while others will profit from this training, and will need much of it in order to make them independent. Phonic training should always be taught according to the needs of each child. Early phonic words should be very simple and familiar, and only the phonetic elements actually needed by the children should be taught. It is impossible for children to remember all the phonetic elements. An attempt to teach all the phonetic combinations may confuse a child more than it will aid him. Accurate pronunciation and enunciation should be a part of phonetic training. Diacritical marks should not be used. They make the word more difficult for the child. Phonic exercises are an aid to reading, but should not be confused with the reading lesson. They should be conducted at a separate period set aside for this purpose."

Currier and Duguid (5) made an extended investigation of the value of phonic training. From their study it may be implied that although some children profit by phonic training, such daily drills are not essential in the primary grades. This is also another good argument for grouping within the classroom.

b) *Preparatory activities.* Before the attention of the child is called to visual discrimination between word elements, ear training should be given. This type of instruction begins during the preparatory period. First, the child is made aware of the words by calling attention to new words used by various pupils during an informal conversation period. It is not uncommon to find children who run their words together, apparently being unaware of the use of words. For example, "What is it?" may be perceived to be a total language pattern rather than a group of words. Second, rhymes are frequently used for ear training. After a rhyme is recited, games may be introduced for identifying words that rhyme. Following this, the children may be encouraged to suggest other words which rhyme. Additional preparatory training can be given by having the pupils listen for initial sounds, final sounds, and sounds within the word. This noting of similarities or differences in the sounds of words pronounced by the teacher should be a significant part of the program for teaching auditory discrimination. Ear training should be among the items emphasized and continued throughout the primary grades. Attention to word details can be secured by writing class-suggested words that begin or end with the same sounds on the blackboard or a chart. In other words, ear training should lead to both ear and eye training. Some children who have difficulty in word recognition may require extended practice in classifying words according to phonetic similarities and in noting similarities and differences between pairs of word forms. Most teachers' manuals contain excellent suggestions for this type of work.

   c) *Introduction to phonics.* Garrison and Heard (15) concluded that, in the main, phonetic instruction should be postponed until the second and third grades. In the first grade, other methods should be used for forming word discrimination habits. It is interesting to note that the investigators found the phonetically trained pupils to be better spellers and more independent in word recognition. Sexton and Herror (30) investigated the progress of several hundred children through the first grade and the first half of the second grade. Their conclusions were to the effect that instruction in phonetics began to be of some value in the last half of the first grade but was of great value during the first half of the second grade.

By and large, prescription in terms of grade level is avoided by writers in this field. To state that phonetic instruction, however defined, should be introduced the fifth week or the thirtieth week of the first or second grade would indicate failure to recognize individual differences. Not all children learn according to preconceived adult notions. In the first place, children vary in their general readiness for reading regardless of the intelligence. Secondly, pupils vary in their rate of learning. Hence, it is usually stated that phonic training should begin only after children begin to note points of similarities and differences in known sight words. Certainly the mechanics of words should not receive concentrated attention until the pupils have acquired the attitude of reading for meaning.

d) *The program of phonics.* To the student of the history of reading instruction, the evolution of phonic instruction is interesting. Older methods began with the memorization of sounds which were later blended into words. Later instruction called for the analysis of words into their phonetic elements and subsequent practice in fusing or blending these elements. Two types of blending were developed. By the initial blend method, the vowel is joined to the preceding consonant or consonants. Words such as *ca-n, ca-p,* and *ca-t* are listed in columns to teach the *ca* blend. To teach the consonant *t,* such words would be listed as *sa-t, ca-t, ha-t, pa-t,* etc. The initial blend was advocated because it is consistent with syllable division used in the dictionary.

Attention should be directed to the beginning of words, but initial consonants cannot be sounded in isolation.

By the final blend method, the initial consonant sound is recognized in isolation from the rest of the word. The "families" of sounds are taught by such a list of words as *s-at, c-at, b-at, h-at,* etc. A child taught by this method will look first at the end of the word to identify the "family" of final blend (such as "at," "am," etc.), and then to blend the initial consonant sound with the "family." The chief objection that is raised to the final blend method is the difficulty of giving the true initial consonant sound in isolation. Inexperienced teachers confused pupils by distorting the initial consonant sound, saying *buh-at* for *b-at, cuh-at* for *c-at,* and the like.

Dr. Anna D. Cordts (4) found a great variation in the frequency with which different consonant sounds occur before or after the vowel. As a result of her researches, she advocates a word method of teaching phonics (3:224). "By the Word Method of Teaching Phonics the pupil never encounters any phonic elements in isolation; he always sees them in their natural setting—the word as a whole. He not only makes his first acquaintance with the phonic elements in whole words, but in all his practice work he always works with the whole word, never with any isolated part of it. The pupil never sees in isolation such beginnings of words as *sa, pa, ha,* or such endings as *t, n, d;* he always meets them as integral parts of the whole words, *sat, pan, had.* Hence he soon learns to see the word as a unit made up of known parts.

"The unity of the word, therefore, is always preserved. Consequently, the child does not work with material that has one aspect in his phonics and another in his reading.

He responds to whole words in both learning situations, in phonics as well as in reading."

The phonetic instruction which should be given is usually carefully described in the manual accompanying the basal series of readers. What shall be taught should depend upon the frequency of occurrence of the sound combinations in the reading materials. The following is a list of items usually included in a basal-reading program:

(1) The sounds of the consonants (See also Section 5)
     Osburn (28) listed the initial consonant sounds in the order of their importance as: *s, t, c, p, d, f, b, r, m, l, w, g, n, h, v, th, st, pr,* and *ch.* He also listed the following final consonants in the order of their importance: *r, n, l, s, t, d, m, p, nt, re, ce, se, th, nd, st, ve, ng, te, ck, c, ch,* and *f.*

   Cordts and McBroom (4:393) suggest that the following consonant sounds should be taught:

   a) initial sounds: *c, l, b, h, s* (sit), *m, r, p, c* (can), *d, t, f, n, w, sh* (ship)

   b) final sounds: *t, ll* (fill), *n, m, d, p, g, ck* (pick), *sh* (dish), *ng* (sing)

(2) The sounds of the vowels
   a) Vowels are usually short except when modified by position

       a- sat, bat, cat
       e- set, bet
       i- sit, big
       o- dot
       u- gun

b) In a short word ending with a final *e*, the *e* is
   usually silent and the preceding vowel is long
   - a- ate, face   i- fine, five, ride
   - e- mete   o- hole
   - u- use

c) In open accented syllables the vowel is usually
   long
   - a- nation   i- diner
   - e- me   o- so, notation
   - u- futile

d) Vowels followed by *r* have a modified sound
   - ar- star, mar   ir- sir
   - er- her   or- corn
   - ur- churn

(3) The sounds of the diphthongs
   - oi- oil   ou- out, our
   - oy- boy   ow- how, cow

(4) The sounds of the vowel digraphs. In vowel digraphs
   the first vowel usually has its own long sound and
   the second vowel is silent:
   - ai- rail
   - ay- slay
   - ie- tie
   - oa- roar
   - oe- hoe
   - ow- own
   - ue- hue
   - ew- few, dew (note exceptions)
   - ee- sleep
   - ea- plea (in some words *ea* has the short *e* sound,
     as in death, bread, feather)

(5) The sounds of the consonant digraphs

sh- wash, ship	th- this, there
ch- chicken	wh- which
tch- watch	nk- drink
ck- duck, back, trick	ng- sing

e) Methods and devices. How phonetic instructions shall be given is described in the teacher's manual which accompanies a good set of readers. Most good reading systems offer a detailed and carefully prepared plan of word recognition, or word perception. Clarence R. Stone has prepared a series of three workbooks entitled *Eye and Ear Fun,* published by the Webster Publishing Company. The materials were developed for use in grades one to four and can be used according to the needs of the learners. The method involves the use of context clues, visual analysis, and the phonetic knowledge until the whole word is recognized. These materials would also be valuable for remedial reading purposes at higher grade levels. Various devices are used for practice on word recognition where phonics are involved. Some of the procedures are summarized below. It will be noted that other word recognition skills are correlated with the phonetic instruction. One principle should be emphasized throughout; namely, the skill learned in isolation should be practiced immediately in context reading.

(1) Arranging a given list of words according to their initial consonant sounds. The pictured dictionary can be used in this procedure.

(2) In a given list of thirty to forty words, have the pupils indicate, by drawing a circle around the word, or by some similar device, words which rhyme with a given word.

(3) Promote mastery of word elements such as *th* by underlining the element in words such as *this, them, there, nothing, both,* etc. Other phonetic elements can be dealt with in like manner.

(4) Promote mastery of word elements such as *th* by the addition of the element to other real words; for example, *under* (thunder), *an* (than), *in* (thin), *ink* (think), etc.

(5) Pronounce words orally and ask the children to tell whether a given consonant sound is at the beginning or end of the word. For example, for the sound *t* give *bat, Tom, cat, fit, tap, tail,* and the like.

(6) Listing words that rhyme with a given word which contains the sound to be taught. For example, *round, ground, found; fool, stool, cool;* and the like.

(7) Listing words that can be made into new words by adding *er, ed, est, ing,* and *s.* For example, *fast* (faster), *clean* (cleaner), *camp* (camper), and the like. Care should be taken not to introduce words where other principles are involved such as *bat* (batter). One principle at a time should be introduced; otherwise, confusion will result.

(8) List elements from which words can be made by prefixing an initial consonant sound to a phonetic element. For example, *et, ay, ig, op,* and the like can be the basis for the learning of many words by prefixing an initial consonant sound. For *et,* such words as *pet, bet, get,* etc., may be formed.

(9) Change words by substituting class-suggested initial sounds for the initial sound of the words. For

example, changing *cut* to *shut, cute* to *chute, deep* to *sheep, dine* to *shine,* etc.

(10) Changing words by adding final *e.* For example, *cap* to *cape,* hat to *hate,* tap to *tape, not* to *note,* etc.

(11) Use key words to illustrate different soundings. For example, the *oo* sound in *too, boot, cool, coo, food,* and in *book, took, look,* and the like.

(12) Note the effect of changing the vowel or adding a vowel in order to identify certain "short" sounds. For example *rag* and *rig, put* and *pit, sat* and *sit, tap* and *tip, hide* and *hid, bite* and *bit, pine* and *pin,* and the like; *bed* and *bead, led* and *lead, met* and *meat,* and the like.

(13) In a list of words, underlining the parts that are alike. For example, the *ow* in *how, plow, cow* or *ew* in *flew, blew,* etc.

(14) Pronouncing lists of paired words which emphasize given sounds. For example, *bit* and *bite, tap* and *tape,* and the like.

(15) Changing words by substituting double vowels for single vowels. For example *met* and *meet, bet* and *beet, fed* and *feed.*

(16) Arranging words according to use. For example, words might be arranged according to color (white, black, etc.); toys (wagon, top, etc.).

(17) Finding small words within big ones. For example underlining *age* in *cage,* at in *cat,* etc.

(18) Making compound words from given words. Multiple choice exercises are useful in this connection. In one column the words are listed which may be combined with certain words in the second column.

(19) Finding letters in words of a prepared list which have a given sound. For example, the *i* sound of *y* in such words as *why, shy,* and *my*.

(20) Pronouncing words to the pupils, asking them to listen for and identify the element common to the words.

(21) Comparing words containing new elements; for example, *this, that, these* or *little, middle,* etc.

(22) Permitting children to "discover" the principle involved in pronouncing a new word by comparing several words involving the same element; for example, *coat* and *goat, pie* and *tie, cheap* and *leap, cried* and *tied*. Here the phonetic principle, of course, is that the first vowel is long and the second is silent.

f) *Pitfalls*. There are many pitfalls in the teaching of phonetics. First, only about 84 per cent of the commonly used words are phonetic. Second, the many exceptions to each rule may introduce interference factors which cause confusions. The use of phonetic rules is a questionable procedure. Third, the distortion of the sound value of a given phonetic element in a word confuses the beginner rather than facilitates learning. Fourth, overemphasis on mechanical analysis leads to "word calling" rather than "thought getting." Fifth, only elements with a high frequency of occurrence should be taught; otherwise, the knowledge and skills cannot be practiced. Sixth, a disproportionate amount of time may be spent on phonetics which is only one aspect of word recognition. If carried to an extreme, phonetic instruction would include all the confusing rules for syllabication. Such instruction would be, of course, of questionable validity even for high-school pupils.

The teacher who expects to teach primary children or to help pupils retarded in reading at any grade level should have at her command a sufficient knowledge of phonics to give a child specific help. Too frequently teachers rationalize the situation by stating that they follow no systematic procedures but instead supply help when needed. Furthermore, the teacher who follows the second procedure must be as well prepared as the teacher who gives systematic instruction.

6. Analysis of compound words. The analysis of compound words as a skill in word recognition is treated in this chapter in the discussion of phonics and of syllabication. The analysis of compound words involves the extension of practice on the identification of phonetic elements, syllables, and words within a word.

The attention of the learner can be directed to compound words by practice on making them from pairs of words and by the analysis of compound words. Visual analysis of compound words can be achieved by exposing only one of the words or by drills on listing the words found in them.

7. Syllabication. The ability to recognize syllables as word elements is an important word-recognition skill. Many of the pupils will have acquired this ability by the time they are ready for second-grade reading materials, but this should not preclude the necessity for systematic instruction on this item. Teaching the recogniton of syllables is a necessary part of both reading and spelling programs.

Training in syllabication should carry over from the analysis techniques involved in making visual discrimination between word forms. The pupils should first be sensitized to syllabication by listening to words as they are pronounced. This can be followed by visual identification of syllables in the primary grades, and dictionary work in the intermediate grades.

It is advisable to initiate the pupil into syllabication gradually by calling attention to two-syllable words. Words with one accent should also be introduced before more difficult words. Diacritical marks should be used only after dictionary work is begun.

Some pupils will require more help with syllabication than others. For extreme cases, some formal or ready-made materials should be used. The pupil can be given exercises involving the separation of the syllables of given words by vertical lines, or marks. Some pupils appear to profit by reading materials that have been typed so that each syllable is separated by one space and the words are separated by two or three spaces. It is important that the learner establish a "feeling" for syllabication by hearing the syllables as well as seeing them.

The best time to teach an item is when the learner has a need for it. Hence, the best time to teach any specific skill in reading is when the pupil is reading. If a child has difficulty with a word where ability to recognize the syllables is important, the teacher can aid in the identification of the syllables by covering the word so that only one syllable at a time is exposed. Usually the child can get the cue to a given word by exposing only one syllable. Sometimes it is necessary to expose each syllable in left-to-right progression before the child recognizes the word.

Difficulties in Word Recognition

One of the chief difficulties of retarded readers is that they have no system or plan by which they can make an independent identification of a word. The first step is to make sure that the word is in the speaking vocabulary of the learner. The second step involves an inventory of the pupils' word-recognition techniques. Many retarded readers at the junior high-school level have not mastered elementary word recognition skills. If an upper-grade teacher expects to help a retarded reader she should know primary reading methods.

Formal tests of word recognition can be made with the Oculomotor and Perception Slides of the Betts Ready to Read Tests, or certain of the Gates Diagnostic Reading Tests, or the Gray Oral Reading Tests. No test is as valid as a test which requires the child to read from materials within his grasp; hence no analysis procedure is complete until such reading is done. This may involve having a seventh-grade boy read from a first-grade reader. The point is that the reading should be done from materials where few errors are made. The examiner should record the type of error made and the technique used by the pupil for the recognition of the unknown word.

Pupils who guess at words may need more training in the use of context clues as well as word analysis. Guessing may result from a lack of practice in the use of context clues (or reading for meaning) as well as from too great a dependence upon the use of context clues. Some children may be timid about attacking unknown words. In such cases, the teacher may have the problem of changing the attitude of the child through genuine and friendly co-operation as well as through the teaching of word recognition skills.

The "word caller" is as great a teaching problem as the child who has no system of word recognition. Such cases can be helped by teaching them to phrase. Frequently, indi-

vidual help can be given by having the child read orally
while the teachers also read orally. In this way the teacher's
voice aids the child through pacing the eye-movements by
means of an auditory stimulus. The child who resorts to
"spelling out" words may be helped by practice in noting
phonetic elements, syllables, and similarities and differences.
Frequently, this type of case can also be helped by flash-card
exercises. Such exercises should not be introduced until the
child has developed other types of skill for recognizing new
words.

The Vocabulary of Reading Materials

The vocabulary burden of primary and remedial reading
materials merits careful consideration because the child may
become confused if new words are introduced too fast. One
of the chief causes of reading difficulties is a lack of word
recognition power. If beginners are to read more than one
pre-primer before the primer is introduced, care should be
exercised to select a second pre-primer which contains the
greatest number of words in common with the pre-primer
of the basal readers. When certain basal readers are used,
it is much more desirable to introduce the primer of the
series before the pre-primers of other series are used. This
should be done because the lack of agreement among writers
regarding which words should be introduced first results in
almost totally different vocabularies for different pre-
primers. If, after one pre-primer has been read, another
pre-primer with a new vocabulary is introduced, the pupil
will be confused because he has no working knowledge of
the new vocabulary. The pre-primer period should be considered as extending through the first part of primer
reading.

Publishers are meeting this problem by supplying additional pre-primers prepared in terms of the vocabulary and interests of the basal pre-primer and by listing the pre-primers of other series which have the highest percentage of words in common with their basal pre-primers.

Teachers can secure information from publishers regarding the number, distribution, repetition, and social value of the words used in each book of a series. Important considerations relative to vocabulary may be summarized as follows: (1) number of new words; (2) ratio of new words to total words; (3) average repetition of words in each book and the succeeding books; (4) maximum number of new words per page; (5) number of running words in each book; (6) percentage of words in authentic lists, such as the International Kindergarten Union, Gates, Thorndike, Gross, and Stone lists.

SUMMARY

1. Vocabulary studies have been made in order to determine which words are socially useful to learners at different levels.

2. The rate of introduction of new words should be controlled for both beginners and retarded readers.

3. A substantial portion of children with reading deficiencies do not have a system for the identification of new words.

4. The acquisition of a faulty system of word recognition may be prevented by giving systematic and definite instruction in this phase of reading. Specific word recognition drills should be given as preparation for the reading in which they will be practiced immediately.

5. Variations in the general pattern of words provide one clue for the visual discrimination between word forms.

6. The use of context clues should be stressed for retarded readers as well as for beginners.

7. Picture clues can be used to extend word meanings through visual associations.

8. Visual analysis of word forms is an essential skill to be acquired by both beginners and retarded readers.

9. A modified program of phonics which contributes to rapid visual analysis of unknown words is a desirable counterpart of a system of word recognition.

10. Practice in visual analysis should include the "breaking-down" of compound words.

11. Skill in syllabication contributes to both spelling and reading efficiency.

12. Supplementary reading materials for beginners should be selected in terms of overlapping vocabulary.

REFERENCES

1. Betts, Emmett A., and Bontrager, O. Ray. *Research Studies in Elementary School Language,* No. 1, University of Iowa Studies, Iowa City, 1934.

2. Child Study Committee of the International Kindergarten Union. *A Study of the Vocabulary of Children before Entering the First Grade.* Washington: International Kindergarten Union, 1928.

3. Cordts, Anna D. *Manual in Reading and Phonics* (Pre-primer and Primer). Boston: Ginn & Company, 1935.

4. Cordts, Anna D., and McBroom, Maude. "Phonics," *Classroom Teacher,* II (1928), 389-432.

5. Currier, Lillian Beatrice, and Duguid, Olive C. "Phonics or No Phonics?" *Elementary School Journal,* XVII (December, 1916), 286-87.

6. Derrer, Helen M. *A Vocabulary Study of a Series of Four Pre-Primers and Primers.* Bureau of Educational Research (Ohio State University, 1934).

7. Dolch, Edward William. "Combined Word Studies," *Journal of Educational Research,* XVII (January, 1928), 11-19.

8. Dolch, Edward William. "The Efficiency of Primers in Teaching Word Recognition," *Journal of Educational Research,* XXVIII (December, 1934), 271-75.

9. Dolch, Edward William. "Testing Word Difficulty," *Journal of Educational Research,* XXVI (September, 1932), 22-27.

10. Durrell, Donald D. "A Vocabulary for Corrective Reading," *Elementary English Review,* XI (April, 1934), 106-09.

11. Faucett, L., and Maki, I. *A Study of English Word Values.* New York: Oxford University Press, 1932.

12. Fennell, Ethel Luella. "An Analytical Study of the Vocabularies Used in Primary Readers, pp. 111-51. Unpublished Master's thesis, Department of Education, University of Chicago, 1927.

13. Fennell, Ethel Luella. "Recurring Words and Their Relation to Difficulties in Comprehension," *Elementary School Journal,* XXIX (September, 1928), 42-53.

14. Fitzgerald, James A. "The Vocabulary of Children's Letters Written in Life Outside the School," *Elementary School Journal,* XXXIV (January, 1934), 358-70.

15. Garrison, S. C., and Heard, Minnie Taylor. "An Experimental Study of the Value of Phonetics," *Peabody Journal of Education,* IX (July, 1931), 9-14.

16. Gates, Arthur I. "The Construction of a Reading Vocabulary for the Primary Grades," *Teachers College Record,* XXVII (March, 1926), 625-43.

17. Gates, Arthur I. *A Reading Vocabulary for the Primary Grades.* New York: Teachers College, Columbia University, 1926. (Revised and enlarged 1935.)

18. Gates, Arthur I. *Reading for School Administrators,* Bureau of Publications, Teachers College, Columbia University, 1931.

19. Gates, Arthur I. *The Improvement of Reading.* New York: Macmillan Company, 1935.

20. Gray, William S. (Chairman). *Report of the National Committee on Reading.* Twenty-fourth Yearbook of the National Society for the Study of Education, Part I. Bloomington, Illinois: Public School Publishing Co., 1925.

21. Gray, William S., and Liek, Edna B. *Teacher's Guidebook for Elson Basic Readers,* Book II. Chicago: Scott, Foresman and Company, 1931.

22. Gross, Olive E. "A Pre-Primer Vocabulary Study," *Elementary School Journal,* XXXV (September, 1934).

23. Horn, Ernest, and McBroom, Maude. *A Survey of the Course of Study in Reading,* University of Iowa Extension Bulletin, College of Education, No. 99, Series No. 3, February, 1924.

24. Horn, Ernest. *A Basic Writing Vocabulary,* University of Iowa Monographs in Education, 1926.

25. Jackson, Edward. "Developmental Alexia" (Congenital Word-blindness), *American Journal of Medical Sciences,* CXXXI (May, 1906), 843-49.

26. McCluskey, Howard Y. "A Quantitative Analysis of the Difficulty of Reading Materials," *Journal of Educational Research,* XXVIII (December, 1934), 276-82.

27. Ogden, C. K. *Basic English.* London, England: Kegan Paul, Trench, Trubner & Co., 1932.

28. Osburn, Worth J. *The Relative Value of Letter Sounds and Consonants.* Madison, Wisconsin: State Department of Public Instruction.

29. Pennell, Mary E., and Cusack, Alice. *The Teaching of Reading for Better Living.* Boston: Houghton, Mifflin Co., 1935.

30. Sexton, Elmer K., and Herron, John S. "The Newark Phonics Experiment," *Elementary School Journal,* XXVIII (May, 1928), 690-701.

31. Shambaugh, C. G., and Shambaugh, Olive L. "A Core Vocabulary for Elementary School Pupils," *Journal of Educational Research,* XIX (January, 1929).

32. Smith, Nila Banton. *The Unit Activity Reading Series* (Teacher's Guide for the First Year). New York: Silver, Burdett and Co., 1935.

33. Smith, Nila Banton. "The Construction of First-Grade Reading Material," *Journal of Educational Research,* XVII (February, 1928), 79-89.

34. Stone, Clarence R. *Teacher's Guide and Course of Study in Reading.* San José, California: Board of Education, 1935.

35. Stone, Clarence R. "The Second Grade Reading Vocabulary," *Elementary School Journal,* XXXV (January, 1935), 359-67.

36. Storm, Grace E., and Smith, Nila B. *Reading Activities in the Primary Grades.* Boston: Ginn & Co., 1930.

37. *The Vocabularies of Fourteen Pre-Primers.* Chicago: Scott, Foresman & Company, 1935.

38. Thorndike, Edward L. *The Teacher's Word Book.* New York: Teachers College, Columbia University, 1921.

39. Thorndike, Edward L. *A Teacher's Word Book of the Twenty Thousand Words Found Most Frequently and Widely in General Reading for Children and Young People.* New York: Teachers College, Columbia University, 1931.

40. Wheeler, H. E., and Howell, Emma A. "A First-Grade Vocabulary Study," *Elementary School Journal,* XXXI (September, 1930), 52-60.

41. White, Margaret L., and Hanthorn, Alice. *Teachers' Manual for Do and Learn Readers.* New York: American Book Company, 1930.

CHAPTER XII
Emotional Factors

Faulty pupil attitudes toward the work of the school grow out of distaste for the work, failure to progress satisfactorily, and unwholesome personal relationships between teacher and pupil.—Leo. J. Brueckner (2:7)

Emotional Aberrations

The writer's attitude is that every child would learn to read if it were in his power to do so. Many factors, enumerated in other chapters of this book, contribute to a given case of reading disability. One of the characteristic symptoms of a remedial case is a dislike for reading sometimes manifested in a reading fear or tenseness. Although such an emotional reaction may be only a symptom of reading disability, it is essential that the emotional aspect of learning be recognized in the remedial treatment. There is enough social pressure in the school and community to cause most children to want to learn to read; therefore, it is the teacher's task to create a desirable attitude toward the contents of reading matter.

Hincks (4:85) found, "the reaction of unpleasantness toward the content of books was probably a conditioned reflex, since the content had always been experienced together with the difficult psychological processes of reading it." Ladd (1:18) reported: "No marked relationships were found between reading ability and gross scores on socio-economic status of the home, play interests, and general personality adjustments."

Durrell (3:92) summarizes the situation by stating: "The confidence which a child gains as he progresses through a well-planned remedial reading program has an alleviating effect on emotional difficulties, if such are present. We need not delay our remedial program while waiting the development of techniques in the analysis and correction of emotions or in the gentle art of remodeling parents."

From the conflicting research reports, there appears to be no data to show that good readers rate higher than poor readers on desirable personality traits. Too frequently have the causes of reading difficulties been ascribed to emotional instability, lack of confidence, inability to concentrate, unwillingness, and the like. Other things being equal, the personality of the teacher probably has as much or more to do with a learning situation than the personality of the learner. If other learning conditions are fulfilled, the child will learn to read if he can be sufficiently interested.

Awareness of Success

"Nothing succeeds like success" is an old adage which is no exception in academic learning. Some children like to read because it affords enjoyment and is a comfortable processs. It is the intrinsic or personal satisfying reward. This type of pleasure can best be achieved by giving the learner a large quantity of easy materials of high personal interest as he reaches each level of reading difficulty.

Motivation, by and large, should be intrinsic and come from the desirable relations among the three factors of motivation—the child, the teacher, and the setting. However, the objections to extrinsic rewards have of late become less pronounced. Certainly, there is no objection to the use of book charts when used under controlled conditions. Tests constructed for the purpose of measuring small increments of growth in reading skills and information are excellent devices for making the pupil aware of his success. One sure way to dampen the spirits of an eager young learner is to require him to read material which offers excessive vocabulary, sentence structure, and meaning difficulties. Such procedures create a distaste for reading and make the process generally uninteresting. Rhythmical reading habits are not fostered in such circumstances.

Attitudes

Once a learner has been permitted to fail to achieve in any learning situation, an emotional problem is created. The biggest obstacle to overcome in any remedial teaching situation is the system of undesirable attitudes acquired by the learner. In addition to the often deep-seated feeling that he cannot learn to read, the retarded reader often rationalizes the situation by insisting that he does not like to read. Aversion to reading on the part of children is built up by forcing them into situations for which they are too immature, by questionable teacher and parent attitudes, by failure on the part of teachers to analyze learning gaps and make necessary provisions, and by a general lack of understanding of the problems encountered by a child with a language disability. In the past, those supposedly concerned with the learning handicaps of children have been entirely too prone, consciously or unconsciously, to "dub" them as dull. In other instances, a change in handedness or some other one factor has been used to account for all language difficulties, forgetting that after all the child can and must be taught to read. Rationalization of a problem does not solve it. Leading classroom teachers the country over are and have

been teaching the so-called "word-blind" to read with satisfaction. Each year educators and phychologists are being
offered additional and improved techniques for the analysis
of the difficulty.

Several attitudes should be acquired by the remedial
teacher: (1) The prognosis of a reading disability case is
hopeful. Through enthusiastic and intelligent persistence on
the part of the teacher, children are being taught to read.
(2) Many difficulties can be more easily remedied by solicit-
ing the co-operation of health specialists. (3) Many retarded readers (as defined in Chapter I) have either normal or superior intelligence. (4) By and large, the most
effective procedures are those which are readily applied and
easily understood. (5) Nothing succeeds like success. The
learner can be helped by being made aware of small increments of growth. (6) Any learner should be approached
through his own specific interests. (7) Remedial instruction
should be regarded as a privilege extended to the child.

Those teachers who appear to achieve most are those who
are constantly improving their own skills, information, and
attitudes. Not the least of these is the attitude of the
worker. The deficiencies of children with reading difficulties
are being removed by persistent and enthusiastic workers.
Undoubtedly, many of the analysis procedures are crude and
the remedial procedures are inefficient, but only the integrated efforts of research workers in many fields can provide data which will permit children to achieve with less
difficulty. The writer raises many questions regarding the
procedures operative in his reading clinic, but the work must
go on for out of it all children are being taught to read
and new possibilities arise each day from such work. The
big task ahead is to cause present data to be translated into

schoolroom practice. The type of program which should be initiated depends, to a degree, on the type of teacher. Any method mechanically used cannot be expected to produce results.

SUMMARY

1. Every child would learn to read if it were in his power to do so.
2. The first task of the teacher is to create a learning situation in which the content of books is pleasurably anticipated.
3. Undesirable emotional reactions are frequently symptoms of learning difficulties and may impede progress.
4. The child should be continually aware of his success.
5. Teacher enthusiasm, attitude, and persistence are important elements in the learning situation.
6. Desirable attitudes are acquired when reading power is developed.
7. Pupil interests should be inventoried as a part of the analysis procedure.
8. The teacher should endeavor to interest the learner by attending to the "readiness" factor at all grade levels.

REFERENCES

1. Betts, Emmett A. "Reading Disabilities and Their Correction: National Conference on Research in Elementary School English," *Elementary English Review,* XII (March, April, May, June, 1935), 69-73, 106-10, 131-41, 157-65.
2. Brueckner, Leo J. (Chairman). "Educational Diagnosis," *Thirty-fourth Yearbook of the National Society for the*

Study of Education. Bloomington, Illinois: Public School Publishing Co., 1935.

3. Durrell, Donald D. "Tests and Corrective Procedures for Reading Disabilities," *Elementary English Review,* XII (April, 1935), 91-95.

4. Hincks, Elizabeth M. *Disability in Reading and Its Relation to Personality,* p. 92. Harvard Monographs in Education, No. 7. Cambridge, Massachusetts: Harvard University Press, 1926.

CHAPTER XIII
The Program of Prevention

In nearly all, if not all, schools a considerable per cent of the children acquire unfortunate attitudes and improper habits in reading during the first three grades.—Clarence R. Stone (10:48)

A Preview

A program for prevention of reading difficulties deals with first-teaching and readiness for reading. Removing a reading deficiency appears to be the chief concern of teachers, school administrators, and parents, but planning for the future avoidance of difficulties should receive first consideration. Far too much has been written on remedial programs as contrasted to the number of publications on prevention.

Throughout this book the emphasis has been placed on the need for data on general reading readiness and a program for first-teaching in which individual differences are recognized in practice. Most authorities in this field believe that reading difficulties can be prevented. No one precautionary measure can be discussed in isolation.

The program of prevention involves:

1. Re-evaluation of typical promotion policies.
2. Correction of physical defects.
3. Identification of the prospective "non-readers."
4. Development of a program of legitimate reading-readiness activities which are valuable beyond the kindergarten.

237

5. Development of a program of first-teaching in which both general readiness for reading and varying rates of learning are recognized.

6. Providing adequate reading materials.

7. Development of a staff philosophy that reading is a tool rather than a subject.

8. Providing proper external conditions for reading.

9. Re-evaluation of the total school program in terms of the maturation levels of the learners.

10. Raising standards of teacher education.

Promotion Policies

The matter of non-promotions and promotion policies was discussed in Chapters I and IV. The basis of promotion and the care of individual differences depend to no small degree on the philosophy of education in operation in a given school system. Needs vary from one community to another, depending upon the type of population and other factors. Hence, the promotion policies for a given community should be determined in terms of the particular problems. After general administrative policies have been determined, there will always be border-line cases which require individual consideration. No one factor contributes to the large number of non-promotions in any one situation. The preparation of the teachers, entrance age, quality of kindergarten instruction, time of introduction of formal arithmetic, type of primary-reading program, grade standards of achievement, adequacy of health service, co-operation of parents, type of population, size of classes, and kindred factors should be considered in establishing policies of promotion.

From the meager data available, there appears to be a relationship between entrance age to first grade and the percentage of failures in that grade. Other things being equal, the higher the entrance-age requirement, the lower is the percentage of failures. Since some normal children are not ready to read until they are six and one-half to seven years of age and since children below normal intelligence are not usually ready for reading until an even older age, the policy of promoting children, who have been admitted to the first grade at six years or younger, to the second grade on the basis of reading achievement is very questionable.

Many school systems are eliminating the grade classification of children in the primary grades and are grouping on the basis of progress in reading. This, of course, necessitates careful planning of the whole school program and the re-grading of school activities, such as arithmetic. There is unquestionably a trend toward the re-evaluation of traditional activities.

Correction of Physical Defects

No one would question the value of an adequate health program in public schools. Every child has the right to all that health specialists can give. The National Society for the Prevention of Blindness and the Volta Bureau (dealing with work for the deaf and the hard of hearing) have contributed generously in sensitizing the public to the need for precautionary health measures. The researches of Betts (3), Bond (4), Eames (4), Fendrick (4), and others have brought out many of the educational implications of physical defects.

Health problems other than visual and hearing defects

may contribute to learning difficulties. Some children are handicapped by toxic conditions which may be caused by infected tonsils, adenoids, kidneys, and the like. These infections in turn may be reflected in visual and hearing difficulties. The family and school doctor should always be consulted in such cases.

Neither good readers nor poor readers should work under physical handicaps which can be corrected. Teachers are trained in a very short period of time to detect visual and hearing handicaps. The problem then appears to be one of supplying teachers and nurses with the necessary materials which will aid them in discriminating between pedagogical and health problems. All cases requiring such service should be referred to the proper specialists through the parents and the family physician. Only in this way can physical handicaps for learning be properly cared for from the standpoint of the school. Further discussion of these important aspects of the problem can be found in Chapters VIII and X.

Identification of the Prospective Non-Reader

After the program of initial reading instruction is determined, procedures should be initiated for the identification of candidates who are not ready for the program. This is necessary because individual differences in level of maturity and rate of maturation do exist. The reading readiness tests described in Chapter V are designed to provide an index to the child's level of readiness for the typical reading program. After the pupils are classified on this basis, the variation in rates of learning can be recognized by varying the amount of repetition and the rate of introduction of new work for the various groups within the class. In brief, the prospective non-reader can be fairly accurately identified although border-line cases will always exist.

Reading-Readiness Activities

One of the purposes of the program of activities in the kindergarten and early first grade is the preparation of the child for reading. Such instruction cannot be expected to overcome general immaturity or low intelligence. Neither can individual differences be decreased; instead, individual differences may be expected to be greater after instruction but the general level of readiness for the whole group should be raised. In brief, the reading-readiness activities are usually planned to develop interests and facility in use of the English language and to provide and extend needed experiences. The provision of legitimate reading-readiness activities is, then, a significant aspect of a program of prevention. This problem is discussed at greater length in Chapter II.

The First-Teaching Program

If pupils were not permitted to proceed from one level of learning to a higher level until each individual were ready, there would be few reading difficulties on succeeding grades. A significant part of the program of prevention is the administration of the activities in each classroom in terms of individual needs. This philosophy would not necessitate wholesale non-promotion because each child can be permitted to progress at his own rate by grouping the children within the room. The first-teaching of new skills and information in reading should not take place until the teacher is assured that preceding basic skills and information have been acquired.

Adequate Reading Materials

Variation in individual rates of learning makes it mandatory for the teacher to expect a wide range of ability in a given activity at any grade level. Adequate reading materials for a given grade will include levels of difficulty from three or more grades below the grade in question to five or six grades above. For example, a third-grade teacher should provide books ranging from pre-primers to sixth-grade science books. In many schools fewer than one-third of the children can profit from reading well-graded third-grade materials. Some will be confused because of the difficulty of the materials and others will be uninterested because the materials are too easy.

Supplying adequate materials does not mean buying copies of the same readers for every child. In the past, many schools have provided as many as seven or ten sets of readers on a given-grade level. By the expenditure of the same amount of money, more books could have been provided by purchasing from three to five copies of each set of supplementary readers. In addition, books written for use below and above the grade level could have been added. In this way, the proper use of adequate material could be used to prevent confusion in reading.

The Teacher's Philosophy

In the past, reading has been regarded too much as a drill subject. In the first place, reading is only a tool and not a subject to be studied as such. Secondly, reading is the key to arithmetic, science, social studies, and literature. From the very beginning, reading should be a part of an activity where the pupils want to learn something in particular; that is, reading should be taught from the reading-to-learn point of view. As indicated in other chapters, there may be occasions for learning specific items about the reading process, but this should be in a meaningful and interesting situation.

It is also erroneous for the teacher to have the philosophy that reading instruction should be given only during the reading class. If reading difficulties are to be prevented, each teacher must assume the responsibility for furthering practice in situations where reading is involved. If everyone looks to the so-called reading teacher to do that task, reading deficiencies are certain to persist because there are specific reading skills and information which can be taught functionally only through activities connected with the content subjects. Every teacher should be a teacher of reading.

External Conditions

Precautionary measures should include proper lighting, seating which fosters good posture, adequate ventilation, and kindred items. Too frequently, time is spent in correcting physical defects which could have been prevented. In other words, everyone is interested in remedial procedures and few are concerned with preventive measures. Many children are bending over flat-top desks and working in one to four foot-candles of light for four to five hours per day. After pupils have acquired visual defects, they are placed in well lighted rooms and are provided with slant-top desks so that it will be unnecessary for them to crane their necks in order to read or write. The question one might ask is, "If this situation is desirable for the handicapped, why not provide for the well in like manner so that difficulties of this nature will not arise?"

Review of the School Program

A plan for the prevention of reading difficulties necessitates the re-evaluation of the school program. If data to the effect that reading retards general educational progress are valid, then for immature groups the substitution of an enriched non-reading curriculum for a reading program necessitates a regrading of the content subjects. Some children at eight years of age are still struggling with elementary-reading skills, which means that the introduction of formal arithmetic and spelling in the second or third grade only complicates their problems.

Standards of Teacher Education

Of the many factors which contribute to reading deficiencies, poor teaching is not the least. Although there is urgent need for extension of the pre-service training period, there is probably a greater need for the training of teachers in service. The instructional leadership of the school administrator is one of his most important functions. Professional teachers require very little direction, for their schoolroom is their laboratory and up-to-date professional libraries of books and magazines are their chief sources of help. During the last ten years the research output has increased to the extent that teaching has been made more nearly scientific. The teacher who was certified ten years ago, finds today more economical methods for teaching of a changed subject matter.

Many problems related to reading deficiencies have been made less ominous for the classroom teacher who has kept up. There can be no changing of the retarded reader's attitude until the teacher first tries to understand the problems surrounding his difficulties. This is not likely to happen until she has studied professional literature on the topic.

SUMMARY

1. Most reading difficulties can be prevented.

2. The prevention of reading deficiencies merits first consideration.

3. Promotion policies should be developed in terms of the problems peculiar to a given community.

4. Physical defects have direct educational implications.

5. Prospective non-readers can be identified with a fair degree of reliability.

6. The validity of reading-readiness activities should be appraised.

7. First-teaching is effective to the degree that preparatory skills and information have been acquired by the learner.

8. Reading materials are adequate to the degree that they meet the needs and interests of the learners.

9. Reading is a tool, not a subject.

10. Improper external conditions contribute to learning difficulties.

11. A modification of the reading program entails a complete reviewing of the curriculum.

12. In the final analysis, reading difficulties can be prevented to the degree that the teacher has a professional understanding of her work.

REFERENCES

1. Betts, Emmett A. "Bibliography on the Analysis, Prevention, and Correction of Reading Difficulties." Meadville, Pennsylvania: Keystone View Co., 1935.

2. Betts, Emmett A. "Is Reading Related to Growth?" *Progressive Education,* XI (December, 1934).

3. Betts, Emmett A. "A Physiological Approach to the Analysis of Reading Disabilities," *Educational Research Bulletin* (Ohio State University), XIII (September, 1934).

4. Betts, Emmett A. "Prevention and Correction of Reading Disabilities," *Elementary English Review,* XII (February, 1935), 25-32.

5. Betts, Emmett A. "Reading Disabilities and Their Correction: National Conference on Research in Elementary School English," *Elementary English Review,* XII (March, April, May, June, 1935), 69-73, 106-10, 131-41, 157-65.

6. Betts, Emmett A. "Teacher Analysis of Reading Disabilities," *Elementary English Review,* XI (April, 1934), 99-102.

7. Betts, Emmett A., Everett, Mabel, and Rodewald, Frances. "Remedial Reading Based on First-Teaching," *Journal of Exceptional Children* (February, 1936).

8. Caswell, Hollis L. *Non-Promotion in Elementary Schools,* x-100. Division of Surveys and Field Studies, Nashville, Tennessee: George Peabody College for Teachers, 1933.

9. Reed, Mary M. *An Investigation of Practices in First Grade Admission and Promotion.* Teachers College Contribution to Education, No. 290. New York: Teachers College, Columbia University, 1927.

10. Stone, C. R. *Teacher's Guide and Course of Study in Reading.* San Jose, California: Board of Education, 1935.

CHAPTER XIV
The Program of Correction

Cases of discouragement and distaste for reading may be remedied only by starting with the child at the point where he can achieve enough success to find satisfaction in his reading experiences.
—Clarence R. Stone (28 : 50)

A Preview of the Program of Correction

Many implications regarding the program of correction are set forth in other chapters. In this chapter the pedagogical procedures are described in more detail, while the other aspects of the problem are only summarized. Failure to achieve in reading can usually be quickly analyzed. Success in any learning situation depends upon how adequately learning conditions are met. In Chapter III a detailed outline of factors which appear to be related to reading deficiencies was offered. At this point in the book, it probably would be well to review the factors which appear to be related to reading difficulties, for from these a remedial teacher can secure a total picture of the relative elementary conditions which must be met.

In most cases of reading deficiencies, the learners will respond readily. Extended analyses are seldom necessary. Likewise, elaborate and involved corrective procedures should be tried only when other plans have proved inadequate. The essential learning conditions to be met are adequate mental age, freedom from physical defects, genuine interest in improvement and in the reading content, material within the grasp of the learner, and kindred items. The teacher should have some knowledge of mental hygiene, clinical psychology, primary-reading methods, phonetics, and remedial reading procedures. If the remedial teacher expects to lead the individual to achievement, she must have a thorough understanding of where she is leading him. In this case, the blind cannot lead the blind. It is probably a truism to state that blind first-teaching contributes largely to reading difficulties. Given intelligent and enthusiastic instruction, adequate reading materials, opportunity for individual rather than mass progress, proper physical care, and general readiness for reading, most, if not all, reading difficulties could be prevented. When proper conditions are met, teachers and parents are usually astonished by the progress of the learner.

Reading is not just a general ability, instead it is a complex pattern of skills, knowledges, and attitudes. The particular combinations practiced vary with the purpose which motivates the reading. The analysis procedure discussed in preceding chapters was offered for the appraisal of educational achievement and for the diagnosis of the defects in the physiological and psychological processes which contribute to speed and comprehension. It is a truism to state that the remedial procedures should meet the needs of the individual as found through the analysis. Since the analysis is made on the basis of specifics, the remedial measures should be designed to provide training on specific items contributing to the retardation in reading.

The reading program embraces the teacher, the learner, and the instructional materials. The teacher is the key to the situation. Through her the door to enjoyable reading can be opened. Her philosophy, attitude, and insight are the chief determiners of success. It is through her intelligent understanding and tireless efforts and through her careful selection of interesting reading materials that the learner acquires a new attitude and reading power, and a satisfaction in his achievement.

Primarily the remedial reading teacher should be a pragmatist. Regarding procedure, the final question should be "were results achieved?" The next question follows: "Was this the most economical means of achieving results?" Since each case presents a peculiar set of circumstances, no one theory and no one pattern of remedial instruction should be adopted for all cases. No magic is involved. Success has been claimed by many investigators reporting a variety of procedures.

There are few techniques peculiar to remedial reading. In the main, remedial procedures for extreme cases are more highly individualized than ordinary classroom processes. Also more attention is given to the reinforcement of various types of imageries. The remedial teacher is primarily concerned with (a) the correction of physical handicaps by a specialist, (b) the establishment of desirable attitudes toward reading, and (c) the development of efficient, rhythmical reading habits. Remedial instruction differs from first-teaching in that each specific situation must be canvassed more thoroughly.

Gray's (11:174) challenge to those engaged in remedial work is contained in the following statement: "It is an interesting fact that many teachers and supervisors think at first that the chief aim of improving reading is to increase the achievement of pupils in tests of speed and comprehension. Valuable as good habits of silent reading are, the major aims to be achieved are enriched experiences and

wholesome interests acquired through wide reading in each
school subject or activity."

Basic Principles and Assumptions for the
Remedial Program

1. Most reading difficulties can be prevented by good first-
   teaching.

2. Severely handicapped readers and non-readers require
   individual instruction.

3. Pupils evidencing a deficiency in only a few specific
   reading skills can be effectively helped in small
   groups.

4. Desirable mind set or attitude is essential to economical
   learning. One of the most significant tasks for the
   teacher is the change of pupil attitude.

5. Remedial reading should be based on the specific needs
   and interests of the learner.

6. Awareness of success is a significant factor in the
   progress and achievement of a retarded reader.
   Measures of small increments of growth, not provided in typical reading tests, are necessary for motivation as well as for continuous inventory. Usually
   graphs of achievement on specific items will cause the
   learner to compete with his own record.

7. Health problems should be identified and referred to
   specialists for help. The correction of physical handicaps is important, but will not give the learner
   needed reading skills.

8. The co-operation of the home should be solicited.

9. Large size type with suitable spacing should be used in the construction of corrective materials. This is especially significant for cases experiencing visual or eye co-ordination handicaps. For first- and second-grade children such material written in manuscript on the blackboard or charts is highly desirable.

10. The work should begin with the child's special interest. Practical arts, art, music, social science, and other science activities may be used as avenues of approach to the content of books.

11. Specific vocabulary building should be a definite part of the reading program, remedial or otherwise. Reading vocabularies are as specific as reading skills. Special attention should be directed to science, social studies, arithmetic, and literature vocabularies.

12. The remedial materials should be at the child's grade level of achievement. Frequently, it is necessary for ten-year-old boys to begin with primer level material. Here the type is larger, the vocabulary required is small, and the sentence structure and punctuation is not difficult to interpret.

13. The learner should not be graduated from one level of reading to another until he has acquired rhythmical habits of reading for meaning at the preceding level. Extensive and interesting reading materials should be provided at each level.

14. Reading for meaning, or reading to learn, should always be emphasized. A close check on comprehension should be maintained throughout the period of instruction. Learning to read by reading implies that there shall be a minimum of drill in isolation.

15. Reading methods where phonetics are emphasized will not prove fruitful for children with hearing handicaps, such as low-auditory acuity or a narrow auditory frequency range.

16. Visual, auditory, and kinaesthetic imageries should be caused to reinforce one another. In cases of severe disabilities, the learner can establish a feeling for the written word by seeing, hearing, writing, and subsequently meaning associations.

17. The learner must acquire a system for the independent recognition of new words. The system will include the use of phonics, context clues (meanings), picture clues, syllabication, total configurations, and the noting of similarities and differences.

18. The learner must have confidence that the teacher will help him learn to read.

19. The learner should not have the remedial reading forced on him as a disciplinary measure. Remedial instruction should be a privilege, not a hardship.

20. Remedial reading instruction should be given when the learner is not fatigued or missing some other activity enjoyed by the group.

21. Remedial instruction should be definitely scheduled. Two periods per day of fifteen or twenty minutes each for the younger pupils are more profitable than one longer period.

22. Specific errors should be corrected.

23. The teacher should be contagiously enthusiastic.

24. Remedial instruction techniques should be varied from day to day. Certain word games have been worked until some children appear to acquire "game nausea."

25. Early in the work, the child should frankly be made aware of the specific nature of his difficulties.

26. Severely handicapped readers are usually low in written spelling, although spelling disabilities are frequently not accompanied by reading disabilities.

27. Learners without physiological hearing handicaps should have a definite program of auditory training with special attention to speech habits.

28. Reading should not be divorced from composition, either oral or written. This will permit the reading of material that is interesting to the learner and the building of a functioning vocabulary (contributing to word recognition).

29. Drill on a word in isolation should always be followed by emphasis on the meaning of the word through use in the context.

30. The program of remedial instruction should be attacked with vigor by both teacher and learner.

31. A definite program should be established for the fostering of left-to-right reading habits.

32. All writing should be done with the preferred hand.

33. The remedial teacher should know in detail the facts revealed by the analysis of the difficulty. No one remedial procedure should be recommended for all cases. Children have been taught to read by a variety of methods. Individual instruction and a definite goal are elements common to the many procedures reported in the literature.

34. In so far as possible, teacher time should be conserved by grouping within the classroom.

The Correction of Physical Defects

There is some controversy over the relationship between certain physical defects and reading achievements. The pragmatist cares little for such discussions, for the fact remains that every child has the right to all the aid that health specialists can give. Comfortable vision, normal hearing, and freedom from toxic conditions certainly should make otherwise tedious school activities more enjoyable.

The researches of Betts (1), Dearborn (1), Eames (1), Farris (6), Fendrick (1), Selzer (25), Wagner (32), and others justify the contention that visual difficulties and ocular anomalies should be listed as possible correlates of reading difficulties. It should not be thought that the correction of such disabilities will teach the individual to read. However, after the proper health precautions have been taken, psycho-educational procedures can be applied more safely and surely. Hence, it may be assumed that one of the first steps in a remedial program is the proper treatment of visual difficulties. Comfortable vision is essential to sustained reading.

The Visual Sensation and Perception slides of the Betts Ready to Read Tests (described in Chapter VIII and in the Appendix) are designed for use by the teacher and other qualified workers. No special training is required by the teacher in order to detect gross visual defects. If the individual fails to pass any one of the tests, the teacher should secure the co-operation of the family eye-specialist. Both the teacher and the doctor should have some common understanding of the educational implications of physical defects. Until this comes to pass, there cannot be the intelligent co-operation for the benefit of the learner.

Since, in many remedial procedures, auditory imagery is emphasized, hearing should be appraised and if defective the individual should receive medical attention. Although good hearing is important in all school activities, it is of special significance in spelling and beginning reading.

Many other physical conditions may contribute to inattention and learning difficulties. Fatigue may be due to a toxic condition as well as to malnutrition and a lack of rest. Such factors require careful analysis by members of the health department. The health specialist should become the ally of the teacher.

The Program for the Immature Learner

Practically everyone who has contacted reading programs at the primary level has been confronted with the problem of the immature child. Since some investigators have found approximately one-third of the first-grade children in many communities failing at the first-grade level, this is hardly a situation which requires only compromise. The mere postponement of reading instruction will not meet the requirements. Instead, a program including specific and legitimate reading-readiness activities should be developed.

It has been the writer's experience that the substitution of a reading-readiness program (not the sheer postponement of reading) for the typical first-grade reading requirements will forestall difficulties for the immature child. In many cases the claims of success through a given method of instruction for six- and seven-year-old children cannot be substantiated scientifically. In addition to the well motivated individual instruction which characterizes such ventures, the maturation which took place included also simultaneous increase in physical and mental maturity. The question then is, "which contributed more to the achievement, the particular brand of instruction or the increased maturity of the learner?"

One semester of growth at the six-year-old level is of tremendous significance. In short, success could have been more economically achieved by placing the emphasis on reading-readiness activities in terms of the individual's interests and abilities until a level of general readiness had been attained. The child capable of a normal learning rate would then progress normally through the initial-reading levels. Regardless of the amount of formal reading exercises forced upon the immature child, reading-readiness or aptitude tests provide substantial information regarding the six- or seven-year-old child who fails to achieve in reading. Tests are administered so that parallel instruction may be offered in terms of the deficiency. Difficulties brought about by immaturity, or a lack of readiness for reading, must be met by a patient redirection of energies into tasks which will yield success. A child cannot be taught to walk or talk before there is readiness for the process involved. Likewise, the energies of both the teacher and the learner are wasted when reading instruction is forced upon the unprepared. Worse yet, poor attitudes are learned.

Chapters II and XIII contained more extended discussions of progress for the immature learner.

Deficiencies in Specific Reading Skills

In Chapter V tests were enumerated for the analysis of reading achievement. Such tests are useful for the identification of deficiencies which can be readily corrected by providing practice on the specific skills and information involved. These tests, however, provide the examiner with little evidence regarding the psychological and physiological procedures involved in the reading process. If the typical pedagogical procedures do not remove the deficiency, further and more detailed analyses are required. Tests for the analysis of extreme reading disability were outlined also in Chapter V.

Either teacher-made or standardized reading tests may be used for the analysis of deficiencies in specific reading skills. In any event, there are few commercial remedial materials which parallel the types of skills analyzed.

It is advisable to provide practice on skills in which deficiencies exist by controlled assignments and class discussions rather than by commercially prepared materials. Diagnostic tests for grades one and two usually include tests over word recognition, phrase recognition and paragraph comprehension. Some tests also include specific items on following directions, anticipating meanings, and organization of ideas.

The correction of specific difficulties in reading is frequently more of a first-teaching than a remedial proposition. In most cases it is a matter of giving more practice on the specific items involved. The materials for remedial instruction usually include workbook drills and commercial remedial exercises. For the overloaded teacher commercially prepared materials are a great help. The literature of the subject, however, contains few, if any, references to the use of ready-made drills. The teacher who groups her children within the classroom will find the material which has functional value to be most economical. Remedial work must be strongly motivated.

The Gates-Peardon *Practice Exercises in Reading* (7) for each of grades three to six were designed to parallel the

Gates Reading Tests. The following important types of reading are provided:

Type A. Reading to Appreciate the General Significance of a Selection.

Type B. Reading to Predict the Outcome of Given Events.

Type C. Reading to Understand Precise Directions.

Type D. Reading to Note Details.

Teachers interested in the prevention and correction of specific reading difficulties should own a copy of Nila B. Smith's *One Hundred Ways of Teaching Silent Reading,* published by Ginn and Company. She describes exercises to improve the following important aspects of reading: speed, comprehension, selection, organization, retention, and skimming. Hovious, *Following Printed Trails,* published by D. C. Heath and Company, is another excellent book for use at the secondary-school level. Cues for types of exercises needed for the correction of specific difficulties can be secured from workbooks and standardized tests.

The following suggestions are offered for the correction of specific deficiencies in reading:

1. **Vocabulary.** Ways and means of developing skills in word recognition are described in Chapter XI. In Chapter II, the administration of a reading program to provide for individual needs is discussed. The problem of materials and methods are presented in this chapter.

2. **Location of information.** Many children are deficient in the ability to locate information. In order to appraise various aspects of this important study ability, tests have been devised to check on the knowledge and skills required in alphabetizing, use of index and table of contents.

Pupils will be unable to locate information quickly if they cannot alphabetize. Individuals with reading difficulties are notorious in their inability to recognize letters in isolation. Following the initial reading period practice should be emphasized on use of table of contents, finding pages by number, and finding answers to specific questions. Incidental to this, of course, will be practice on skimming.

The reading of third-grade materials requires knowledge of skills in skimming and the use of a glossary and dictionary. At about the fourth-grade level, the reading activities will require of the pupil some knowledge and skill in the use of chapter headings, paragraph headings, maps, charts, graphs, reference books, and indexes. Later in the reading program, practice should be given on the use of appendixes, cross references, keys, and footnotes. All of these skills can best be taught through class or small group activities. Undoubtedly some of the skills such as alphabetizing can be more economically presented to the class as a whole. The skills must be built up a step at a time; otherwise, some pupils will be confused. For example, the pupils should be given practice in arranging words in alphabetical order according to the first letter of each word. Subsequent practice can be given on alphabetizing words according to the second letter, such as *acorn, alarm, clever, crab;* according to the third letter, such as *frisky, frolic, hail, hardly,* and so on until the pupils at each grade level can make accurate and quick use of the indexes found in their books. All this work may be preceded by interesting class activities wherein the pupils discover the alphabetical arrangement of words and topics in indexes, dictionaries, and encyclopedias.

The ability to locate information quickly by skimming can be practiced in the study of science, social science and the like. During class discussions there may arise specific questions to which the answers can be found by the scanning of a chapter or a page. In other instances, the specific words used to describe an incident or a character may provide the occasion for skimming. Frequently, it is advisable to have the class list three or four questions on the blackboard which requires skimming in order to answer. The difference between "incidental" and "accidental" instruction lies in the degree to which the teacher has planned to insure the coverage of specific skills.

Practice on the reverse side of the situation should not be omitted. When class or individual booklets are prepared as a part of the class activities, there will be some children who will suggest that they make a "real" book, including a table of contents and an index. In other words, new type assignments and class discussions rather than a reciting-to-the-teacher process can be used to motivate and insure practice on needed skills.

3. Comprehension. Tests used to measure level or power of comprehension are enumerated in Chapter V. In the same chapter, tests are described for the analysis of reading achievement which are valuable for determining underlying and contributory deficiencies. All such measuring devices are helpful for the analysis of comprehension difficulties. Comprehension and other reading skills, information, and attitudes are highly interdependent. It is not uncommon for some individuals to get the meaning of a paragraph although they have faulty mechanical habits of reading. The attitude of reading for meaning should be emphasized from the beginning, even during the preparatory period. Standardized tests can be used to locate the deficiencies which contribute to a low rate of comprehension.

Satisfaction and a rapid rate of comprehension are more or less the end results of reading. Items contributing to comprehension difficulties may be summarized as follows: (a) meager vocabulary, (b) word-by-word reading (inability to phrase), (c) inaccurate perception, (d) failure to note punctuation, (e) low intelligence, (f) lack of interest, (g) reading material too difficult, and (h) inadequate mechanical habits.

One of the first considerations for remedial work in comprehension is that of difficulty of material. It is common to find third-grade children with only first-grade reading ability attempting to read third-grade materials. Rhythmical reading habits and a rapid rate of comprehension cannot be fostered in situations where the reading materials are not within the grasp of the learner. One rule should be followed rigidly; namely, regardless of his grade classification, provide the child with materials which he can read, even though they are pre-primers. It is the usual case that difficulties have arisen because the teacher has failed to begin with the learner's level of ability. Even fifth-grade children may have to begin with materials at the pre-primer or primer level. If the learner is of normal mentality, progress will be rapid and it will not be necessary to spend more than a week or two with such easy materials. It is essential to practice at each level of difficulty for a sufficient time to insure mastery of word-recognition techniques, rhythmical reading habits (phrasing and the like) and the attitude of reading for meaning. Comprehension cannot be stressed when the mechanical difficulties are insurmountable.

The second consideration in building comprehension techniques is that of practice on material within the experience of the learner. The chief limitation of using first- and second-grade reading materials for individuals with reading deficiencies is the difficulty in locating stories which interest the troubled learner. It has been the writer's experience, however, that most normal children have a strong desire to remove their deficiency and that this interest properly recognized will carry them through the initial stages. Pupil-dictated compositions about subjects of their particular interest can be used entirely or as supplementary-reading material. If the problem is mainly one of building for comprehension, the material should be largely ready-made.

The appraisal of the learner's powers of comprehension should be the third important consideration. This can be done through the type of assignment made and through carefully planned class activities. The purpose of the reading and the type of material read determines the type of comprehension skills which are practiced. In a properly motivated situation, the check on comprehension will be a means for stimulating the learner to further effort and to acquiring a desirable mind set or attitude.

Checks on comprehension commonly used are:

a) Following of written directions.

(1) For beginners, action cards can be used, such as *sit, stand, walk,* etc. If such work is introduced as games, considerable enthusiasm can be injected into the situation.

(2) Directions in Boy Scout, Girl Scout handbooks and the like can be used to provide excellent comprehension exercises which require very little artificial motivation.

(3) Written directions for playing reading games in small groups are usually well received.

(4) Blackboard or bulletin board notices can be used effectively. The teacher should take every practical opportunity to substitute written for oral directions.

b) Securing answers to specific questions. (Described above under the heading "Location of Information.")

c) Preparing oral and written summaries for a class report.

d) Outlining.

e) Preparing original oral or written illustrations or application of the information gained from reading.

f) Finding the main idea in a sentence or paragraph.

g) Supplying omitted words in prepared comprehension exercises.

h) Guessing the answer to written riddles.

i) Answering "yes" and "no" to true-false exercises.

j) Preparing questions on the assignment for the class.

Sentence and paragraph comprehension is usually emphasized in standardized tests. The teacher should also provide opportunties for summarizing larger thought units and books. Other types of exercises in this chapter should be caused to contribute to an increase in comprehension.

4. Organization. The development of the ability to organize, select, and evaluate what is read contributes directly to an increase in comprehension. How the reader organizes what he learns from reading depends upon what use we expect to make of this information; hence, the particular organization skills practiced will be modified by the nature of the assignment. Practice in organization usually includes outlining, identification of the central idea, arranging topics in sequence, summarizing, planning dramatizations and similar program activities, classifying materials and ideas, preparing bibliographies, debating, etc.

5. Oral reading. Oral reading should not be omitted from the program of remedial instruction in the elementary school. Sections of the Betts, Gates, and Gray tests described in Chapter V were designed to analyze various types of oral-reading difficulties. In much of the initial remedial instruction, oral reading should be emphasized. From such reading, the teacher can detect reversal tendencies, word-by-word reading, inadequate phrasing, speech difficulties, faulty word recognition habits, inaccurate perception, omissions, substitutions and insertions. The establishment of rhythmical reading habits should be one of the products of reading instruction. Rugg and Shumaker (24: 158-159) wrote: "Sears has pointed out that irregular activity or unrhythmical movements are in a much greater sense consumers of energy (than rhythmic activity) in that every new operation demands a new action of the intellect. In a word, rhythm lightens and facilitates labor. . . . The best readers are those whose eyes make the longest and most regular sweeps, with fewer fixations or pauses across the lines and down the page."

The child should be caused to have both auditory and visual feeling for reading phrases by calling his attention to their existence. This can be done by having him listen to the teacher's oral reading as she points to the phrases. A good arithmetic teacher never initiates a class into percentage without first explaining the processes involved. In like manner, the process of rhythmical reading should be explained and demonstrated. Reading instruction involves more than providing practice on skills. Insight into the processes involved can be given, in part, through information.

Rhythmical reading cannot be achieved if the vocabulary

burden is too great. The preparatory period usually includes the building of experience charts, formal drill on a sight list of words, or practice on rhymes. After the child has a sufficient sight vocabulary, he is given materials on which he can begin to acquire rhythmical habits of perception. If new words and more difficult sentence structure are introduced too rapidly, attempts to maintain rhythmical reading are frustrated.

To a degree, habits of proper phrasing can be developed by heightening the child's interest in the story and by emphasizing context clues and reading for meaning. Occasionally the reader can be urged to re-read a paragraph and repeat with feeling what one of the characters has said. Most children have rhythmical speech patterns. It is the obligation of the teacher to cause such speech habits to carry over into oral reading. Strained, high-pitched, and monotonous voices can be corrected in like manner.

The primary teacher initiates the child into written language skills when she first introduces him to the printed page. There is one general use for punctuation; namely, to facilitate reading. Duffy (1) found the highest percentage of errors in third-grade reading was caused by ignoring punctuation. Reading for meaning is to a degree dependent upon attending to punctuation. Breathing habits, voice control, and phrasing are modified by punctuation marks. All these items should be explained and demonstrated by the teacher.

Some successful teachers prepare materials in either manuscript or in typewritten form, so that each phrase is set off from the rest of the sentence by additional spacing. Although such a procedure is without scientific justification, it has been used successfully in the writer's clinic. This type of material provides a visual aid to phrasing. Some teachers also use the same technique for teaching the children to break down words into syllables.

Pedagogical Plans for the Care of Extreme Cases of Reading Deficiency

Many plans have been advocated for the correction of the deficiencies of severely retarded readers or non-readers. By and large, each of the plans offered is a modification of some one system used either in the United States or Europe. It is interesting to note that success has been claimed for most of the cases taught by each investigator. Individual or small-group instruction is usually advocated for extreme cases. The remedial teacher should be familiar with a number of definite plans for the correction of reading difficulties. With such knowledge, the teacher has a greater opportunity to deal effectively with individual differences. Success usually characterizes the venture when learning is directed to the specific difficulties of a learner who is mature enough to profit by instruction. No one is a protagonist of incidental methods for remedial cases.

1. Tracing method. In 1921, Fernald and Keller (5) reported success with a remedial teaching plan which was based on the tracing and writing of words. The procedures may be summarized briefly as follows:

a) Selection by the pupil of the word to be learned.

b) The seeing, saying, and tracing of the script form of the word by the child.

c) The writing, without copy, of the word by the child, saying the syllables to himself.

d) Presentation of the word in print form.

f) Use of words in context or story selected by the child.

e) The writing of sentences from memory.

(1) Before reading, the child learned the new words in the paragraph by the method described above.

(2) The words which the child failed to recognize in the context were learned in the manner described above.

(3) The words and phrases in each paragraph were drilled on by means of rapid-flash card exercises.

(4) The paragraph was re-read by the child who then reported the content.

(5) As soon as possible the child was encouraged to read by himself.

The investigators emphasized the value of kinaesthetic training. They attributed the success largely to the lip and hand kinaesthetic elements which supposedly reinforced the visual cues to the words. This report was one of the important early contributions to remedial reading. The work was characterized by individual instruction, attention to word details, emphasis on left-to-right progression in reading and spelling, simultaneous improvement of spelling and reading, and a goal to be achieved.

The limitations of the plan were obvious. Such procedures would require super-motivation because the reading-to-learn approach was not made. In addition, the writers reported that "the motor tendency is still obvious after the children become fluent readers." No one should adopt such a plan for the care of all remedial cases. If such were true, all analysis procedures could be discarded and an elaborate set of remedial material could be prepared to execute the plan. Individual differences could be disregarded. Fortunately, a great many retarded readers can be helped by more interesting and economical methods. The writer has found, however, that the Fernald-Keller plan is of high value for subnormal children with reading deficiencies. For other cases, the writer uses a modified form of the procedure. In short, the investigators offered a definite plan for the correction of extreme reading difficulties. The plans of many other investigators are vague and fragmentary. The success of any procedure lies more or less within the control of the teacher.

   2. Phonetic procedures. In 1932, Marion Monroe (16) summarized her analysis and remedial procedures. Her remedial method was largely what she termed as "sounding-tracing." In addition to the tracing method developed by Fernald and Keller, a heavy load of phonetic instruction was offered. The remainder of the work was given over to considerable oral reading.

   Miss Monroe (16: 111, 112) summarized her selection of remedial methods as follows: "We tried to teach the children who had trouble in learning to read to utilize the possible secondary or vicarious steps in word-recognition which are not usually presented in ordinary instruction. For example, the child whose visual discriminations were precise for small patterns, such as letters, but not for large ones, such as words, was taught by a method which began with the small units and built up the larger ones gradually. The child who had trouble in recognizing the spatial orientation of patterns was taught to use a manual cue to give the position of the pattern. The child who failed to discriminate precisely the sounds of words was taught the movements of placing the speech organs to obtain the desired sounds and hence to rely on the kinaesthetic cues of articulation rather than on audition. The child who had difficulty in recalling an auditory symbol (the word as heard) when presented with a visual symbol (the word as seen) was taught to associate each with the same overt response, and hence to build up the desired associations by a secondary link. The child whose motor control of the eyes was inaccurate for keeping the place of reading was taught to utilize a combination of eye-and-hand movement in developing the desired habit."

Specific suggestions were given for each of the following reading difficulties:

a) Faulty vowels and consonants.

   (1) Build up ability to discriminate between certain speech sounds.

   (2) "The associations between the letters and their most frequent sounds were established next. . . . By use of the sounding-tracing method, we tried to combine the separate components of the word into an organized unit" (16:119, 121).

   (3) "As soon as the child had a vocabulary of a number of words he was given stories written in simple phonetic language" (16:124).

   (4) "From this stage on, and while the two-letter vowels were being learned, the children were given the ordinary primers and first readers available in the schools" (16:126).

b) Reversals

   (1) Motor cues to direction were used.

   (2) Tracing-sounding method was used.

   (3) The child wrote words from dictation.

   (4) In extreme cases, the child was taught to read words "printed in very large type, and also raised in pattern by the dots of a Braille writer" (16:128).

c) Addition of sounds.

    (1) Drills were given on lists of words containing *r* and *l* sounds.

d) Omission of sounds.

    (1) The omission of sounds was corrected often simultaneously by the sounding-tracing method.

    (2) Speech training was given.

    (3) For some children emphasis was placed on syllables and sound units.

    (4) In some cases a slower rate of reading was encouraged temporarily.

e) Substitution of words.

    (1) Drill on context clues in easy reading materials.

f) Repetition of words.

    (1) Concert reading by teacher and child was used.

    (2) "Repetitions which accompanied reversals were often eliminated by the process of manual guidance in the direction of reading" (16: 133).

    (3) Others were given a method of attacking new words.

g) Addition of words.

    (1) "When the meaning was confused because of insertions of words, however, we gave drill to prevent the insertions by typewriting the sentence twice, once as given in the text, and again as given by the child. The child read both sentences and was asked to point out the difference in words and in meaning. Addition of words was found to be the least differentiating of any of the error-types in separating the good and poor readers" (16: 134).

h) Omission of words.

(1) Slower rate of reading was encouraged.

(2) Material typewritten with wide spaces between the lines was used to break up the habit of skipping lines.

Dr. Monroe's (16: 113, 114) justification for her procedure is stated: "Although some of the methods which we have used stimulate at first a mechanical approach to reading, we have not discarded them on that basis if they brought measurable improvement in reading without sacrificing comprehension. We have proceeded on the assumption that, although it is desirable to be a speedy reader, it is better to be a slow reader than a non-reader; that, although it is desirable to be able to recognize large thought units, it is better to read sentences word by word, or words sound by sound, than not to read them at all; that, although it is desirable to obtain meaning without the awareness of mechanics, it is better to get the meaning by mechanical steps than not to get the meaning at all."

3. Visual approach to reading. Dr. Arthur I. Gates and his assistants have used successfully several methods for instructing cases with extreme reading disabilities. He describes (8: 450) a method based on the visual study of words: "The writer has applied to a variety of cases, including extreme disabilities, a method which utilizes almost exclusively a visual attack. This method produced admirable results in teaching beginning reading to deaf-mute pupils. It utilizes an outfit of carefully prepared material of various types, many of which are designed to foster constructive, artistic, dramatic, and other enterprises. Words are introduced gradually and re-used extensively. At first, the pupils recognized the words on the basis of general configuration and the more obvious component features. Gradually, assisted and directed by the teacher, the children learn to observe more details, more subtle features and to perceive them more quickly and accurately, to work out the recognition of unfamiliar words, and to acquire familiarity with new words in terms of these visual elements."

Gates (8: 451) also describes a method in which visualization is emphasized: "The writer and his students have employed with disabilities a method which gives particular prominence to experiences in visualizing—or recalling in the mind's eye—the appearance of a word as a whole and part by part. This plan was developed from investigations of spelling in which it appeared that practice in visualizing words helped not only to fix their appearance in mind but also served to produce a better technique of observing words. Just as attempts to recall or recite a piece of prose or verse or a series of nonsense syllables tend to give birth to better techniques of learning by rote than do mere reading and re-reading without active recall, so efforts to recall the look of the word may tend to produce a more effective way of seeing words one wishes to recognize later.

"The method differed from the preceding one by asking the pupil to close his eyes and see in his mind's eye the word he had observed. He was encouraged to see it part by part, in the left-to-right order, and then as a whole. If the word could be divided into syllables, he was asked to say the syllables softly to himself, while visualizing them simultaneously. Later, as he learned to write, he was asked to visualize the syllables as he wrote and sounded them."

A plan for teaching the child to visualize words is advocated also by Horn and Ashbaugh (12) for the study of spelling. The Horn-Ashbaugh directions to the pupils are:

a) The first thing to do in learning to spell a word is to pronounce it correctly. Pronounce the word, saying each syllable very distinctly and looking closely at each syllable as you say it.

b) With closed eyes try to see the word in your book, syllable by syllable, as you pronounce it in a whisper. In pronouncing the words, be sure to say each syllable distinctly. After saying the word, keep trying to recall how the word looked in your book, and at the same time say the letters. Spell by syllables.

c) Open your eyes, and look at the word to see whether or not you had it right.

d) Look at the word again, saying the syllables very distinctly. If you did not have the word right on your first trial, say the letters this time as you look sharply at the syllables.

e) Try again with closed eyes to see the word as you spell the syllables in a whisper.

f) Look again at your book to see if you had the word right. Keep trying until you can spell each syllable correctly with closed eyes.

g) When you feel sure that you have learned the word, write it without looking at your book, and then compare your attempt with the book to see whether or not you wrote it correctly.

h) Now write the word three times, covering each trial with your hand before you write the word the next time, so that you cannot copy. If all of these trials are right, you may say that you have learned the word for the present. If you make a single mistake, begin with the first direction and go through each step again

i) Study each word by this method. Take special pains to attend closely to each step in the method. Hard and careful work is what counts.

Gates (8:452) believes that it is often worthwhile to spend a moderate amount of time and effort in an attempt to teach the pupils to visualize. He recommends visual methods for cases with auditory handicaps. For other cases, he states that "some degree of phonetic work and of tracing or writing may be highly useful."

Roy E. Keller, Superintendent of Schools in Manchester, Massachusetts, reported unusual success with flash cards. (This report has not been published.) The words for practice were determined by having the pupil read the list of words found in the summary at the back of the reader. The words missed by each pupil were written on small flash cards. In the higher grades, the pupils made their own cards. The child then dictated a short sentence containing the word, which was written on the back of the card. Following the preparation of the cards, the children were paired for "games." If difficulties persisted, several cards were prepared using the word in different sentences. This is a good technique for teaching the recognition of words through meaningful situations.

4. Development method. The developmental method has been used by many successful remedial teachers. In such cases, the teacher usually spends considerable time in conference with the pupil in order to informally inventory his interests and hobbies. Following this, the child is interested in dictating his experiences to the teacher who types them in a primer-size type. Since this procedure capitalizes on the use of context clues, the child usually has little difficulty with the reading of his stories. After a very few days, the child will have acquired a considerable quantity of material which he is usually anxious to take home so that he can "read to his mother."

It will be noted that this method is not unlike the experience charts dictated by the class during the pre-book period of reading. An enthusiastic and alert teacher can capitalize on the learner's interest. The chief consideration in remedial reading is that of change of pupil attitude. No extensive research is needed to define the dominating interests of an individual at any given time in his life, hence the procedure is simple and easily administered.

Word recognition skills can be practiced in the reading of pupil dictated stories to the degree that the teacher finds it necessary. The whole plan, however, can be defeated by the too early introduction of the drudgery and mechanics of word recognition. Such materials provide a unique opportunity for transferring speech patterns (such as phrasing, voice control, etc.) to the reading situation.

The work can be terminated by binding the typewritten pages into one volume, which the rest of the class will find to be interesting reading. Both self-respect and the respect of the class will be the profit to the learner. From the development of his own materials, the child can be interested in reading stories along the same line of interest in other books. The remedial teacher should secure a quantity of pre-primers, primers, and other easy reading materials. Recent pre-primers and primers contain a surprising amount of interesting reading. When these easy books are introduced, the child should have an opportunity to look through several and select the story which is most appealing.

5. **Combination methods.** If the remedial procedures are to parallel the analysis program, the type of instruction given should vary with the needs of the individual. Some of the chief problems for the readers in difficulty are word recognition, left-to-right reading habits, phrasing, and

reading for meaning. Many non-readers have not advanced far enough to have acquired even poor habits of reading. In such instances, a change of attitude is the chief problem. Others are word-by-word readers who require the substitution of both desirable habits and attitudes for faulty reading techniques and a dislike for reading.

About 10 per cent of the remedial cases require definite help in left-to-right reading habits. Some individuals exhibit a tendency to read from the right end of the line to the left. Others may be confused with word forms or word elements. Confusions with word forms are manifested by the reading of *tac* or *cat* for *act, rat* for *art, on* for *no, sag* for *gas,* and the like. Occasionally the order of word elements is also confused, the child reading *ch-we* for *chew, lena* for *lean, peatun* for *peanut,* and so on.

The tendency to reverse or confuse the reading sequence for word forms and word elements can usually be corrected by explanation and demonstration of left-to-right progression and by practice which calls attention to word details. Since many children exhibit a tendency to confuse word forms until they have a mental age of approximately seven to seven and one-half years, the remedial teacher should be assured that the child is ready for reading by administering some such tests as the Betts Word Form Tests and the Betts Visual Sensation and Perception Tests. If the child is ready for reading, rapid progress usually can be expected. Children of normal intelligence or above who confuse such words as *lean* and *peanut* can be helped by calling their attention to words containing the vowel digraphs in question and by having the child suggest and write several words containing similar sound combinations. For example, in the above situation, the following words might be listed:

lean, heap, plea, read, reason, real, sea, steal, tease, etc. From this list of words, permit the child to discover that the first vowel is long, or "says its own name," and the second vowel is silent. Confusions where other vowel digraphs (*ai, ay, oa, ie, ue, ee, oe, ow*) are involved can be taught in like manner. At all times, care should be exercised that the words are not taken apart and that the child is given help only on those sound combinations with which he is having specific difficulty. Confusions with one set of sound combinations do not always carry over to other combinations where the same principle is involved. This type of help is valuable to the extent that the information learned is made to function automatically in practice and to the degree that it causes the individual to be sensitized to word details. Carried to the extreme, such drill may tend to produce "word callers." Each drill on words in isolation should be followed by exercises where the word is read in context. This can be achieved by having the child dictate sentences to be written by the teacher. Left-to-right progression for word forms can also be emphasized by calling attention to the initial sounds of words. This can be done by stimulating the group or individual to give orally a list of words beginning with the same sound. Later, the teacher can write the dictated words on the board. This type of work should usually be followed by interesting the child in writing a list of words beginning with the same sound.

For beginners, an auditory feeling for left-to-right reading can be developed by the use of such materials as the Allard and McCall "Teeny Tiny Rimes," published by the Johnson Publishing Company. The materials consist of a teacher's manual, an individual illustrated booklet, and flash cards, each containing a rhyme. Most children derive considerable pleasure from reading such rhymes as

"My little boat
began to float."

The "fun" with these cards should be followed with opportunities for the child to dictate and later write his own rhymes. The most commonly used word forms are frequently the ones most often confused. In order to overcome confusions, a quantity of easy reading material should be used. By means of tests of reading achievement or by informal reading from pre-primers, primers, and so on, the level of reading achievement can be determined.

When the more reasonable and economical methods described above fail to produce results, the writer makes use of a combination method. This method is valuable not only for those who appear to confuse word forms, but also for those who have difficulty in applying word recognition techniques. The following steps are used:

a) Determination of a reading level (pre-primer, primer, etc.) where the individual misses no more than two or three words per page or paragraph.

b) Selection of a story by the learner.

c) Discussion of the illustrations and of the child's previous experiences related to the story.

d) Using various methods of word recognition. When the child comes to a word which he cannot recognize an attempt is made to cause him to use the context clue to the word. This can be done by discussing the thought up to the point of the difficulty and by encouraging him to suggest an appropriate word. If this fails, the child is asked to write the word in the first column of a previously prepared notebook. (Notebook is prepared by drawing in vertical lines in order to divide the page into three columns.) After the word is copied, the child is then told the word or given an opportunity to identify it by means of previously learned techniques. Following this the child is urged to visualize the word, saying it by syllables if possible. Then he is urged to use orally the word in sentences. He then writes the word in the second column, saying it as he writes. The last step is the matching of the written with the printed form. The paragraph is then re-read. The important aspects of the procedure are that meanings be associated with the word form and that the learner *writes, says, sees,* and *hears* simultaneously.

The above procedure is valuable to the extent that the learner establishes a feeling for the meaning of the word form. The cumulative list of words is also an excellent progress record for motivating the work. If the child is reading a book prepared for his level of ability and constructed so that the rate of introduction of new words is low, he will, after a few times, be able to progress rapidly and with a great deal of personal satisfaction in achievement. In practically every case, it is necessary to write each word only twice under the conditions outlined. After that, recognition is rapid. Small increments of growth are always before the learner, because the list of words which can be quickly recognized increases rapidly.

Confusion of letter forms are usually indicated by the reading of *b* for *d, p* for *q, u* for *n, w* for *m,* and the like. For example, the words may be read as follows: *lamb* for *lamp, bone* for *done, bear* for *dear, put* for *but,* etc. These pupils usually cannot identify letters in isolation.

Smith (26) investigated "Matching Ability as a Factor in First Grade Reading." In addition to finding a high correlation between the ability to match letters at entrance to first grade and ability to read after twelve weeks of instruction, she determined the relative difficulty of matching certain letters. The following four groups of letters are arranged in the order of their difficulty:

Group 1   b, p, q, d (most difficult)

Group 2   r, h, f, i, j, n, m

Group 3   e, v, x, y, k, t, z, l

Group 4   a, c, u, o, w, s, g (least difficult)

Remedial procedures usually include: •

a) Teaching the identification of the letters of the alphabet. This can be functionally achieved by creating an interest in pictured dictionaries. A loose-leaf book, a composition book, or cards made from oak tag may be used. Since meaning is an important element in word recognition, it would be well to have an illustration made above each word.

b) Emphasizing the initial and final sounds of the words, depending upon whether or not the difficulty was with a word such as *put* or such as *top*.

c) Emphasizing context clues.

d) Comparing the word with the confusion, such as *put* and *but, park* and *bark, bear* and *dear, prod* and *drop*.

Remedial work for letter confusions involves the correction of visual difficulties, the teaching of reading after a sufficient level of maturity has been reached, and instruction in quick and accurate perception of letter forms. If an individual is given help on specific difficulties, progress is usually rapid. The chief consideration should be the identification of and practice on the particular letter and word forms which the learner confuses. This requires individual instruction usually over a short period of time.

Sight-Saving Materials

The writer has found that some children with reading deficiencies can read stories printed in sight-saving books twenty words per minute faster than they can read the same stories printed in the smaller type used in first-grade readers. Not enough evidence has been collected to justify the recommendation of large sized type for certain types of reading difficulties. Few would doubt, however, the wisdom of using materials printed in eighteen, twenty-four, or thirty-two point type for children with eye co-ordination or focusing difficulties. Eye co-ordination can be increased by reading type which can be easily fused by the two eyes. Sight-saving materials can be purchased from the Clear Type Publishing Committee, 36 Elston Road, Upper Montclair, New Jersey, and from the Follett Publishing Company, Chicago, Illinois.

Spelling

Many of the individuals with reading difficulties also experience difficulty with spelling. Frequently the spelling difficulty can be corrected simultaneously with the reading deficiency. Davis (4) found the most common difficulties to be (a) faulty techniques in learning how to spell a word, (b) poor quality of writing, (c) faulty pronunciation, (d) undesirable attitude toward spelling, and (e) failure to associate the sounds of the letters or the syllables with the spelling of the words.

Witty (33) studied intensively the difficulties of a group of poor spellers. His general conclusions were: (1) Many of the difficulties could have been avoided. (2) Inability to spell may be due to visual defects. (3) A preponderance

of the errors of each child were specific habit types. (4)
The disabled spellers had strong aversions to spelling. (5)
The learners were interested in the identification of their
specific difficulties. (6) Most of the cases made errors of
associating specific word parts with wrong sound units.

The procedures for correction of spelling difficulties may
be summarized as follows: (1) Teach the child a technique for learning to spell a word. See description of the
Horn-Ashbaugh procedures described above. (2) Correct
reading deficiencies. (3) Correct speech defects. (4) Seek
to change the child's attitude toward spelling. The keeping
of a weekly progress record advocated in most spelling
books is one excellent device. (5) Provide practice in pronunciation. (6) Have child correct misspelling in all written work. (7) Have vision and hearing checked and if
defective secure the assistance of a health specialist.

Individual Versus Group Instruction

The analysis of reading achievement should be a continuous process. Since too frequently formal testing procedures are not functional, it is highly desirable to observe
the difficulties of individual pupils. This obviously cannot
be done if children are being given instruction in large
groups. Children who exhibit mild deficiencies in reading
can be cared for very well in small groups (probably two
to five). The administration of such a plan of grouping
within the classroom is discussed in Chapter II.

Individual instruction is usually recommended for children who are characterized by extreme reading difficulties.
In the first place, individual instruction permits a better
understanding of all the problems of the learner. Second,
for such cases class instruction has been demonstrated to

be ineffective. Third, the individual with such a difficulty usually has developed a reading fear and tenseness which is aggravated when attempts are made to read before the class. These and many other reasons could be advanced in favor of individual or small-group instruction for severely retarded readers.

If the learner is mature enough to profit by the individual instruction, a rapid gain can be made so that the pupil can soon participate in group reading activities. It is not uncommon for a ten-year-old boy to make a gain in reading achievement of two to three years in a period of three months. Exceptional cases may make a similar gain in less time while other cases may require more time. Gains can be anticipated only if the learning conditions are met.

One of the chief disadvantages of individual instruction is the heavy demand upon the teacher's time. It is also very difficult to find suitable periods during the day for individual help.

Rate of Reading

Speed of reading should not be emphasized for the extreme cases. Rate is influenced by the familiarity with the content, interest, proficiency in basic reading skills, vocabulary burden and kindred factors. Since the retarded reader is usually struggling to acquire the elementary skills in reading, his attention should not be diverted from the thought by an over-emphasis on speed. Rhythmical and efficient reading is usually reflected in a satisfactory rate.

Rate of reading varies with the type of material read and the purpose of the reading. Much harm has been done by overemphasizing speed as an isolated factor in reading achievement. Speed of comprehension should be the goal rather than just speed.

Position in the Classroom

Individuals with auditory or visual handicaps should be seated near the front of the room. In the case of children with learning difficulties when no physical defects are found the same procedure should be followed. Connelly (1) concluded that "The position of pupils in the classroom affects their ability to comprehend printed matter on flash cards, charts, lantern slides, screens and blackboards. Pupils seated near the printed matter comprehend significantly more than those seated farther away. Pupils seated in the center section of the room comprehend more, though not significantly more, than those seated in the left and right sections."

This factor should also be considered when the children are grouped before a wall chart. Children can be seated too close as well as too far away. The chart should always be hung at a level with the eyes of the children so that they will not have to bend their necks in order to read it.

SUMMARY

1. Reading difficulties can be corrected.
2. Most reading difficulties could be prevented.
3. Remedial reading instruction should begin with the learner's interests and level of ability.
4. Remedial instruction should be directed at the specific difficulties of the learner.
5. Physical defects should be corrected before the initiation of the pedagogical procedures.
6. Remedial reading should not be attempted until the teacher has sufficient evidence regarding the child's general readiness for reading.

7. About 10 per cent of the reading deficiencies are characterized by reversal tendencies.

8. The remedial procedures should be based on the deficiencies revealed by the analysis program.

9. Word recognition, phrasing, left-to-right progression, and reading for meaning, should receive emphasis in the corrective program.

10. The final criterion for the appraisal of the correction program is the extent to which the pupil enjoys extensive reading.

11. Attention usually should not be called to word elements until a reasonable degree of rhythmical reading has been achieved.

12. A goal, individual attention, and systematic instruction are essential in cases of extreme retardation.

REFERENCES

1. Betts, Emmett A. "Prevention and Correction of Reading Disabilities," *Elementary English Review,* XII (February, 1935), 25-32.

2. Betts, Emmett A., Everett, Mabel, and Rodewald, Frances. "Remedial Reading Based on First Teaching," *Journal of Exceptional Children,* (February, 1936).

3. Davis, Georgia. "Procedures Effective in Improving Pupils of Poor Reading Ability in Regular Reading Classes," *Elementary School Journal,* XXXI (January, 1931), 336-48.

4. Davis, Georgia. "Remedial Work in Spelling," *Elementary School Journal,* XXVII (April, 1927), 615-26.

5. Fernald, G. M., and Keller, H. "The Effect of Kinaesthetic Factors in the Development of Word Recognition in the Case of Non-Readers," *Journal of Educational Research,* IV (December, 1921), 355-77.

6. Farris, L. P. "Visual Defects as Factors Influencing Achievement in Reading," *Junior-Senior High School Clearing House,* IX (December, 1934).

7. Gates, Arthur I., and Peardon, Celeste Comegys. *Practice Exercises in Reading.* New York: Teachers College, Columbia University, 1933.

8. Gates, Arthur I. *The Improvement of Reading.* New York: Macmillan Company, 1935.

9. Gillingham, Anna, and Stillman, Bessie W. *Remedial Work for Reading, Spelling, and Penmanship.* Ethical Culture School, New York City, 1934.

10. Gray, Clarence Truman. *Deficiencies in Reading Ability: Their Diagnosis and Remedies,* pp. 365-409. Boston: D. C. Heath & Company, 1922.

11. Gray, William S. "A Study of Ways and Means of Reorganizing and Improving Instruction in Reading," *Journal of Educational Research,* XV (March, 1927), 166-75.

12. Horn, Ernest, and Ashbaugh, Ernest. *Horn-Ashbaugh Speller.* Philadelphia: J. B. Lippincott Co., 1920.

13. MacLatchy, Josephine H. "Devices Used in Remedial Reading," *Educational Research Bulletin,* II (May, 1932), 263-7.

14. Merton, Elda, "The Discovery and Correction of Reading Difficulties," *The Problem of the Elementary School Principal in the Light of the Testing Movement,* pp. 346-63. Second Yearbook of the Department of Elementary School Principals, Vol. II, No. 4. Washington:

Department of Elementary School Principals of the National Educational Association, 1923.

15. Middlebrook, Pearl M. "Remedial Work in Reading," *Elementary School Journal,* XXVII (December, 1926), 305-6.

16. Monroe, Marion. *Children Who Cannot Read,* pp. xvi-206. Chicago: University of Chicago Press, 1932.

17. Monroe, Marion. "Suggestions for Remedial Instruction in Reading." Institute for Juvenile Research of Illinois. Chicago: Department of Public Welfare.

18. Monroe, M., and Orton, S. T. "Methods of Diagnosis and Treatment of Cases of Reading Disability," *Genetic Psychology Monographs,* IV (1928), 335-456.

19. Moran, Sister Patricia. "The Effect of Definite Remedial Drills on Silent Reading Ability." Master's thesis, Fordham University (1933).

20. Newell, Nancy. "For Non-Readers in Distress," *Elementary School Journal,* XXXII (November, 1931), 183-95.

21. Orton, Samuel T., and Monroe, Marion. *Monroe Methods for Diagnosis and Treatment of Cases of Reading Disability,* Genetic Psychology Monographs, Vol. IV, Nos. 4 and 5. Worcester, Massachusetts: Clark University Press.

22. Otto, Henry J. "Remedial Instruction in Reading," *Elementary School Journal,* XXVIII (January, 1928), 353-61.

23. *Rhythm Reading.* Southbridge, Massachusetts: American Optical Company, 1935.

24. Rugg, Harold, and Shumaker, Ann. *The Child Centered School,* World Book Company, 1928.

25. Selzer, Charles A. "Lateral Dominance and Visual Fusion," p. 119. Harvard Monographs in Education, No. 12 (Harvard University Press, 1933, pp. 119.

26. Smith, Nila B. "Matching Ability as a Factor in First Grade Reading," *Journal of Educational Psychology,* XIX (November, 1928), 560-71.

27. Stone, Clarence R. "A Non-Reader Learns to Read," *Elementary School Journal,* XXX (October, 1929), 142-46.

28. Stone, Clarence R. *Teacher's Guide and Course of Study in Reading,* Board of Education, San Jose, California, 1935.

29. Sultzer, Mary F. "Remedial Measures," *Journal of the National Education Association,* XIX (February, 1930), 43-44.

30. Traxler, Arthur E. "Corrective Reading in University High School," *English Instruction in the University High School,* Publications of the Laboratory Schools of University of Chicago, No. 4 (October, 1933).

31. Tinker, Miles A. "Diagnostic and Remedial Reading," *Elementary School Journal,* XXXIII (December, 1932) 293-307 (January, 1933) 346-58.

32. Wagner, Guy W. *The Maturation of Certain Visual Functions and Their Relationship to Success in Reading and Arithmetic,* Doctor's thesis, University of Iowa, 1935.

33. Witty, Paul A. "Diagnostic and Remedial Treatment of Poor Spellers," *Journal of Educational Research,* XIII (January, 1926), 39-44.

CHAPTER XV

The Reading Clinic

*The foundation of remedial success is careful
observation of the pupil, with thorough diagnostic
analysis, careful tabulation and study of his errors, and ingenuity in applying specific treatment.*
—Marion Monroe (4:228)

Remedial Instruction

Procedures described for the prevention and correction
of reading difficulties are valuable largely to the degree
that they can be made effective in the classroom. The science of education has been developed to a level where
diagnosis of learning difficulties can be made with increasing sureness. The immediate future holds even greater
possibilities. Many of the factors which probably contribute
to reading difficulties are yet to be discovered; hence,
remedial procedures are still in need of extension and re-
evaluation. Although most of the remedial work should
be done in the classroom, there should be a central place
in each school unit where extended analyses can be made
and where individual corrective exercises can be administered for extreme cases. The room called the reading
clinic or laboratory serves this purpose.

Administration of Reading Clinic

Charts I and II are schematic diagrams showing how the
work of the reading clinic is co-ordinated with other school
departments and community agencies. This plan was de-

Chart I

ADMINISTRATIVE PROCEDURE FOR FIRST GRADE ENTRANTS
For Prevention of Reading Disabilities

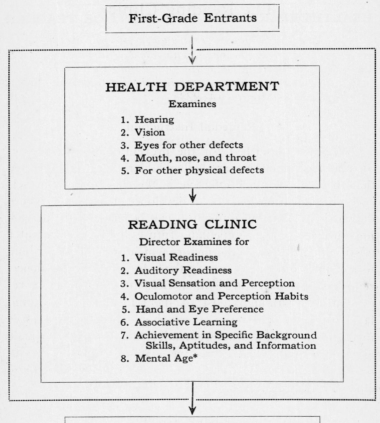

First-Grade Entrants

HEALTH DEPARTMENT

Examines

1. Hearing
2. Vision
3. Eyes for other defects
4. Mouth, nose, and throat
5. For other physical defects

READING CLINIC

Director Examines for

1. Visual Readiness
2. Auditory Readiness
3. Visual Sensation and Perception
4. Oculomotor and Perception Habits
5. Hand and Eye Preference
6. Associative Learning
7. Achievement in Specific Background Skills, Aptitudes, and Information
8. Mental Age*

FIRST GRADE

Provision is made for care of each child in light of above data.

*Even with equal intelligence, not all children are ready to read at six years of age.

Chart II

ADMINISTRATIVE PROCEDURES FOR PUBLIC SCHOOLS
For Remedial Work in Reading

HEALTH DEPARTMENT -OR- PARENT -OR- TEACHER

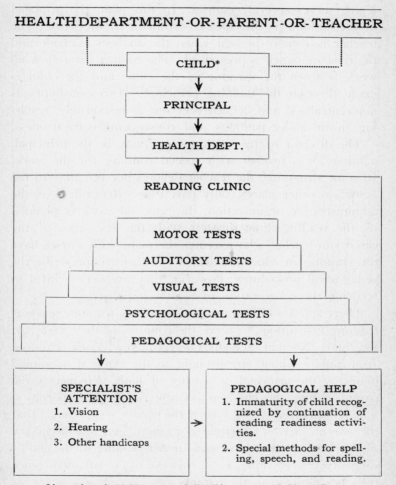

```
                    CHILD*
                      ↓
                  PRINCIPAL
                      ↓
                 HEALTH DEPT.
                      ↓
                READING CLINIC

              MOTOR TESTS
            AUDITORY TESTS
           VISUAL TESTS
         PSYCHOLOGICAL TESTS
       PEDAGOGICAL TESTS
        ↓                        ↓
```

SPECIALIST'S ATTENTION	PEDAGOGICAL HELP
1. Vision	1. Immaturity of child recognized by continuation of reading readiness activities.
2. Hearing	
3. Other handicaps	2. Special methods for spelling, speech, and reading.

*Approximately 10-25 per cent of all children are retarded in reading.

veloped by Dr. Justin A. Garvin, Head of Health Department, Shaker Heights, Ohio, and the writer. It has also been used at the State Normal School, Oswego, New York, which serves several counties. In this plan, the principal of the building is the chief co-ordinator of the work. The teacher is usually present when the analysis is made and the remedial work is prescribed. The contact for follow-up work between the director of the clinic and the child is made through the building principal. If responsibility is not centralized and defined everyone is responsible, resulting in misunderstandings and consequent ineffectiveness.

The director of the reading clinic may be the principal, a nurse, or a teacher with special training for the work. In some situations, the teacher devotes her full time to the work; in other places, only part time. Regardless of the administrative organization, the remedial work is planned by the reading-clinic director with the assistance of the classroom teacher who executes the plan. Few nurses have the training in education which fits them to prescribe the pedagogical procedures; however, they are very helpful in securing the co-operation of health specialists.

There appears to be a growing tendency for state teacher-training institutions to serve the counties in their area. At the State Normal School, Oswego, New York, children from public schools are brought to the clinic at appointed hours by the principal or teacher or both. Frequently the parents bring the children because of the transportation liability involved. It has been the writer's experience that the parents are in a better position to give the necessary co-operation, if they have some understanding of the child's difficulty. Everything with the exception of intelligence tests is explained to the parents.

The reading-clinic materials are usually kept in the health clinic or a small room designated as the "Reading Clinic." It is not advisable that the analysis materials be kept in a classroom where they are likely to be handled by the pupils. In some places a portable unit has been prepared so that the materials can be transported easily from one school to another. District or county superintendents in rural areas use the centralized schools as reading-clinic centers for the one- and two-room rural schools. In schools of more than three hundred pupils, it is advisable to have one small room set aside for individual testing and remedial work. As a part of the administration of a clinic, the principal should hold a series of conferences with his teacher for the purpose of intensively studying preventive and remedial procedures. The number of retarded readers in each school usually makes it advisable for the classroom teacher to assume the responsibility for remedial work. Since reading is involved in most school activities above the first grade, the efforts of an outside remedial teacher frequently would be frustrated. The functions of a full-time remedial teacher should be those of developing a preventive program which insures adequate first-teaching, analyzing learning difficulties, prescribing and preparing the remedial work with the help of the teacher, demonstrating the care of variations in reading ability by grouping within the classroom, and developing a program of community-school relations.

In the principal's office there should be a file of individual pupil folders containing cumulative information and test data. Ordinary letter-size manila folders are very satisfactory for this purpose. The information outlined in Chapter V should be accumulated over a period of years, beginning with the child's first entrance to the school. This information becomes indispensable for parent conferences and for the understanding of the child's progress and difficulties.

Equipment of Reading Clinic

Equipment for the reading clinic varies according to the size of the school and the extent of other services, such as health. Every school unit should have some means by which the difficulty may be defined and a few materials suitable for remedial purposes. Success can be expected to the degree that the problems are identified.

1. **Analysis materials and equipment.** In order to make essential analyses the equipment should include the Betts Ready to Read Unit, Gates Diagnostic Tests, Gray Oral Reading Tests, at least one series of well-graded readers, general achievement tests, reading achievement tests, and reading-readiness tests. Supplementary equipment would include the Ophthalm-O-Graph or reading materials for the Miles peep-hole technique, a tachistoscope or rapid exposure device, and materials for the administration of the Stanford Revision of the Binet-Simon Tests. All of these materials and equipment are described in Chapters V, VI, VII, VIII, and X.

2. **Remedial materials.** Remedial materials are described in Chapter XIV. The essentials would include several series of readers, one complete set of sight-saving books, a typewriter with sight-saver type, several reading workbooks of various types, and a chart holder and flashcards. The Metron-O-Scope should be included in the equipment for larger school systems. Provision should be made for ready reference to all materials prepared locally. Many schools have built up files of remedial materials which

have been mimeographed or printed for local use. This should be encouraged. Some systems have provided for an exchange of materials between buildings and with other school systems.

SUMMARY

1. The reading clinic should be housed in a separate room.
2. The supervisor or director of the reading clinic should be prepared for both the testing and the corrective work.
3. The building principal should be the chief co-ordinating agent.
4. The parents should be informed regarding the preventive and remedial procedures.
5. The classroom teacher should assume the responsibility for the correction of reading difficulties.
6. The remedial reading has at least two functions: (1) to assist in planning the reading program in the content subjects at the elementary- and secondary-school levels; and (2) to provide systematic instruction in reading at scheduled periods for all students.

REFERENCES

1. Carter, Homer L. J. *Clinical Service at Western State Teachers College,* Michigan Academy of Science, 1934.
2. Clowes, Helen Coe. "A Reading Clinic," *Educational Research Bulletin* (Ohio State University), IX (May 14, 1930), 261-68.
3. Cobb, Percy W., and Moss, Frank K. "The Fixational Pause of the Eyes," *Journal of Experimental Psychology,* IX (October, 1926), 359-67.

4. *Educational Diagnosis.* "Diagnosis and Treatment of Reading Disabilities," Chap. XII. *Thirty-fourth Yearbook of the National Society for the Study of Education.* Bloomington, Illinois: Public School Publishing Co., 1935.

5. Stevens, Avis C. "The Administration of a Reading Clinic." Unpublished, filed in Carl Hamann Library of Anatomy, School of Medicine, Western Reserve University, 1934.

6. Woods, Elizabeth T. "Special Classes for Non-Readers," *Fourth Yearbook of the Psychology and Educational Research Division,* pp. 99-105. School Publication No. 211. Los Angeles, California: Los Angeles City School District, 1931.

CHAPTER XVI
Reappraisal

One of the encouraging signs of the times is that investigators are pursuing given types of cases until the problems which they present are reasonably well understood.—William S. Gray

Increased Interest in Reading Problems

About 1870 the first scientific reference to the problem of reading appeared. Most of the research findings which modify present school practice have been reported in the last fifteen years. Among the reports, the Twenty-fourth Yearbook of the National Society for the Study of Education, Part I, presented in 1925, has probably had the greatest influence on this phase of American education. The research summaries so generously contributed by Dr. W. S. Gray of the University of Chicago have been a means for speeding up the translation of research into schoolroom practice. Because there is a great time lag between the reporting of researches and actual practice even in the best of schools, we can expect during the next decade to experience further highly significant changes in the reading program.

A great number of research workers have been at work upon the psychological, physiological, and educational aspects of the problem presented by the retarded reader. Few of the data gained are final or conclusive. In fact, a careful inventory of the readings reveals very little specific and helpful information for the administrator and classroom teacher. The multiple approaches made to the problem leave the uninitiated quite overwhelmed. Furthermore, the terminology and concepts developed by the various classes of investigators in specialized fields of interest make the integration of the findings a task of no small magnitude. The prognosis of a case has been improved through the efforts of interested and better trained teachers, administrators, psychologists, health specialists, and lighting engineers.

Equally impressive is the great range of problems studied. In 1897 Javal first reported his observations regarding discontinuous eye-movement in reading. Since then, eye specialists, psychologists, and physiologists, have added much to our concept of two-eyed vision and its relation to the reading process. Others have initiated studies of the rôle which hearing plays in learning-to-read. Maturation, especially the physiological and psychological implications in readiness for reading, has been caused to stand out in bold relief by most of the investigators. The emotional aspects of the problem have proved to be fruitful for research. Many external items, more easily controlled, also have been under suspicion. Significant among these are typography, lighting conditions, and administrative policies. Such is the array which confronts the one who would interest himself in the study of reading disabilities.

Teachers at all levels of education are showing an increasing interest in the problem of the retarded reader. For proof, one needs only to survey the increasing number of tests, corrective materials, and articles from the field.

Reviewing the Problem

The prevention and correction of reading difficulties requires the co-operation of all those concerned with the wel-

fare of the learner. There is no one panacea for the
correction of all types of reading ills because the causes are
many and varied. It is quite generally agreed that no one
factor contributes to all types of reading difficulties. A
review of the problems discussed in this book follows:

1. Incidence of reading difficulties. From 8 to 25
per cent of the children in the elementary schools fail to
achieve in reading although they adequately learn in certain
other school activities. A reading deficiency retards general educational progress.

2. Word blindness. During recent years the term
"word blindness" has been used less frequently when certain learning conditions are met. So-called word-blind
children can be taught to read.

3. Intelligence. There is a preponderance of individuals with normal or superior intelligence who are retarded in reading. The misuse of intelligence tests has confused the issue. Group tests of intelligence, which usually
involve reading, are inadequate criteria for rating the
intelligence of retarded readers. In any event, the remedial
teacher should be concerned with mental age rather than
the I. Q. The writer assumes that a mental age of six and
one-half to seven years is essential for beginning reading,
especially in the case of children experiencing difficulty.
Likewise, a mental age of eight and one-half to nine is
assumed for success with third-grade vocabulary, meanings,
and sentence structure. Many cases are working up to the
limit of their mental ages. This does not refute the statement that some children may be ready for reading at six
years of age.

4. Reading program. The reading program should
be planned to care for individual differences in specific

readinesses for reading and in rates of learning. Reading
for meaning should be emphasized from the beginning.
Progress from one reading level to another should be based
on the adequacy of previous learnings. By and large, very
little should be left to incidental learning. The skills, attitudes, and knowledges at each level of instruction should be
carefully outlined and plans made for providing reading
situations in which they may be practiced. A program
planned and administered in terms of individual requirements would reduce significantly the percentage of retardations at each succeeding level.

5. Reversal tendencies. The tendency to reverse letter and word forms accounts for about 10 per cent of
reading difficulties. In the early literature of the subject,
the matter of reversals attracted major attention. It is the
writer's contention that when a child who is generally mature enough for the reading process is given specific training in word perception, the reversal tendency is no longer
an obstacle in reading. Many children at six and one-half
years of age tend to reverse word and letter forms. Some
children persist in this tendency until they reach an age of
seven and one-half years. On the other hand some do not
confuse letter forms at five years of age.

6. Symptoms and causes. Throughout this book an
attempt has been made to differentiate between symptoms
and causes. Faulty eye movements, undesirable attitudes,
reversal tendencies, and the like are symptoms of reading
difficulties. A noting of the symptoms is desirable only
to the degree that the causes can be identified more easily.
In brief, the analysis procedure should be directed toward
the possible causes of the deficiency. The causes may be
designated as psycho-educational and physical.

7. **Reading readiness.** Our concept of reading readiness has been enlarged. The term is no longer a general one; instead, specific physical, mental, and emotional readinesses are identified. Intelligence tests as measures of reading readiness are being replaced by tests of the specific functions involved in reading aptitude.

8. **Sex differences.** It is a well established fact that boys experience more difficulty with reading than girls. Although many theories have been advanced, there is not a satisfactory explanation for this situation.

9. **Failures in grade one.** The highest percentage of failures occurs in the first grade. Since a majority of pupils are promoted to grade two on the basis of reading achievement, this one item should be of major concern to both parents and school workers. It is interesting to observe that an increase in the age required for first grade admission is accompanied by a decrease in first-grade failures.

10. **Vision.** The Snellen Chart Tests and similar tests have proved to be inadequate as a test of vision of school children. Cases of farsightedness or astigmatism could not be reliably tested. Heretofore, the problem of eye co-ordination has not been under suspicion, but the need for checking such items is becoming increasingly evident because herein lies one possible explanation of the difficulties of a slow reader. Research workers of the Dartmouth Medical School have injected a new element into the situation by their work on differences in size and shape of ocular images. Good two-eyed vision, excluding certain types of cross-eyedness, is the right of every child and it is essential to sustained reading effort.

11. **Eye-movements.** Faulty eye-movements are symptoms of inadequate reading habits although some indi-

viduals who have inefficient eye-movements may read with understanding. Rate of reading may be increased largely by decreasing the duration of the fixation pause. The learning of accurate habits of word perception and a feeling for phrasing contributes directly to a decrease in perception time. Other things being equal, efficient eye-movements will be developed to the degree that the learner has acquired rhythmical and left-to-right habits and word-recognition skills. The problem, however, is not entirely a matter of skill because the reader's background of experience, rate of association, and mind set are significant factors.

12. Hand and eye preference. The relation of dominance, as determined by hand and eye preference, to reading difficulty is still an unsettled question. Although the writer believes that a child should be permitted to use the preferred hand for school activities, he contends that it is not a factor of major importance. The study of dominance as a possible factor in retardation in reading does not merit the consideration of classroom teachers until there is sufficient research to justify the hypothesis.

13. Typography. Large size type for remedial materials, especially in the primary grades, is recommended. Pupils needing this type of material can be identified by means of the Visual Sensation and Perception Tests of the Betts Ready to Read Tests. Until suitable materials are prepared, sight-saving books printed in twenty-four and thirty-two point type are satisfactory. If changes in size of type are to be made in the future, the type probably will be larger. To date no one has studied scientifically the relationship between size of type and ocular fatigue. Until this is done the safe decision for retarded readers with visual difficulties is to use eighteen to twenty-four point type.

14. Hearing. With certain type of reading programs which emphasize the oral-phonetic approach to word analysis, hearing handicaps may frustrate learning. If such cases do not respond to phonetic readiness activities, a visual approach to reading should be used. In order to distinguish between sound values or to identify certain sounds in a given blend, the child probably should have certain capacities for hearing which have not been adequately investigated. A lack of auditory acuity (keenness of hearing) and perhaps a narrow auditory frequency range do not entirely account for the difficulty. Pupils with hearing difficulties should be seated in the front and center of the room.

15. Vocabulary. For both the beginner and the retarded reader, speaking, reading, and writing vocabularies merit further study. To a degree, reading difficulties can be prevented (a) by insuring the adequacy of the speaking vocabulary, (b) by the development of a beginning reading program wherein the learner is introduced gradually to symbols representing the words in his speaking vocabulary, and (c) by giving the learner control over a system for the identification of unknown words.

Reading-readiness activities in which speaking vocabularies are enlarged, both quantitatively and qualitatively (i.e., enrichment through meanings), are valuable at all grade levels as well as in the kindergarten. The immature learner or the one with a slow learning rate can be confused with materials in which new words are introduced too rapidly. Likewise, the retarded reader at any grade level should have access to materials which are within his grasp, from the point of view of both vocabulary and concepts. A substantial portion of retarded readers show a lack of control over word-recognition skills. In the chapter on vocabulary burden, these problems were discussed in detail.

16. Emotional responses. One of the first tasks of the teacher is the utilization of situations in which desirable attitudes toward reading are developed. It is only human for a child to like to do the thing that he can do well; hence, the learner should be made aware constantly of small increments of growth. It is most important that the remedial teacher inspire confidence on the part of the learner in her ability to help him enjoy reading. It is the writer's contention that undesirable emotional reactions in the reading situation are symptoms rather than causes of reading difficulties. In other words, if the learner is given proper instructions and help to increase his reading power and to make reading a comfortable and enjoyable process, the reading deficiency can be removed. A reading difficulty is seldom corrected by psycho-analysis or any other mysterious analysis of the learner's emotional life.

17. Prevention. The prevention of reading difficulties should be the chief concern of teachers. This involves the correction of physical handicaps, the substitution of a program of reading-readiness activities for formal instruction in reading until each child is mature enough to profit from the help, the development of a beginning reading program in terms of the learner's needs, and instruction on specific reading skills and information in the content subjects at succeeding reading levels. Difficulties in reading retard general educational progress. In short, the program of prevention is the responsibility of all public-school teachers. There can be little hope for the development of preventive measures described in this book until teachers are professionally prepared to accept the challenge which is theirs.

18. Correction. Remedial procedures described in the literature and summarized in this book are neither mysterious nor difficult to administer. They consist largely of providing materials within the learner's interest and grasp and of instruction in terms of individual needs. The identification of the learning problem requires only those techniques which are within a well-trained teacher's professional province. There are few, if any, procedures which are peculiar to remedial reading. Since most retarded readers are deficient in elemental-reading skills, the remedial instruction is based largely on modern primary methods.

19. Reading clinic. In some centralized, consolidated, and large school systems, administrators are designating a small room, called the reading clinic or laboratory, for central use by teachers who wish to use specific analysis and remedial materials. Frequently, some one in the school system, who is charged with the chairmanship of the reading committee, serves as director or counselor. By and large, the corrective work should be done within the classroom.

20. Individual differences. Variations among retarded readers are probably as great as differences among any other group. Each reading case usually is characterized by a peculiar combination of difficulties, hence no one pattern of corrective reading can be prescribed. Learning is not just a mechanical process. Investigators in the future will probably uncover many other factors which contribute to difficulties in specific learnings. As the problems are more clearly defined, the corrective procedures for individual cases will be more economically applied. However, there is no need for waiting; it behooves the educator of today to reappraise his care of individual differences in reading.

APPENDIX A

PUBLISHERS AND DISTRIBUTORS OF EDUCATIONAL MATERIALS MENTIONED IN THIS VOLUME

Allyn and Bacon, 11 E. 36th Street, New York City

American Book Company, 88 Lexington Avenue, New York City

American Educational Press, Columbus, Ohio

American Optical Company, Southbridge, Massachusetts

Bacon and Vincent Company, Buffalo, New York

Beckley-Cardy Company, 17 E. 23rd Street, Chicago, Illinois

Benjamin H. Sanborn Company, 185 Madison Avenue, New York City

Bobbs-Merrill Company, 462 Fourth Avenue, New York City

Bureau of Educational Measurements and Standards, Kansas State Teachers College, Emporia, Kansas

Bureau of Educational Research, University of Illinois, Urbana, Illinois

Bureau of Educational Research and Service, University of Iowa, Iowa City, Iowa

C. A. Gregory, Inc., 345 Calhoun Street, Cincinnati, Ohio

Carl Fischer, Inc., Cooper Square, New York City

Charles Merrill Company, 381 Fourth Avenue, New York City

Charles Scribner's Sons, 597 Fifth Avenue, New York City

C. H. Stoelting, 424 N. Homan Avenue, Chicago, Illinois

Clear Type Publishing Committee, 36 Elston Road, Upper Montclair, New Jersey

Courtis Standard Tests, Detroit, Michigan

D. Appleton-Century Company, 35 W. 32nd Street, New York City

D. C. Heath Company, 180 Varick Street, New York City

Denoyer-Geppert Company, 5235 Ravenswood Avenue, Chicago, Illinois

Department Superintendence of National Education Association, 1201-16th Street, Washington, D. C.

Doubleday, Doran and Company, Garden City, New York

D. Van Nostrand Company, Inc., 250 Fourth Avenue, New York City

Educational and Personnel Publishing Company, Washington, D. C.

Educational Test Bureau, Minneapolis, Minnesota, and Philadelphia, Pennsylvania

E. P. Dutton and Company, 286 Fourth Avenue, New York City

Farnum Press, Minneapolis, Minnesota

Farrar and Rinehart, 232 Madison Avenue, New York City

F. E. Compton Company, 1000 N. Dearborn Street, Chicago, Illinois

Follett Publishing Company, 1255 S. Wabash Avenue, Chicago, Illinois

Frederick Stokes Company, 443 Fourth Avenue, New York City

Ginn and Company, 70 Fifth Avenue, New York City

Greenberg Publishing Company, 449 Fourth Avenue, New York City

Hall and McCreary Company, 434 S. Wabash Avenue, Chicago, Illinois

Harper and Brothers, 49 E. 33rd Street, New York City

Henry Holt Company, 1 Park Avenue, New York City

Houghton, Mifflin Company, 2 Park Street, Boston, Massachusetts

John C. Winston Company, 1006 Arch Street, Philadelphia, Pennsylvania

John Day Publishing Company, 386 Fourth Avenue, New York City

Johnson Publishing Company, 381 Fourth Avenue, New York City

J. P. Lippincott Company, 227-231 S. Sixth Street, Philadelphia, Pennsylvania

Junior Literary Guild of America, 244 Madison Avenue, New York City

Keystone View Company, Meadville, Pennsylvania

Laidlaw Brothers, 36 W. 24th Street, New York City

Little, Brown and Company, 34 Beacon Street, Boston, Massachusetts

Longmans, Green and Company, 114 Fifth Avenue, New York City

Lyons and Carnahan, 76 Ninth Avenue, New York City

Macmillan Company, 60 Fifth Avenue, New York City

McGraw-Hill Book Company, Inc., 330 W. 42nd Street, New York City

McKinley Publishing Company, 1021 Filbert Street, Philadelphia, Pennsylvania

Newson and Company, 73 Fifth Avenue, New York City

Oxford University Press, 114 Fifth Avenue, New York City

Peckham Little and Company, 140 W. 21st Street, New York City

Prentice-Hall Company, 70 Fifth Avenue, New York City

Public School Publishing Company, Bloomington, Illinois

Rand McNally and Company, 111 Eighth Avenue, New York City

Reynal and Hitchcock, Inc., 386 Fourth Avenue, New York City

Row, Peterson and Company, 1911 Ridge Avenue, Evanston, Illinois

Russell Sage Foundation, 130 E. 22nd Street, New York City

School Arts Magazine Company, Printer's Building, Worcester, Massachusetts

Scott, Foresman and Company, 623 S. Wabash Avenue, Chicago, Illinois

Silver, Burdett and Company, 41 Union Square West, New York City

Southern California School Book Depository, 3636 Beverly Blvd., Los Angeles, California

Teachers College Bureau of Publications, Columbia University, New York City

Thomas Crowell Publishing Company, 393 Fourth Avenue, New York City

University of Chicago Press, 5750 Ellis Avenue, Chicago, Illinois

University of North Carolina Press, Chapel Hill, North Carolina

University of Texas Press, Austin, Texas

Wallace Publishing Company, Des Moines, Iowa

Warwick and York, Baltimore, Maryland

Webster Publishing Company, 1808 Washington Avenue, St. Louis, Missouri

Wheeler Publishing Company, 2831-35 South Parkway, Chicago, Illinois

Wilcox and Follett Publishing Company, 1255 S. Wabash Avenue, Chicago, Illinois

Winnetka Educational Press, Horace Mann School, Winnetka, Illinois

World Book Company, Yonkers-on-Hudson, New York

APPENDIX B

Betts Ready to Read Tests

(1936 Edition)

All of the tests developed and edited by the writer are distributed by the Keystone View Company, Meadville, Pennsylvania. The basic unit consists of the following:

1. Visual Readiness Tests
2. Auditory Readiness Tests
3. Visual Sensation and Perception Tests
4. Oculomotor and Perception Tests

Four supplementary sets of tests have been added. These additional tests have been prepared for research centers and for schools where the basic unit is already in use. It is suggested that the supplementary tests should not be used until the technique for the administration of the basic tests has been learned. The four supplementary sets of tests include:

1. Tests of Fusion. (See Appendix C.)
2. Reliability Check Tests. (See Appendix D.)
3. Tests for Agility of Visual Blending. (To be released later.)
4. Tests of Eye Co-ordination for Context Reading. (To be released later.)

A discussion of the administration and interpretation of all the tests is included in the following pages. In so far as possible, descriptive terms more easily understood have been substituted for the technical terminology used in the professional literature on the subject. The *Manual* for the 1934 edition of the tests is published by the Keystone View Company, Meadville, Pennsylvania.

SECTION I

Directions for Administration and Interpretation of the Betts Visual Readiness Tests

Foreword

Several tests of the ability to discriminate between letter, phonetic element, word, phrase, and sentence forms were developed. The Betts Word Form Test proved to be the best instrument of the battery for the purpose of identifying the prospective retarded reader. The Betts Letter Form Test and Betts Phonetic Elements Test were retained so that border-line cases could be checked further. *For survey purposes, only the Betts Word Form Test should be used.*

Test V-1a and V-1b—Betts Letter Form Tests

Purpose. The Betts Letter Form Test is a matching test. The letter in the left vertical column is matched with one of the five succeeding letters in the horizontal row to the right. No correction of the score for guessing is required. Two aspects of validity are considered: (1) The type approximates that found in typical first-grade reading materials. Test V-1a is composed of commonly confused capital letters; Test V-1b, of lower case letters. (2) The kindergarten child is confronted not with hieroglyphics or figures of little or no future social value but with the letters between which he must make visual discriminations when learning to read.

This test can be administered to any kindergarten child. Previous training by any reading method will have little, if any, effect upon a child's performance. For kindergarten children and first-grade entrants *this is not a reading test;* it is a test of one phase of readiness to read. The test is one for the evaluation of the child's ability to make visual discriminations between total letter *forms,* not *meanings.* One who has a severe

Equipment for the Betts Ready to Read Tests

visual defect or who is immature will not be able to make the required visual discriminations, hence he usually is not ready to attempt reading.

The tests are valuable for securing an index to the visual readiness of first-grade entrants for reading. In addition to this use, the tests permit the study of the symptoms of reading disabilities on higher grade levels.

Normal performance. Children who are ready to read should match *all* the forms correctly.

Procedure. The examiner should be seated facing the subject. A small table or classroom desk is the only other equipment needed. Place the card marked "V-1a" in the guide, or mask, so that the first horizontal row of letters will be seen in the aperture. The guide should always be used, for it prevents the possibility of finger marks which would suggest the correct response. Say, **"Here is a letter** (pointing to the isolated letter at the left). **Point to a letter in this line** (pointing to the five letters at the right) **which is like this one** (pointing again to the isolated letter)."

Go over the examples until the subject thoroughly understands the testing technique. Proceed with the test items in like manner. No normal cases will experience difficulty with the procedure; however, for some children it may be necessary for the examiner to point always to the letter in the left-hand column and say, **"Match this one,"** or **"Find one like this."**

Proceed with Test V-1b in like manner. On very few occasions will the examiner find it necessary to repeat the instructions of V-1a for V-1b.

Recording. In the record blank check the correct responses and record the incorrect answers. The total score is the sum of the scores for both parts, V-1a and V-1b. The score for each part is the number of correct responses.

Interpretation. Children who are ready to read on the first-grade (entrance) level or above give correct responses on all items. Failure to pass the test, i.e., the incorrect matching of two items or more, may be caused by defective vision or immaturity. A visual disability may be checked by means of the Visual Sensation and Perception Tests. If the child is too immature for the reading process, he should be placed in a situation where preparatory or reading readiness activities are stressed. (See Chapters II and XIV.)

Test V-2—Betts Word Form Test

Purpose. The test is used for determining reading readiness and for the analysis of the symptoms of retarded readers. It is obvious that before an individual can learn to read readily, he must be able to discriminate rapidly and accurately between word forms. *No knowledge of reading is necessary for successful performance on this test.*

The testing technique employed is that of finding the unlike word. Four words are alike; one is different. No correction of the score for guessing is needed.

The subject may get the cue to the unlike word through:

1. The length, e.g., *not* and *none*

2. Variation within the word, e.g., *sled* and *said*

3. The reversal of the total configuration, e.g., *lap* and *pal*

4. A reversed part, e.g., *dark* and *park*

The words for the test as a whole are not arranged in the order of their difficulty; instead they are grouped according to the above types and arranged within each group in the order of their difficulty.

Normal performance. Upon entrance to Grade II, children identify all the items correctly. It is the writer's opinion that in the near future superior performance will be required of all pupils before initiation into typical reading activities. The following are standards for first-grade entrance:

Score	Rating
28-30	Superior
24-27	Good
17-23	Mediocre
9-16	Poor
1- 8	Failure

Administration of the Word Discrimination Test

Procedure. The examiner should be seated in front of the subject. Place Card V-2 in the guide, or mask, so that the first row of "Examples" can be seen through the aperture, or window. Say, **"Here are five words. Four of them are the same. One is not like the others. Point to the one that is not like the others."** If the subject has difficulty in discriminating between the reversed word forms of the "Example," explain, **"Some of the letters are turned around or are upside down in the word that is not like the others."**

After the subject understands the testing technique on the five examples, proceed with the test. The examples are included for the purpose of familiarizing the subject with the testing technique. It is permissible to correct the responses on the examples, but the examiner should refrain from *suggesting* anything but encouragement on the test items. In other words, the subject should not be told if he makes an incorrect response on the test items. If an incorrect response is given, proceed to the next line of test items and emphasize, **"Point to the word that is not like the others."** Present all the test items on each side of the card. For kindergarten children it may be necessary to repeat the instructions for various items. However, do not permit a second chance. Allow about thirty seconds on each test item.

Recording. On the record blank check the correct responses. The score is the total number of correct responses.

Interpretation. A low score on the test for first-grade entrants may be due to a visual disability or immaturity. The data should always be interpreted in the light of the findings from the Visual Sensation and Perception Tests. In general, children tend to reverse words and letters, e.g., *p* for *q* and *saw* for *was* less to the degree that they are mature.

Children who fail to discriminate between the word forms which are reversed or which have reversible letters should be watched carefully and checked frequently during the initial learning-to-read stage. If there is evidence of immaturity from the other tests, especially the Auditory Span Test, the child should continue with the reading-readiness activities of the kindergarten for another semester. (See Chapters II and XIV.) In systems where kindergarten groups are not maintained, an I-C classification (three semester group for first grade) may be developed. *Preventive* measures should be emphasized in a program designed to provide for the care of reading difficulties.

Test V-3—Betts Phonetic Elements Test

Purpose. The Betts Phonetic Elements Test is a matching test. The letter group in the left vertical column is matched with one of the five succeeding letter groups in a horizontal row to the right. No correction of the score for guessing is required.

Previous training in reading is not necessary for success with the items. This test is one for the evaluation of a child's ability to discriminate between configurations. This permits a re-check on children who fail on the Word Form Test.

Normal performance. Children who are ready to read should match all the forms correctly.

Procedure. The examiner should be seated at a small desk, facing the child. Place the card marked "V-3" in the guide so that the first horizontal row of test items may be seen in the aperture. The guide should be used always because it eliminates tell-tale finger marks. Say, "**Here are two letters** (pointing to the isolated sound at the left). **Point to the two letters in this line** (pointing to the five sounds at the right) **which are like these** (pointing to the isolated sound again)." Make certain that the subject understands the testing technique for the examples.

Recording. On the record blank check the correct responses. The score is the total number of correct responses.

Interpretation. Children who are ready to read give correct responses to all items. Failures may be due to defective vision or immaturity. The test is also valuable for studying the *symptomatic* responses of retarded readers.

Test V-4—Betts Letter Recognition Test

This test is to be used for case studies. It is a convenient instrument for checking children who have been allowed to go beyond the first semester of the first grade without being able to read.

Many retarded readers in the second or third grade cannot identify certain letters of the alphabet in isolation. It is not implied that such pupils should "learn the alphabet"; instead, it is recommended that procedures described in Chapter XI should be used.

SECTION II

Directions for the Administration and Interpretation of the Betts Auditory Readiness Tests

Test A-1—Betts Auditory Span Test

Purpose. Recent researches indicate that the tendency to confuse and reverse letters and words decreases with an advance in the maturity of the child. Aside from good vision and hearing, general maturity is probably one of the most important single elements in readiness to read. The Auditory Span Test provides an index to this important phase of maturity. This test has a reasonably high correlation with success in first-grade reading classes.

Normal performance.

Score	Rating
21-25	Superior
17-20	Good
13-16	Mediocre
8-12	Poor
1- 7	Failure

The average score for a typical class will be fifteen. The middle 50 per cent of the cases will lie between the score of nine and eighteen. A first-grade entrant who falls below a score of seven has little chance of success in the typical reading activities of that grade. The above data were secured on children in systems where a chronological age of six years was required for first-grade entrance.

Procedure. The examiner should be seated facing the subject. Say, "**I am going to tell you something. After I have finished, you say it.**"

1. Use the examples to insure an understanding of the testing technique by the child.

2. *Do not phrase.* Say the words at the rate of about one per second with a slight, but definite, pause after each word.

3. Do not repeat. If a child fails on an item, say, **"Let's try the next one."** With some children it may be necessary to remind them, **"Listen carefully and say it just as I do."**

4. Continue until *one* or more errors are made in each of *five* sentences.

5. Pronounce each word distinctly and clearly in a normal speaking voice.

The items are arranged in the order of their difficulty. An examiner after limited experience, will find that most children will reach a point in the scale where they can go no further. The writer has found that few children will fail on any of the sentences until they near their limit. Erratic results are evidence of questionable testing technique.

Recording. On the record blank check the correct responses. In order to be correct, a response must be repeated as printed in the test. No substitution of words or changing of verb tenses is permitted. The score is the total number of sentences correctly repeated.

Interpretation. This test should be interpreted in terms of the data secured from the other tests of Auditory Readiness. Inadequate performance may be indicative of short memory span, meager vocabulary, lack of facility in the use of language, narrow background of experience, or auditory defects. (See Chapters I, II, and IV.) If there is no auditory defect, a low score on the test is indicative of immaturity. Maturity is essential to reading success.

Test A-2—Betts Auditory Fusion Test

Purpose. The Auditory Fusion Test was constructed to secure an index to an individual's ability to fuse sounds into words. The words included in the test are broken down into the isolated sounds. This test has no predictive value in situations where synthetic systems of phonics have been discarded. The present tendency in beginning reading programs is to place the emphasis on visual discrimination of words or on the word method of teaching phonics. Short words were used in the test in order to minimize the influence of auditory span on the scores. It is suggested that this test be used only in rare instances.

Normal performance. All second-grade entrants should be able to fuse all the sounds into words without the loss of identity of any of the sounds. Children entering first grade should not fail on more than seven items.

Procedure. The examiner should be seated facing the subject. Say, **"I will give you some sounds which make a word. Listen carefully for the sounds and tell me the word they make."** Make sure the testing technique is understood by going over the examples until the subject can give the correct response. Practice giving the test until each sound is presented at a rate of about one per second. As far as possible, avoid vocalizing the voiceless stops such as *p, b,* and *t.* Articulate each sound distinctly and separately, but do not exaggerate, or distort, the true sound. The success of the examiner will depend upon his ability to present the true sound values which *can* be fused or blended into a word.

Recording. On the record blank check the correct responses. The total score is the number of correct responses.

Interpretation. The incorrect responses may be classified under three headings: omissions, substitutions, and addition of sounds. It is still a debatable question whether or not all children who fail on this test can be trained in this function. For some kindergarten children, this may be a good instrument for prognosis of success with certain types of phonetic training. Some children in the elementary school never acquire this ability to fuse sounds into words, and it is not essential to reading success that they should.

Many subjects may have normal visual acuity in each eye, but have little or no fusion which is essential for the formation of desirable two-eyed reading habits. In like manner, an individual may pass satisfactorily an auditory acuity test and lack the power to fuse sounds into words. In such cases, a visual approach to beginning reading should be made.

Test A-3—Betts Auditory Perception Test

Purpose. This test is designed for use with retarded readers. In certain types of beginning reading programs much stress is placed upon auditory patterns, therefore this test is significant. The child is required not only to perceive the correct sound but also to repeat it. Many children *spell* incorrectly because they spell what they have fallen into the habit of hearing and speaking. In like manner, they *pronounce* words as they habitually hear and speak them. The purpose of this test is to appraise, in part, the individual's powers and habits of auditory perception. This test, along with the Betts Phonetic Elements Test, may also be used for appraising the phonetic ability of children with second-grade reading ability. When used for the purpose, the child should be asked to look at each phonetic element and give the sound equivalent.

Normal Performance. All normal first-grade children are able to respond correctly to the sounds given.

Procedure. The child should be seated in front of the examiner. The subject should be at a distance of about three feet. Say, **"I am going to give you some sounds. After I have**

given each sound, you repeat it." Give the true sound. All first-grade teachers should be qualified examiners. Although credit is given only for the correct response to the *first* presentation of each sound, the examiner should attempt to have the subject repeat the sound correctly after a failure on a given item.

Recording. On the record blank check the correct responses on the first attempt. The score is the total number of items correctly repeated.

Interpretation. A low score (failure to repeat correctly all but six items) may be due to a narrow auditory frequency range, defective hearing, or inadequate auditory perception. Not all cases can be taught to respond correctly to all the items of the test; hence, it is questionable whether such cases can profit by certain phonetic types of training.

Test A-4—Auditory Acuity

Request the subject to stand at a distance of twenty feet from the examiner. The subject should turn his back to the examiner and close the ear not being tested by pressing on the tragus with the forefinger. Repeat the numbers in the order given in the record blank with a very low voice, not a whisper. Although this test is not as reliable as an audiometer test, it is practical. The degree of success will depend upon the experience of the examiner.

Test A-5—Auditory Frequency Range

This test can be given only in clinics where an audio-frequency oscillator is available. The instructions for the administration of the test accompany the instrument. The Bell Telephone Laboratories of New York City have announced an inexpensive audiometer which should be available in 1936.

SECTION III
Betts Visual Sensation and Perception Tests

General Instructions

1. Make certain that the bottom edge of each slide rests snugly in the holder. The slides must be level; otherwise, the tests are of little value.
2. Adjust the instrument to a height comfortable for each subject and make sure that the head is rested firmly in the instrument.
3. Note the two markings on the top surface of the Telebinocular shaft. In setting the slide holder, the *front* or inside edge (side next to the barrels or between slide holder and barrels) of the slide holder should be at the black line. (See page 163 for the Telebinocular.)

This shows how the slide should *not* be held

The 1936 model of the Keystone Ophthalmic Telebinocular has only two markings on the shaft; namely,
Reading Distance and .00_∞. The reading distance
mark corresponds to the 2.50_16 reading on the 1934
model. All slides used at the 3.00_13 and 2.50_16 settings on the 1934 model can be used when the slide
holder on the 1936 model is set at Reading Distance.
Infinity (.00_∞) markings are the same on each model.
Slides used at 1.00_40 and .00_∞ settings on the 1934
model can be used when the slide holder on the 1936
model is set at .00_∞. Without sacrificing validity and
reliability, these changes were made in order to simplify
the testing procedures. The 1934 model is valuable for
research purposes, but is no longer available for public
school use. For the purpose of detecting crucial visual
disabilities, the 1936 model meets the same standards as
the 1934 model. In no case should the use of the 1934
test slides be discontinued, for they can be used on
either instrument. Likewise, the 1936 edition of the test
slides may be used on the 1934 model Telebinocular.

4. Keep the lenses clean with a soft cloth.

5. The light may be connected to any 110 to 120 volt circuit
   (D.C. or A.C.). Extra bulbs may be secured from the
   Keystone View Company, Meadville, Pennsylvania.

6. Do not touch the glazed surface of the slides with the
   hands. Use the pointer provided with the set. When the
   slides become soiled, secure new ones. Never use a lead
   pencil or a pen for pointing.   .

7. The examiner should check himself before testing others.

8. To the School Doctor: If a subject is wearing a correction, he should be tested with and then without his
   glasses. The subject should wear his distance correction
   for the tests when the slide holder is set at .00_∞, and

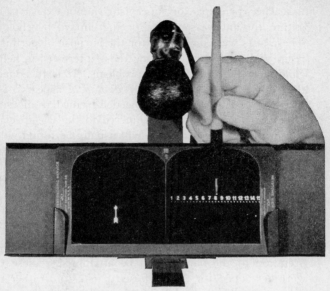

This illustrates the use of the pointer

his reading correction when the slide holder is set at Reading Distance. In such instances, a pencil with a different color lead can be used to record the readings with glasses.

9. Do not permit children to see the slides out of the instrument, with the one exception of Test 1 slide.

10. The examiner should familiarize himself with the instructions. *These tests are as simple to administer and to interpret as the usual standardized tests for school purposes.* It is true that the more experienced examiner will be rewarded with more nearly consistent results. Follow the directions and establish rapport with the subject.

11. The teacher, principal, or supervisor cannot expect to substitute for an eye-specialist or the clinical psychologist. These tests were developed for the purpose of permitting reciprocal co-operation among those interested in helping children over their reading problems. It is the duty of the educator to identify the *pedagogical* aspects of the problem and to apply the needed remedial measures. Other problems should be referred to the eye-specialist, auralist, or pediatrician who will usually be found willing to co-operate with the school authorities. It is important for the educator not to recommend doctors, but instead to suggest that the parents consult specialists of their choosing for such advice. *The principal should be in a neutral position to co-ordinate the efforts of those involved.*

12. If a teacher or psychologist administers the test, no interpretation of the data should be attempted. These tests were developed for the purpose of *detecting* rather than *diagnosing* visual disabilities. In no way are these tests to be regarded as a substitute for the diagnosis by a competent eye-specialist. In a great many cases, the tests can be given in as short a period of time as the Snellen Tests. (See Chapter VIII.)

13. Many cases requiring the aid of an eye-specialist can be detected in thirty seconds. Unless the data are being recorded for research purposes, there is no need for using any more of the Visual Sensation and Perception Slides after the first test failed has been recorded.

14. Inexperienced examiners should study the illustrations before attempting to administer the tests.

15. All tests used with the Telebinocular should be given only when the subject is seeing with both eyes. The chief value of these tests is study of the co-ordinate functioning of the eyes.

16. Refer your questions regarding the tests to the Research Bureau, Keystone View Company, Meadville, Pennsylvania.

Test 1. Introductory (Slide DB-10)

Purpose. This test serves two purposes:

1. Younger children are immediately interested in the "pictures."

2. The examiner may detect the presence of one-eyed vision.

Normal performance. Normal two-eyed vision will permit the subject to superimpose the two images so that one composite picture will be formed. In brief, the dog should be seen jumping through the hoop.

Procedure. The whole series of tests can be introduced by the statement: **"I am going to show you some pictures. See this picture?** (Show Test 1 slide outside the instrument.) **Let us put this picture in this** (pointing to the instrument) **and see if we can make the dog jump through the hoop."** Set the front of the slide holder at .00_∞ and insert Test 1 slide. Be sure the slide rests snugly in the holder. The pig with the ring on his back will be seen with the left eye and the running dog will be seen with the right eye. Say, **"Tell me what you see in this picture."** The typical or normal report of the subject is, "A dog and a pig." If the pupil reports seeing only the right eye picture (the dog) or the left eye picture (the pig), say, **"Do you see anything else?"** If only one side (the right or the left) of the slide can be seen, the child does not have two-eyed vision; he is seeing with one eye only. In all probability the visual acuity in the non-seeing eye is low or the subject is ignoring the vision in it.

Recording. On the record blank, record as follows:

1. If the subject sees the dog jumping through the hoop, place a check mark after "Both."

2. If subject sees the dog only, place a check mark after "Right."

3. If subject sees the pig only, place a check mark after "Left."

Interpretation. If the subject sees with one eye only, he cannot be expected to pass Tests 2, 4, 5, 6, and 7. The subject also will fail on either Test 3b or Test 3c, depending on which eye is causing the difficulty. A subject who is using one eye which functions normally probably experiences little difficulty with reading so far as vision is concerned.

Test 2. Distance Fusion (Slide DB-4)

Purpose. Normal reading or seeing of fine detail is accomplished by one small part of the retina called the *macula,* the most highly sensitive area of the retina. Both the right and left eyes have macular areas. In order to fuse two images into one, it is necessary for them to fall upon corresponding points of the retina of each eye; that is, both eyes must be pointed precisely toward the object of regard. This is achieved by the subject's desire for single images and the subsequent reflex action incident to seeing. As stated on authority:[1] "If our contention is correct, 84.5 per cent of the patients who consult us complaining of ocular fatigue have some disturbance of the neuromuscular functions, which, if not the sole cause of their complaint, at least adds to their discomfort. We are convinced that we are not giving our patients the benefit of our best

---

[1] Berens, Conrad, M.D., Losey, Ray R., M.D., and Hardy, Le Grand H., M.D. "Routine Examination of the Ocular Muscles and Nonoperative Treatments," *American Journal of Ophthalmology* (December, 1927).

judgment, if we neglect the examination of the ocular muscles in clinic and office practice."

This test is used to appraise the individual's fusion power for isolated letter-size images. This is an important test for retarded readers, except in situations where the individual has learned to compensate for the difficulty.

Normal performance. The subject with normal eye co-ordination for distance seeing will fuse quickly the four balls into three. His reply as to the color of the three balls will depend upon his ability to discriminate between colors.

Procedure. Set the front of the slide holder at .00_ ∞ and insert Test 2 slide. Be sure the slide rests snugly on the bottom of the holder. Ask, **"How many balls do you see?"** The normal response is "Three balls." After the subject's report, ask, **"What color are the balls?"** A normal case may reply, "Red, white, and blue," "Red, yellow, and blue," or "Red, blue, blue." The subject may report seeing four balls at first, then, while naming the colors, report seeing only three balls. Such a response (four balls, then three balls) is questionable, for the response should be immediate.

Recording. On the record blank check the response given.

Interpretation. The seeing of four balls, then their fusion into three, indicates sluggish fusion; therefore, the case is questionable and should be watched carefully for future difficulty. If the child sees four balls and cannot fuse them into three, his fusion power is at a low level. If only two balls are seen, there is evidence of one-eyed vision. In either of the last two instances, the need for thorough eye examination is indicated.

The reliability of the subject's report may be checked by asking, **"What colors are the balls?"** If two are seen, the reply will be, "Red and blue," or "Yellow and blue." In this case, the same eye will probably be used for Test 1 and the other tests. In further study of this phase of the problem, the examiner is referred to the Betts Tests of Fusion.

A check on the reliability of the report can be made in two other ways. First, the subject can be asked to point to each ball. If the number of balls pointed to is not equal to the number of balls reported to have been seen, ask the subject to count them again. Second, insert the Test 7 slide (Slide DB-5) and ask the subject to state the number of balls seen. Most cases cannot fuse the four balls of this slide into three. Cases failing the Test 2 slide should be referred to a specialist who will determine whether glasses or eye-training exercises are required.

Test 3a. Two-Eyed Efficiency (Slide DB-1)

Purpose. This is a test of the visual efficiency (keenness of visual powers) of both eyes.

Normal Performance. A score of 100 per cent may be considered normal on Test 3a.

Procedure. Set front of slide holder at .00_ ∞. Insert Test 3a slide which is used to test two-eyed visual efficiency. Be sure the slide rests snugly in the holder. On this slide dots appear in each of the signs before each eye and normally are fused into one dot for each sign. Using the pointer, point to the first and largest sign and say, **"There is a black dot in each of the signs. Tell me whether you see the black dot in the right, the left, the top, the bottom, or the center of the sign"** (pointing to each white square mentioned). If the subject has difficulty in mastering the technique, use the same procedure and point to the first sign before the *left* eye. Always point downward toward the top edge of the sign, never across the slide. Should further difficulty be encountered, show the location of the first dot. In very rare instances a fusional difficulty prevents the subject from seeing the details of the picture clearly. This is a problem for the doctor and will be identified on the other tests.

Point to the upper edge of each sign; never to the dot in the sign. Children express themselves in various ways; any response which indicates their knowledge of the location of the dots should be counted as correct. Some preschool children have difficulty in differentiating between right and left. With these younger children, the tests for visual acuity will have more appeal if called "The Game of Finding the Black Dot." They may indicate their responses by a motion of the right or left hand. Do not allow them to point at or otherwise touch the slides with their hands.

For survey work, especially with older subjects, it is permissible to jump from the first sign to the seventh sign. This will lower the administration time of the test without lowering the reliability.

For an individual with normal depth perception each succeeding sign will appear to be at an increased distance from the first one. This facilitates the administration of the test by making it easier for the subject to continue with the signs in their proper sequence. However, depth perception is not essential for the validity of this test.

When surveys are made, time can be saved by preparing groups of pupils for the tests of visual efficiency. This can be done by drawing the first sign on the blackboard and instructing the class in the proper way of designating the location of the black dot. Also, a chart prepared for this purpose can be secured from the Keystone View Company, Meadville, Pennsylvania.

Recording. On the record blank, check the correct responses. "R" refers to right; "L," left; "C," center; "B," bottom; and "T," top. On the blank line after the word "score" record the per cent of vision as indicated under the *last correct response*. For example, if the last dot correctly located by the subject is on the ninth sign (in the center, "C"), the score will be 100 per cent. The response should be immediate and effortless. Do not permit the subject to struggle or prolong his efforts.

Interpretation. For Test 1 the dots are in the following positions:

Position of sign	Per cent A.M.A.	Position of dot
1	20	Right
2	30	Left
3	40	Center
4	50	Bottom
5	60	Top
6	70	Center
7	80	Left
8	90	Bottom
9	100	Center
10	105	Left
11	110	Right

Reading from near target to far target

An individual registering a visual efficiency of 90 per cent or lower should be referred for a thorough eye examination. A score of 110 per cent is doubtful, but the subject should not be referred to a specialist unless he fails on one of the other tests.

Test 3b. Visual Efficiency of Left Eye (Slide DB-2)

Purpose. The purpose of this test is to check the sharpness of the vision of the left eye. Test 3b differs from test 3a in two respects:

1. There are no dots before the right eye; therefore, the visual efficiency of the left eye is checked *while both eyes are seeing as habitually*. This test is not available elsewhere. In all other tests of visual efficiency it is necessary to occlude, or cover up, one eye while testing the other eye, thereby inviting it to perform at a higher level of efficiency than is habitual. Reading is not accomplished normally with one eye covered; therefore,

the validity of this test lies chiefly in the appraisal of the efficiency of one eye while both eyes are functioning. The subject usually is unaware of which eye is being tested.

2. The sequence of dots is changed in order to forestall memorization of their respective locations. On the Test 3b slide the dot on the first sign is at the top.

Normal performance. A score of 90 or 100 per cent may be considered normal on this test.

Procedure. Set front of slide holder at .00_ ∞ and insert Test 3b slide. Be sure the slide is snug and level in the holder. Usually no difficulty with the testing technique is encountered on Test 3b because, with a few exceptions, the subject will have mastered it on Test 3a. Proceed with Test 3b as with Test 3a. Point to the signs before the *right* eye. *Always point downward toward the top edge of each sign, never across the slide.* If the pointer is used across the slide so that it can be viewed with both eyes, the double images seen will confuse the subject.

The chief advantage of this test over other procedures for the checking of visual efficiency is that of testing one eye while both eyes are seeing; therefore, the examiner should *always* point to the signs on the half of the slide where there are no dots in order to insure the use of both eyes while one eye is being tested. If this is not done, there is very little need for using all three slides for testing visual efficiency. The right and left half of the slides normally are blended into one, so that the subject mentally superimposes the sign containing the dot over the sign to which the examiner is pointing. It is suggested that the examiner should experiment with this phenomenon before administering the test to others.

Recording. On the record blank check the correct responses. The score is the per cent of efficiency indicated under the last correct response; for example, if the dot is seen in the center (C) of the ninth sign the score is 100 per cent. The position of the dot is abbreviated as follows: "T" means top; "B," bottom; "C," center; "R," right; "L," left.

Interpretation. For Test 2 the dots are in the following position:

	Position of sign	Per cent A.M.A.	Position of dot
	1	20	Top
	2	30	Bottom
Reading	3	40	Center
from	4	50	Right
near	5	60	Left
target	6	70	Center
to	7	80	Bottom
far	8	90	Right
target	9	100	Center
	10	105	Bottom
	11	110	Right

The subject may report the alternate seeing and non-seeing of the dots, the dots "dancing," or no dots at all. During the period when the dots have vanished, there is evidence that the eye has ceased to see, which usually is called ignoring of or the psychological blocking of the vision of that eye. "Dancing" dots are evidence of unstable control of the left eye during the two-eyed seeing process. Low visual efficiency or ignoring the visual image is evidenced when no dots are seen. The manifestation of this may be re-checked by covering the front of the Telebinocular tube for the right eye with a piece of black cardboard. Then the efficiency of the eye in question may be tested. If this is necessary, however, the subject should be referred for a thorough eye examination.

The advantage of using a test of visual efficiency which permits the checking of one eye while both eyes are seeing is obvious after a few cases have been tested. Sometimes an individual with a 20 per cent visual efficiency in one eye while both eyes are seeing can be made to use it with 80 per cent efficiency when the companion eye is covered. And again, an eye registering 50 per cent visual efficiency can be caused to register 100 per cent efficiency if the other eye is covered. It is the principle of checking each eye separately while both eyes are seeing that gives this series of tests high value for checking individuals who experience reading difficulties. This type of case is not detected by typical wall chart tests. Individuals who completely ignore the vision in one eye seldom experience discomfiture during reading. It is those who report the dots as dancing or alternately appearing and disappearing that may be expected to have difficulty which interferes with efficient and comfortable reading. However, all such cases should be referred for a thorough eye examination.

Test 3c. Visual Efficiency of Right Eye (Slide DB-3)

Purpose. The purpose of this slide is to check the sharpness of the vision of the right eye *while the left eye is seeing also.* It differs from Tests 3a and 3b in that the dots before the left eye are omitted.

Normal performance. A score of 90 per cent or 100 per cent may be considered normal on this test.

Procedure. Set front of slide holder at .00_ ∞ and insert Test 3c slide. Be sure the slide rests snugly in the bottom of the holder. Proceed with Test 3c as with the two previous tests, *pointing to the signs before the left eye.* Always point downward toward the top of each sign, but never across the slide.

Recording. On the record blank check the correct responses. The score is the percent of efficiency indicated under the last correct response.

Interpretation. For Test 3c the dots are in the following positions:

	Position of sign	Per cent A.M.A.	Position of dot
	1	20	Right
	2	30	Left
Reading	3	40	Center
from	4	50	Bottom
near	5	60	Top
target	6	70	Center
to	7	80	Left
far	8	90	Bottom
target	9	100	Center
	10	105	Left
	11	110	Right

See interpretation section of Test 3b for interpretation of this test. The same principles which apply to the interpretation of Test 3b also apply to Test 3c. It will be noted that a score of 90 per cent or above on this test is satisfactory.

Test 4. Vertical Imbalance (Slide DB-8)

Purpose. The purpose of this test is to determine whether or not the eyes function in the same horizontal plane. The condition in which one of the eyes deviates upward is called a vertical imbalance.

Normal performance. A subject with normal vertical eye-muscle balance, will see the line superimposed upon the center meridian of the ball. If the line falls upon any part of the ball, the condition is acceptable.

Procedure. Set the front of the slide holder at .00_ ∞ and insert Test 4 slide. Be sure the slide rests snugly in the bottom of the holder. Ask, **"Does the line go through the star, diamond, ball, cross, or box?"** To check on the reliability of the subject's report, slide the pointer down the *left* eye side of the slide, asking the child to say **"Stop"** when the pointer touches the line. After the technique is understood by the subject, slide the pointer down the *right* eye side. Have the pointer come down in vertical alignment with the right-side edge of the ball, rather than through the ball. Ask the child to say **"Stop"** when he sees the pointer touch the line.

Recording. On the record blank indicate the response given by drawing a line as seen in relation to the ball.

Interpretation. An individual without two-eyed vision will see either the ball or the line, depending upon which eye is used. If such a condition exists (it will have been discovered by means of the previous tests of Visual Sensation and Perception), the case should be referred for a complete eye examination. A serious vertical imbalance exists when the ball lies entirely above or below the line. This latter condition should also be referred for attention.

The line should be projected upon the center of the ball. The range of tolerance is the diameter of the ball; that is, normally the line should fall on some part of the ball. If the line falls at the extreme upper or lower edge of the ball, the case should be recorded as questionable. Some adults may see certain sections of the line alternately appearing or disappearing. This is not alarming.

Luther C. Peter[2] says: "Low degrees of hyperphoria (vertical imbalance) are often ignored as negligible. When stereoscopic slides are scientifically constructed, the difficulty of fusing in the presence of vertical imbalance becomes apparent, and points to the necessity for the proper correction of hyperphoria to obtain comfortable single binocular vision."

---

[2] Peter, Luther C., M.D., *Book of Stereoscopic Technic,* Keystone View Company, Meadville, Pennsylvania, 1932.

Test 5. Eye Co-ordination Level (Slide DB-6)

Purpose. The purpose of this test is to measure the individual's level of eye co-ordination power by the use of a depth perception test, which is graduated in difficulty. Although depth perception is not required for reading on the usual flat surface, the degree of eye co-ordination required to pass this test is essential to efficient and comfortable reading habits, providing the individual has not established certain compensations. Wells[3] states: "When the facts are known, it is quite possible that visual tests will not stop with measuring the acuity of each eye and testing the color sense, but that a certain standard of stereopsis (depth perception) will be required."

Ralph I. Lloyd[4] states: "Stereoscopic vision is vision with an appreciation of three dimensions. As the third dimension is appreciated only when two eyes are used, it follows that successful binocular vision is stereoscopic vision. There are those who use both eyes part of the time or depend on one entirely, or alternately on one and then the other. The more carefully patients are examined, the sooner will one realize that it has not been the custom during the course of an ordinary examination of the eyes to determine whether or not binocular vision is present, and if present, whether for both near and far."

Man is probably the only animal with the degree of eye co-ordination which permits depth perception. Without co-ordination, a high degree of true depth perception is not possible. This test, therefore, measures the co-ordination level of the two eyes. The examiner can prove this to himself by closing one eye and noting the absence of depth. A disparity of 20 per cent or more in the visual efficiency of the two eyes usually causes an individual to fail this test.

---

[3] Wells, David W., M.D., *The Stereoscope in Ophthalmology,* E. F. Mahady Company, 1928.

[4] Ralph I. Lloyd, M.D., *Archives of Ophthalmology* (June, 1932).

Normal performance. All should pass this test with the rating of 100 per cent. *A score of 100 per cent on this test is equivalent to approximately 50 per cent on the tests used by specialists.*

Procedure. Set front of slide holder at .00_∞ and insert Test 5 slide. Call the attention of the subject to the figures in the top row and while pointing from left to right say, **"Here is a star, a box or square, a cross, a diamond, and a ball** (pointing to each figure with the pointer). **Which one stands out nearest to you? Which one looks as though it is standing out from the others?"** "The cross," is the correct response for Row 1. Some subjects may have to look at the figures for about ten seconds before the phenomenon appears. Proceed with each of the remaining horizontal rows as with Row 1. After the reading of the first row, the responses should be immediate. If the subject has difficulty with a given row, check on his knowledge of the characters by naming each one in the row. With older children and adults, time may be saved by skipping from Row 1 to Row 8. There is no real need for checking on the reliability of the report, because each row of targets presents five possible responses only one of which can be correct.

Recording. The total score is the per cent of eye co-ordination for the *last* row read promptly and correctly. On the record blank check the correct responses.

Interpretation. The following standards apply to Test 5 only. It should be remembered that the percentages on this test are not comparable to the scores derived from tests used by the specialist.

An individual who fails to pass the test should be referred to the family specialist who can determine whether or not the condition can be improved. The teacher should not concern herself with the diagnosis of the visual disability because that is the responsibility of the specialist.

Test 1. Introductory (Slide DB-10)

Test 2. Distance Fusion (Slide DB-4)

Courtesy, Keystone View Co.

Test 3a. Two-eyed Efficiency (Slide (DB-1)

340

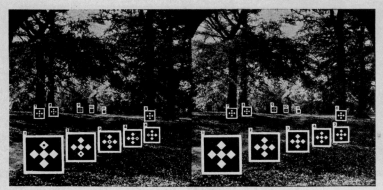

Test 3b. Visual Efficiency of Left Eye (Slide DB-2)

Test 3c. Visual Efficiency of Right Eye (Slide DB-3)

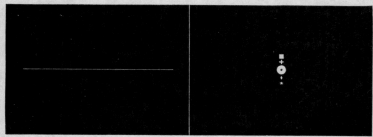

Courtesy, Keystone View Co.

Test 4. Vertical Imbalance (Slide DB-8)

341

Row	Correct Response	Per Cent
1	Cross	10
2	Ball	20
3	Star	30
4	Ball	40
5	Box	50
6	Box	60
7	Diamond	70
8	Cross	80
9	Star	90
10	Cross	100

Test 6. Lateral Imbalance (Slide DB-9)

Purpose. The purpose of this test is to determine the tendency of the eyes to turn in or out or to remain normally parallel for distance seeing and to converge normally when viewing targets at Reading Distance. In other words, it determines the tone of the extrinsic eye muscles as well as the status of the convergence reflexes. If there is a lateral muscle imbalance, the visual axes of the eyes tend to deviate outward or inward from the normal position.

Normal performance. Position 1. When the front of the slide holder is set at .00_∞, the range of tolerance is indicated by the line underscoring the numbers in the following row:

1 2 3 4 5 6 <u>7 8 9 10 11</u> 12 13 14 15

It will be noted that the tolerance ranges from a reading of 7 to a reading of 11. About two-thirds of the cases will report seeing the pointer from 8 to 9½.

Position 2. When the front of the slide holder is set at Reading Distance, the range of tolerance is indicated by the line underscoring the numbers in the following row:

1 2 <u>3 4 5 6</u> 7 8 9 10 11 12 13 14 15

The range of tolerance is from 3 to 6½. About two-thirds of the cases will report seeing the pointer between 4 and 6.

Procedure. Insert Test 6 slide. Be sure it is level and snug in the holder. Readings are taken with the front of the slide holder set at two different positions:

Position 1—.00_ ∞

Position 2—Reading Distance

The order of administering the tests requires only two settings of the slide holder for their administration. The sequence of testing also makes it unnecessary to remove any of the test slides during the test.

For subjects ten years or older, a reliable response can be secured by asking, **"To what number does the arrow point?"** For younger children, the pointer should be used. Teach the child the technique by sliding the pointer laterally across the *left-eye half* of the slide, saying, **"Say 'stop' when the pointer gets to the middle of the arrow."** After the examiner has assured himself that the child says "stop" at the correct position, slide the pointer along the horizontal line of numbers on the *right-eye half* of the slide, repeating the same instructions. The pointer should be moved alternately from left to right and right to left.

Recording. After 3 consecutive readings with the same response and with the slide holder in each of the two above mentioned positions, record the response by drawing a vertical line showing the *position of the arrow.*

Interpretation. These tests determine the general tone of the eye muscles by indicating whether or not the eyes normally converge when the target is moved from .00_ ∞ to Reading Distance position. Any variations of the readings from the tolerance allowances (see above section on "Normal Perform-

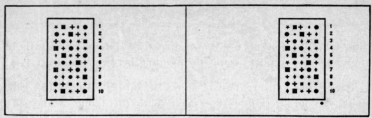

Test 5. Eye Co-ordination Level (Slide DB-6)

Test 6. Lateral Imbalance (Slide DB-9)

Test 7. Reading Distance Fusion (Slide DB-5)

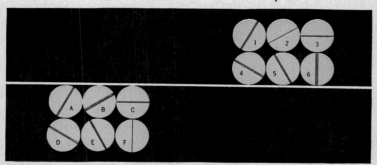

Test 8c. Sharpness of Image (Slide DB-7c)

ance") is a problem for the specialist[5] and not for the teacher. The hour of the day, the presence of farsightedness, nearsightedness, and astigmatism, and the general status of health are important factors contributing to faulty oculomotor control. A subject with symptoms of visual disturbances should be checked in both the forenoon and afternoon. Presence of farsightedness will usually cause the subject to over-converge slightly, i.e., register readings below 7 when the slide holder is set at .00_∞ and below 4 when set at Reading Distance.

Maximum results can be achieved by the experienced examiner if this battery of tests is interpreted as a whole. This is particularly true of the lateral imbalance test. Some subjects may exhibit a lateral imbalance but compensate for the difficulty without effort. It is therefore important to remember that if the individual is successful in both the fusion tests (Tests 2 and 7), he should not be referred to a specialist for help.

Test 7. Reading Distance Fusion (Slide DB-5)

Note: Do not confuse the two fusion tests (Tests 2 and 7).

Purpose. This test provides an index to the individual's fusion ability at reading distance. The time required by the subject to fuse provides an important clue to visual comfort and efficiency during sustained reading. When the visual efficiency in each eye is normal, a high level of two-eyed vision is essential for rapid perception during the fixations or pauses of the mechanical reading process. Wells[6] states: "A recent review of one thousand cases of eye strain shows that 25 per cent needed treatment because of some failure of the two eyes

---

[5] Guibor, George P., M.D., "Some Possibilities of Orthoptic Training," *Archives of Ophthalmology,* II (March, 1934).

[6] Wells, David W., M.D., *Book of Stereoscopic Technic,* Keystone View Company, Meadville, Pennsylvania, 1932.

to work together properly. Since each person is obliged to learn the art of using the two eyes together as a part of his own experience, and has no instruction whatever, some of us learn it well and some of us learn it quite imperfectly."

Normal performance. The subject with normal fusion at Reading Distance will fuse the four balls into three instantly. His reply as to the color of the three balls will depend upon his ability to discriminate between colors.

Procedure. Set the front of the slide holder at Reading Distance and insert Test 7 slide. Be sure it is level and snug in the holder. Ask, **"How many balls do you see?"** After the subject's report, ask, **"What color are the balls?"** The normal response is, "Three balls." With such a normal case, the reply to the question, "What are the colors of the balls?" may be "Red, white, and blue," "Red, yellow, and blue," or "Red, blue, and blue." The subject may report seeing four balls at first, then, while naming the colors, report seeing only three balls. Such a response (four balls, then three balls) is questionable.

Interpretation. The seeing of four balls then their fusion into three and the seeing of three balls which "break" into four are indications of fusion difficulty; therefore, the case is a questionable one and should be carefully watched for a visual disability in the future. Slow function at Reading Distance, such as seeing four then three balls, also may account for the increased number of fixations per line of some retarded readers. If the child sees four balls and cannot fuse them into three, his fusion power is at a low level. If only two balls are seen, there is evidence of one-eyed vision. In either of the two instances the child should be referred for a thorough eye examination.

The reliability of the subject's report may be checked by asking, **"What colors are the balls?"** If two are seen, the reply will be, "Red and blue," or "Yellow and blue." In this case, the same eye will probably be used for Test 1 and the other tests. The subject's report can be checked also by having him point to each of the balls, counting them as he points.

Test 8. Sharpness of Image (Slides DB-7c and DB-7d)

Purpose. These tests are used to detect errors of focus which interfere with efficient vision. Common errors of focus which blur or otherwise distort the image on the retina of the eye are called farsightedness, nearsightedness, and astigmatism. Such errors can be corrected with glasses. It is the purpose of these tests to detect errors rather than to diagnose the difficulty; hence, their use is entirely within the professional province of a teacher, psychologist, nurse, or school doctor. Examiners can be assured that failure to pass this test is a definite indication that the subject should be referred for a thorough eye examination. The correction prescribed by the specialist may not be great; nevertheless, failure to pass this test proves that the subject cannot compensate for the difficulty. The amount of focusing error which a given subject can tolerate is entirely an individual matter. Some can accept without discomfort large errors while others are incapacitated to a degree by the presence of relatively small ones. These tests therefore are especially valuable for the detection of focusing errors for which the individual does not compensate readily.

The tests of sharpness of image are mounted on two standard stereoscopic slides. The twelve golden balls on each slide are divided so that six balls above the white line are seen with the right eye and the six balls below the white line are seen with the left eye. In the 1934 edition, each ball had three lines. In order to forestall guessing, the 1936 edition of these tests has been revised so that only three balls before each eye contain three lines each. This necessitates the use of two slides in order to test the six principal meridians of each eye by means of a ball containing three lines. The use of three lines for the *test balls* is necessary in order to insure comparable and consistent results.

The *dummy balls* have one, two, or four lines. *Only the responses on the balls containing three lines are recorded.*

Normal performance. When the slide holder is set at .00_ ∞ and at Reading Distance, the subject should see three lines in the test balls. In Test 8c, the test balls A, D, and E are before the left eye and test balls 1, 4, and 5 are before the right eye. In Test 8d, the test balls B, C, and F are before the left eye and test balls 2, 3, and 6 are before the right eye.

Procedure. *Position 1.* Set the front of the slide holder at Reading Distance and insert Test 8c slide. The slide should be level in the holder. Point to ball A and ask, **"How many lines do you see?"** Point to B, C, D, E, and F in their order and repeat the question. The balls on the left-half of the slide are seen with the left eye. In like manner, proceed with balls 1 to 6 which are above the white line and before the right eye. Only the number of lines seen in the test balls should be recorded. Each ball contains one, two, three, or four lines, only the *test balls* contain three lines. The number of lines in each ball is varied to forestall guessing. *At no time during the testing should the examiner give a clue to the correct response.*

The number of lines in each ball on the Test 8c slide is as follows:

	Left Eye	Number of Lines	Right Eye	Number of Lines
Test Ball . . .	A	3	1	3
Dummy Ball . .	B	4	2	1
Dummy Ball . .	C	2	3	2
Test Ball . . .	D	3	4	3
Test Ball . . .	E	3	5	3
Dummy Ball . .	F	1	6	4

One-half of the balls on Test 8c slide contain three lines while on Test 8d slide the other half of the balls contain three lines. In short, the use of the two slides is equivalent to using one slide with three lines in each of the twelve balls.

The number of lines in each ball on the Test 8d slide is as
follows:

		Left Eye	Number of Lines	Right Eye	Number of Lines
Dummy Ball	. .	A	4	1	1
Test Ball	. . .	B	3	2	3
Test Ball	. . .	C	3	3	3
Dummy Ball	. .	D	2	4	2
Dummy Ball	. .	E	1	5	4
Test Ball	. . .	F	3	6	3

Position 2. Set the front of the slide holder at .00_∞ and
insert Test 8c slide which should rest level and snugly in the
holder. Administer Tests 8c and 8d at the .00_∞ position of
the slide holder in the same manner as when the slide holder
was set at Reading Distance.

Recording. In the record blank, record the number of lines
seen in the test balls, those containing three lines. Make no
record of the number of lines reported seen in the dummy balls,
those not containing three lines. Space is provided in the record
blank as follows:

Slide holder set at Reading Distance.

                             Left Eye   Right Eye
Test 8c:
   No. of lines seen in A__D__E__   1__4__5__
Test 8d:
   No. of lines seen in B__C__F__   2__3__6__

Slide holder set at .00_∞.

                             Left Eye   Right Eye
Test 8c:
   No. of lines seen in A__D__E__   1__4__5__
Test 8d:
   No. of lines seen in B__C__F__   2__3__6__

Interpretation. The normal eye should see three lines in all the test balls. If the subject cannot see three lines in all the test balls, he should be referred for a thorough eye examination. If the three lines in some of the test balls are blurred, the subject may report seeing one or two blurred lines or four or more fine lines. *It is important that significance be attached only to the responses on the test balls.* The dummy balls containing one, two, and four lines are used only to minimize opportunities for guessing. It is also important that subjects wearing bifocal glasses should look through the lower segments when the slide holder is set at Reading Distance and through the upper segments when the slide holder is set at .00_∞.

Each response should be immediate and effortless; otherwise, the subject may invalidate the results by prolonging the examination or by turning his head or squinting his eyes while attempting to clear up the lines in certain test balls. It is also important that the subject should rest his head on the instrument which should be adjusted to a comfortable height.

SECTION IV

Oculomotor and Perception Habits

Purpose of tests. This series of tests is used for the study of the subject's habits of word perception and two-eyed reading tendencies. In addition to this, these tests are used as the basis for the determination of the remedial reading needed. When the type used in these tests is viewed through the lens system of the instrument, it is magnified approximately two and one-half times.

Faulty oculomotor behavior and perception habits are reflected in the number and nature of eye movements. Inefficient readers make many fixation pauses of long duration and frequently many regressive movements. Cases with faulty oculomotor control can be detected on the Visual Sensation and Perception Tests. The Tests of Oculomotor and Perception Habits are valuable for the study of word recognition skills. The reversal or confusion of letter and word forms accounts for about ten per cent of the difficulties of retarded readers. The specific nature of the letter and word recognition difficulties can be determined by means of the tests of Oculomotor and Perception Habits. The identification of words in isolation is a more severe test than recognition of words in context.

Some cases appear to go through a period where they confuse letter and word forms. In their efforts to co-ordinate their eye movements, these subjects sometimes reverse the words before one or both eyes. Other cases evidence spatial orientation of the words; that is, do not reverse, etc., on the slides requiring depth perception, but fail of this control on the slides which do not require eye co-ordination. The writer has recorded data to the effect that some individuals are more efficient readers when using one eye than when using both eyes.

Occasionally the vowels *a, e, o, u*, and the consonant *c,* when printed in the lower case (or small letters), appear to present a difficulty for subjects with focusing anomalies. Sometimes where faulty fusion is experienced at Reading Distance, difficulty will be experienced with such consonants as *p, b, d, g, u, n,* and sometimes *w* and *m*.

The reading involved in the Series 1 and 2 tests requires only the lowest level of eye co-ordination; Series 3, superimposition (the image before each eye is superimposed without depth perception), and Series 4, depth perception, a high degree of fusion. The fourth series capitalizes on the fusion function to insure eye co-ordination during the reading fixations; that is, depth perception is possible only when the two eyes are working together normally.

The following is a summary of the tests:

Series 1—Unskilled Two-eyed Vision
    Slide DB-20—Word Perception—Level 1
    Slide DB-21—Word Perception—Level 2
    Slide DB-22—Word Perception—Level 3

Series 2—Unskilled Two-eyed Vision
    Slide DB-40—Letter Perception—All grades
    Slide DB-41—Number Perception—All grades

Series 3—Superimposition
    Slide DB-60—Word Perception—Level 1
    Slide DB-61—Word Perception—Level 2

Series 4—Depth Perception requiring eye co-ordination and an
    appreciation of third dimension seeing
    Slide DB-80—Word Perception—Level 1
    Slide DB-81—Word Perception—Level 2
    Slide DB-82—Word Perception—Level 3

Selection of words. The words used in these tests were
checked against the Durrell, Gates, Gross, Horn, Stone, and
Thorndike lists. For example on Slide DB-20 all of the words
are found in the first 500 of the Gates list; fourteen of the
twenty are found in the Gross list; all with the exception of
cat are in the Thorndike and the Horn 1A lists; and fourteen
are in Durrell's first level words. On Slide DB-21, 75 per cent
are in the Stone second-grade list. A complete report on the
selection of the words may be secured from the Keystone View
Company, Meadville, Pennsylvania.

Normal performance.

Series 1
    Slide DB-20—At the end of the first grade, children normally
    can give correct responses to all the words.

Slide DB-22—Represents third grade performance.

Slide DB-21—Represents second grade performance.

Series 2

Slides DB-40 and DB-41—Children above first grade normally are able to give correct responses to all items.

Series 3

Slide DB-60—Represents first grade performance.

Slide DB-61—Represents second grade performance.

Series 4

Slide DB-80—Represents first grade performance.

Slide DB-81—Represents second grade performance.

Slide DB-82—Represents third grade performance.

Procedure. Subjects who have failed the fusion or eye coordination tests of the Visual Sensation and Perception series may have difficulty with these tests. Set front of the slide holder at Reading Distance for all tests of Oculomotor and Perception Habits. Give the tests in the order indicated in the record blank. The reliability of the report can be checked by asking the subject to point to each target as he reads. Always use the pointer.

Insert Slide DB-20 and ask, **"Where is the star?"** If the subject sees the star in the circle, proceed with the tests. If the subject reports seeing the star outside the circle move the slide holder out until the star is seen in the circle.

1. Begin with Slide DB-20 of Series 1 and proceed with Slides DB-21 and DB-22 until ten errors are made on a given slide. Read words downward beginning with the left column.

2. Insert Slide DB-40 and ask, **"How many stars do you see?"** If the subject sees two stars, move the slide holder out until the two stars are blended into one.

Slide DB-40 should be read from left to right, beginning at the top; DB-41 downward beginning with the left row. Present Slides DB-40 and DB-41 consecutively. The slide holder should be adjusted for slide DB-41 until the star is seen in the circle.

3. Insert Slide DB-60 and ask, **"Where is the star?"** If the subject sees the star in the circle, proceed with the test. If the subject reports seeing the star outside the circle, move the slide holder out until the star is seen in the circle. Begin with Slide DB-60 of Series 3 and proceed with Slide DB-61 until ten errors are made on a given slide. Read words downward beginning with the left column.

4. Insert Slide DB-80 and say, **"Point to the cross. Point to the star."** The content of the right and left halves of the slide should be blended so that a cross appears on one side and a star on the other. For some cases it may be necessary to move the slide holder out in order to secure the desired response. After the slide holder is adjusted, the subject should report that the words appear to be recessed. The words should appear to be printed on the bottom of two boxes which are estimated to be 3 to 12 inches deep, depending upon the subject's interpretation of the phenomenon. Begin with Slide DB-80 of Series 4 and proceed with Slide DB-81 and DB-82 until ten errors are made on a given slide. Read words downward beginning with the left column.

Recording. Check the correct responses and record the incorrect. Record an omission with an "o."

Interpretation. Subjects ignoring the vision in one eye will omit all or a part of the words before that eye on Series 1 and 2 tests. Individuals with a low level of eye co-ordination may see double or indistinct words on Series 3, while on Series 4 they may have depth perception. The seeing of three or four columns of words indicates faulty eye co-ordination. The above mentioned behavior is the problem of the specialist. The following interpretations are of pedagogical significance:

1. *Reversal of word forms.* To a degree, a lack of normal two-eyed vision may contribute to this difficulty. However, the child must be taught to recognize words after the visual difficulty has been corrected. In Chapters XI and XIV, suggestions are given for building word-recognition skills

2. *Reversal of letter forms.* Suggestions for the correction of reversal difficulties are given in Chapter XIV. Some cases can profit by practice on initial and final consonant sounds.

3. *Inadequate word analysis skills.*

   a) Difficulty with words beginning with *th* and *wh* indicates a need for drill on visual analysis, as suggested in Chapter XI.

   b) Failure on Slides DB-20, DB-60, and DB-80 indicates a need for extended practice on a list of sight words.

   c) The reading of *hope* for *hop, pine* for *pin,* and the like indicates a need for practice involving the phonetic principle; namely, a final *e* is silent and makes the preceding vowel long.

   d) The reading of *hop* for *hope, dean* for *den, note* for *not, pean* for *pen,* and the like indicates a need for practice involving the phonetic principle that the vowel is usually short except when modified by the position of some other vowel.

   e) The reading of *ro-ad* for *road, pad* for *paid, met* for *meat,* and the like indicates a need for practice on vowel digraphs.

f) The reading of *wear* for *war, frame* for *form, dirk* for *dark,* and the like probably indicates a need for practice on the "murmur" diphthongs.

All the above practice should be given in terms of the learning conditions outlined in Chapters II, XI, and XIV. the writer advocates the use of the analysis method of teaching phonics, with the emphasis on noting similarities and differences between word forms. Meaning should be emphasized both before and after practice on words in isolation.

Pupils who have been given certain types of practice in word analysis may make *systematic* errors; that is, they repeat the same error with certain word elements. In such instances, very little help on the specific items involved will be required. When *random* errors are made, there is usually evidence that systematic instruction in word analysis should be given.

4. *Low level of performance.* It is advisable to supplement these tests with other reading tests or reading from a well-graded series of readers. Failure on Slides DB-20, DB-60, and DB-80, usually indicates that the child is not ready for second grade reading material. In such cases, extended practice should be given in pre-primers, primers, or first readers—depending upon the achievement level of the pupil. Failure on Slides DB-21, DB-61, and DB-81 is a fairly reliable indication that the pupil is not ready for third grade reading materials. It is extremely important that retarded readers—and all other pupils—should read at their own achievement levels, otherwise earnest attempts may be frustrated. *Typical incorrect responses for each of the test items follow on the next page.*

Slide DB-20

Test Word	Typical Incorrect Responses
1. and	an, dan, nad, nod
2. no	not, on
3. put	but, pit
4. these	the, there, this, those, tree
5. very	every, over, worry
6. for	of, ten
7. did	bid, dib, dip, do
8. on	know, no, not
9. was	saw
10. over	even, ever, every, or
11. how	hot, now, won
12. this	them, there, these
13. who	how, oh
14. the	dog, this
15. big	by, dig, gip, pig
16. ten	hen, net, then, time
17. done	didn't, does, don't, down, drop
18. bad	bag, back, dab, dad, did
19. saw	sad, sat, some, was
20. cat	at, sat, tac

Slide DB-21

Test Word	Typical Incorrect Responses
1. read	dear
2. father	far, farther, rather
3. horse	home, house
4. dry	day, tired
5. farm	arm, farmer, frame, from, funny
6. dog	bag, bog, hog
7. hop	hoop, hope, pooh, shop, top

8. drop	broke, did, drope, hope, dop, prod
9. cup	but, cap, pup, sup
10. never	even, ever, near, nearly, very, over
11. dig	big, did, dog, dug, gib, gip, pig
12. before	forb
13. ever	even, every, eyes, over, very
14. send	said, sand, second, seen, sent, sound, spend
15. left	after, felt, laid, leaf, let, life, lip
16. short	horse, sat, shirt, shoot, shore, shot, should, show, sport, store
17. own	cow, draw, now, on, one, only, or, who, whoon, won, too
18. dark	bank, bark, dig, drink, park
19. pin	bin, nip, pail, pain, pine, pink
20. lap	lake, lamp, let, lip, pal

Slide DB-22

(For a reproduction of this slide see page 167.)

Test Word	*Typical Incorrect Responses*
1. meat	met, team
2. build	barn, beld, blue, building, built, butter, did, pulled
3. den	ben, dean, done, don't, eat, pen, ten
4. part	pat, pet, puss, tarp, trap
5. hope	heep, hoop, hop, pony
6. card	crad, dark, hard, pad, sand, saw

7. war   raw, ware, was, way, wear, were

8. reason   sooner, run

9. copy   carpen, catch, clop, coop, cop, cope, cover, crop, soap

10. strange   stand, starb, stare, start, strap, strong, sun

11. quiet   cute, peet, pet, quick, quickly, quit, quite

12. paid   pair, part, pay, ped, pen, prayed, put, said

13. pond   bond, pony, pound, put

14. push   brush, bush, pull

15. dust   bust, damp, desk, does, push

16. lamp   camp, laid, lamb, palm

17. sort   rots, short, shot, sorry, starb, start, steal, store

18. pit   big, bit, pig, pint, pitch, put

19. chew   carry, chair, cheap, cherry, chose, ch-we, cow, crew, crow, shoe, show, then

20. split   bell, slip, slit, split, while

Slide DB-40

Test Letter	Typical Incorrect Responses
1. b	d, p, q
2. n	h, u
3. p	d, q, b
4. u	n
5. p	b, d, q
6. d	b, g
7. q	g, p
8. h	n, u
9. h	n, u
10. u	n

11.	b	d, p
12.	n	h, u
13.	d	p, q, b
14.	h	n, p
15.	p	b, d, q
16.	q	g, j, p
17.	q	g, j, p
18.	w	u, y
19.	b	d, p
20.	u	n
21.	p	b, d, j
22.	b	d, p
23.	h	n
24.	d	b, p
25.	u	n
26.	q	g, j, p
27.	d	b, p
28.	m	n, w

Slide DB-41

Test Number		Typical Incorrect Responses
1.	12	21
2.	9	6
3.	3	8
4.	12	21
5.	9	6
6.	24	42
7.	6	9
8.	23	32, 33
9.	5	9, 8
10.	8	6
11.	32	22
12.	8	6
13.	5	9, 8

14. 42	24
15. 13	31
16. 21	12
17. 3	9
18. 14	4
19. 21	12
20. 6	9

Slide DB-60

Test Word	Typical Incorrect Responses
1. up	pup
2. do	down, odd
3. good	dog, go, god
4. day	bag, dry, pay
5. not	hat, no, ton
6. that	these, this, what
7. but	be, pat, put, tub
8. now	how, no, own, won
9. their	theirs, this, with
10. been	barn, be, bean, beer, den, pen
11. two	tow, wot
12. we	em, en, eu (you), that
13. them	met, then, when
14. show	no, should, slow, snow, wash
15. am	an, aw, ma
16. bed	bad, bird, deb
17. of	fo, for, off
18. seem	mess, see, sleep, some
19. dear	dark, drop, dry, read
20. pig	big, dig, gip

Slide DB-61

Test Word	Typical Incorrect Responses
1. house	home, horse
2. morning	moan

3.	road	read, ready, red
4.	top	pot, toop, toy
5.	oh	ah, ho, how, on
6.	brown	barn, been, born, down, dry
7.	pick	kip, part, pig, pink, pitch, think
8.	round	around, drown, ralled, ran, red, road, rund
9.	rat	fat, tar, tra
10.	kind	can, cant, din, kid, kin, king
11.	even	ever, every, never, over, ven
12.	knew	kew, knick, know, now, when
13.	number	numbers, umbrella
14.	catch	cat, cats
15.	middle	marbles, meal, mild, mittle, mud, needle, nibble
16.	ink	in, kin, nik
17.	mouth	met, month, most, mother, mount, mouse, nor
18.	pen	hen, nip, pin
19.	tap	pat, take, tape, top, trap
20.	park	bank, borak, karp, pack, pike, play

Slide DB-80

	Test Word	*Typical Incorrect Responses*
1.	be	been, eb
2.	then	there, when
3.	said	days, siad
4.	man	an, nam
5.	so	saw, some
6.	one	eon, once
7.	from	farm, for, form, of
8.	us	is, you
9.	know	how, no, now, won
10.	boy	bob, they

11.	my	man, may, me, why
12.	there	them, then, these, this
13.	in	is, us
14.	they	the, there, this, why
15.	an	and, on
16.	does	chop, done, don't, dose, dress
17.	open	nepo, orange, up
18.	off	for, of, over
19.	stop	pots, stook, top, tops
20.	mother	moth-er, rather

Slide DB-81

Test Word		Typical Incorrect Responses
1.	pretty	better, betty, part, partly, party
2.	where	dart, there, went, were, when
3.	keep	hept, kane, keek, kept, peek
4.	ride	dire, rain, ran, red
5.	ship	house, push, sap, shop, skip, sprinkle
6.	bear	beer, bread, dar, dear, door
7.	seen	sa, sun
8.	pull	apil, built, bull, push, put, sew
9.	ball	bull, dall, doll, dool
10.	wood	woods, wool, world
11.	nine	and, any, mine
12.	pay	bay, day, par, pie, play, put
13.	through	that, there, these, thought, throwed
14.	busy	be, bees, bise, blue, bush, bushes, buzz, dizzy, push, us
15.	heard	bread, had, hard, hand, head, hear, heart, higher
16.	afternoon	noon
17.	miss	mars, mines, misses, mister, mix, muss, sim

18.	began	bank, beg, begin, big, darn
19.	quick	pick, puck, queen, quickly, quiet, quits
20.	queer	pea, poor, queen

Slide DB-82

Test Word		*Typical Incorrect Responses*
1.	bit	pit, put, tib
2.	supper	rubber, subber, suffer
3.	beat	bee, best, bet, bit, brat, brit, peat, pet
4.	month	more, moth, mouth, north, nothing
5.	though	thought, through
6.	touch	taught, thrush, ton
7.	evening	even, evering, every, everything, over
8.	quite	picked, quiet, quit
9.	trip	lip, pirt, pit, put, tear, top
10.	sad	ads, days, send, siad, staid
11.	pound	bound, pond, pous, proud
12.	step	pest, pets, peet, snip, sted, steep, stip, tip
13.	stamp	start, stump, ten
14.	gray	gary, gay, get, grave, pay
15.	lead	deal, laid, lay, learn, led, leg
16.	spot	post, short, show, soap, spats, step, stop, tops
17.	straight	start, strange, strength
18.	net	mat, meat, met, neat, need, nets, ten
19.	team	mate, mean, meat, stream, theme, then
20.	prod	bro, drop, paul, pete, pork, poured, pound, proud

APPENDIX C

Instructions for the Administration and Interpretation of Betts Fusion Tests

Keystone View Company, Meadville, Pennsylvania

1936

Purpose. The fusion tests of the Betts Ready to Read Unit have been expanded into a battery for the determination of the smallest target which an individual can fuse or blend readily into one image. These tests, used in the writer's clinic for the past three years, have been found valuable as checks on the two fusion tests of the basic set.

The Series 2 tests are used for testing when the slide holder is set at .00_∞, the Series 7 tests when the slide holder is set at Reading Distance. The Series 2 tests differ from the Series 7 tests in the spacing between the right eye and left eye targets. When viewing a target at twenty feet or beyond, the visual axes of the eye are normally parallel. When an object at normal reading distance (10 to 16 inches) is viewed, the eyes converge or turn in. For this reason the targets on the Series 2 tests are spaced farther apart than the targets on the Series 7 tests in the spacing between the right eye and left eye targets. the eyes of individuals is provided in the optical construction of the Keystone Ophthalmic Telebinocular, the targets can be spaced permanently for all subjects. The variable on each series of tests is the size of the targets. Both series of tests have been prepared with targets of equivalent sizes.

Under the lens system of the Keystone Ophthalmic Telebinocular, the targets are magnified about 2.5 times. Without magnification, the diameters of the targets for each series are as follow on the next page.

Slide	Diameter (Millimeters)
A	1
B	2
C	4
D	6
E	8
F	10
G	15
H	20

The writer has initiated an extended investigation of the relationship between the size of the target which can be fused and the optimum size of letters for efficient *mechanical* reading habits. By means of these tests, the size of isolated targets required for fusion can be determined. However, in a true reading situation more than the fusion measured by these tests is involved because the peripheral vision aids in maintaining eye co-ordination. During the fixation pause, a number of letters command focal attention while the remainder of the line and the other lines on the page serve to stabilize the fusion process. This test of the ability to fuse isolated targets is, therefore, a more severe test than the Betts Tests of Eye Co-ordination for Context Reading. Eye co-ordination can be developed, to a degree, by practice on large sized targets which can be easily and comfortably fused by the two eyes. If the teacher or psychologist can secure a crude index to the size of target which a given individual can fuse easily, then he can supplement the efforts of the specialist by providing reading materials printed in type of a more nearly suitable size, and by the use of stereographs. These tests are being made available with the understanding that continued research is necessary for the validation of tentative conclusions regarding these tests as a possible physiological approach for the determination of size of type.

Normal performance.

1. On Test 2B an individual should report seeing three balls, when the front of the slide holder is set at .00_ ∞.

2. On Test 7B an individual should report seeing three balls, when the front of the slide holder is set at Reading Distance.

It is important that these tests should not be used if the subject has failed to see more than two balls on the fusion tests of the Visual Sensation and Perception Tests. If only two balls are seen, the subject is using only one eye or has a serious vertical imbalance. Since this is a test of two-eyed vision, there is no need for the school worker to make a further analysis of this phase of the problem.

Procedure.

1. Series 2 tests.

Set the front of the slide holder at .00_ ∞. Insert Test 2A slide and ask, **"How many balls do you see?"** If the subject reports seeing three balls, further examination with the Series 2 tests is unnecessary. The reliability of the report can be checked by having the subject point (with the pointer provided with basic Betts Ready to Read Tests) to each of the balls. If all three balls are not indicated as being in a vertical line, steps should be taken to "double cross" the subject or to explain that four balls were pointed out. This can be done in most cases by inserting Test 7A slide which usually cannot be fused at the .00_ ∞ setting of the slide holder. If the subject still reports the seeing of three balls, he should be asked to point to each ball, counting them as he points. With very little practice, the examiner can secure consistent results.

On Test 2A the subject will report the seeing of two balls, three balls, or four balls. A response of "three balls" indicates immediate fusion. The reporting of "two balls," indicates that the subject is using only one eye. This situation is created if

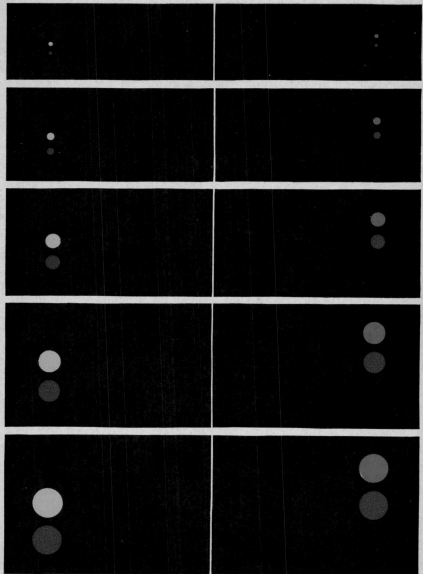

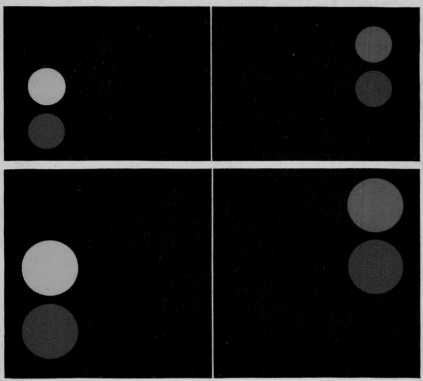

Courtesy, Keystone View Co.

The slides illustrate the fusion tests of the Betts Ready to Read Unit. Their purpose is to determine the smallest target which an individual can fuse or blend readily into one image. Examiners should exercise extreme caution when administering these tests because the "2" series may be confused with the "7" series. Since the dots on the "2" series have a greater lateral spacing than the dots on the "7" series, a subject would be required to relax the convergence in order to fuse the targets on the "2" series at Reading Distance. Few cases would be able to achieve this. It is important, therefore, that the "2" series should be used when the slide holder is set at .00_∞ and the "7" series when the slide holder is set at Reading Distance.

one eye is closed or if the vision in one eye is unconsciously ignored. A vertical imbalance might cause the subject to fuse the four balls into two. If the subject is closing one eye, the examiner should say, **"Look with both eyes."** *At no time during the administration of the tests should the subject be told how many balls he should see.* If four balls are seen, the examiner should replace Test 2A with Test 2B. The targets should be fused quickly for normal performance. If the targets on Test 2B slide are not fused into three balls, then 2C, 2D, and so on should be used until one is reached which permits visual fusion indicated by the immediate seeing of three balls.

2. Series 7 tests.

Set the front of the slide holder on the point marked Reading Distance. (On the 1934 model Telebinocular, Reading Distance is equivalent to 2.50_16.) For the Reading Distance position use the Series 7 tests. Insert Test 7A slide and proceed as with the Series 2 tests.

Subjects wearing bifocal glasses should be certain that they look through the upper segment when viewing Series 2 tests and the lower segment for Series 7 tests. The examiner should be sure that such a subject is not looking through the division line of the two segments.

Recording. On the record blank, record the number of the test on which visual fusion (the immediate seeing of three balls) was first reported. Separate entries should be made for each of the series of slides. For example, an individual may report visual fusion on Tests 2A and 7E.

Interpretation. Several types of responses are possible on the two series of tests.

1. *Failure to see more than two balls on either Series 2 or Series 7.* This, of course, indicates one-eyed vision or a vertical imbalance. Such a case should be referred for an eye examination.

2. *Failure to see three balls on both Tests 2A and 7A.* This situation is not serious unless the subject also fails to see three balls on Tests 2B and 7B. The ability to see three balls on both Tests 2A and 7A indicates superior fusion.

3. *Failure to see three balls on both Tests 2B and 7B.* The seeing of four balls only on Tests 2B and 7B indicates a need for the attention of a specialist who probably will prescribe glasses, stereoscopic eye-training exercises, or both. The presence of eye-muscle imbalance, astigmatism, nearsightedness, or farsightedness may contribute to faulty fusion indicated by the seeing of four balls or the slow fusion of four into three on Tests 2B and 7B. Faulty oculomotor control may also be a significant factor in failure on Tests 2B and 7B. Such a case can be helped if the teacher will provide reading materials printed in a large size type and interesting stereographs until the condition has been corrected. The use of large size type requires less effort for the maintenance of eye co-ordination.

4. *Failure to see three balls on Test 2B and the seeing of three balls on Test 7B.* This is an indication of faulty fusion for distance seeing and of normal fusion at reading distance. Such a case should be referred for a thorough eye examination. This type case may benefit by the use of stereographs.

5. *Failure to see three balls on Test 7B and the seeing of three balls on Test 2B.* This indicates faulty eye co-ordination at reading distance and the case should be referred for a thorough eye examination. As indicated by the lateral imbalance test, some cases may overconverge. If the individual also has a focusing difficulty, it may be necessary for the specialist to prescribe

glasses. It has been the experience of the writer that this type of case can profit by reading blackboard and chart material as well as books printed in large size type. Stereoscopic pictures also can be used to an advantage.

6. *Failure to see three balls on test slides with targets larger than those of Tests 2B and 7B.* Failure to see three balls on either Tests 2B or 7B indicates faulty fusion. Some cases may have varying abilities for fusing the Series 2 and Series 7 targets. Of course, all cases fusing the targets on Tests 2B and 7B usually can fuse the targets on succeeding tests. The purpose of the tests with the larger targets is to determine the smallest size target which can be fused immediately and from the results to secure a clue regarding the size of type which can be read most comfortably. No one has determined the percentage of perception time during reading that is required for the focusing and co-ordination of the eyes. Neither has anyone determined the percentage of perception time during reading that is required for the focusing of the eyes. Undoubtedly, the rate of eye co-ordination and focusing is related in some degree to the duration of the fixation pause and the number of fixation pauses. However, it has been pointed out elsewhere by the writer that reading is largely a matter of conditioning the central processes.

Reliability of report. Fatigue and general body tone is one factor sometimes contributing to a variation in test results from one testing period to another. An individual's responses in the late afternoon may vary slightly from those given in the morning.

Suggestion of the response expected by the examiner is another factor contributing to variation in results. Children should not be tested when there are others waiting in the same room.

In view of the above statements, every precaution should be taken to insure accurate results. There are two ways to check on the reliability of the subject's report. In the first place, the subject can be asked to point to each target. If he points to three balls, they should be in vertical alignment. On the other hand, if four balls are designated, each pair only should be in vertical alignment. If the subject persists in reporting the seeing of three balls and in pointing to four, have him count the balls as he points. A second method of checking on the accuracy of the response is that of using the Series 7 tests when checking the responses on the Series 2 tests and the Series 2 tests when checking the responses on the Series 7 tests. The individual usually will not be able to fuse the targets on both series of tests when set at either of the two positions.

This set of tests should be administered only by an examiner who understands the use of the basic Betts Ready to Read Tests. The validity of the results will depend upon the examiner's skill in securing the co-operation of the subject.

APPENDIX D

Betts Check Tests on Reliability of Report
Keystone View Company, Meadville, Pennsylvania,
1936

In the directions for the administration of tests in the basic
Betts Ready to Read Unit, suggestions are made for checking
the reliability of the subject's report. Borderline cases, however, always exist. It is the purposes of these tests to provide
additional means for checking the accuracy of the response.
The check tests consist of:

Test 1. Slide DB-1a—Two-eyed Visual Efficiency

Test 2. Slide DB-2a—Left Eye Visual Efficiency

Test 3. Slide DB-3a—Right Eye Visual Efficiency

Test 4. Slide DB-5a—Eye Co-ordination Level (Reading
Distance)

Test 5. Slide DB-7e—Sharpness of Image

Test 1—Two-Eyed Visual Efficiency

Purpose. This is a check on Test 3a (Slide DB-1) of the
basic Betts Ready to Read Tests. The dots in the signs have
been rearranged to forestall guessing.

Normal Performance. A score of 100 per cent is normal
for this test.

Procedure. Follow the same procedure as outlined for Test
3a (Slide DB-1) of the basic Betts Ready to Read Tests.

Recording. Record the correct responses on the supplementary record blank provided for this purpose.

Interpretation. For Test 1 the dots on the signs are in the following positions:

	Position of sign	Per Cent A.M.A.	Position of dot
Reading	1	20	Left
from	2	30	Top
near	3	40	Center
target	4	50	Right
to	5	60	Bottom
far	6	70	Center
target	7	80	Right
	8	90	Top
	9	100	Right
	10	105	Top
	11	110	Bottom

See "Interpretation" section of Test 3a (Slide DB-1) of the basic Betts Ready to Read Tests for interpretation.

Test 2—Left-Eye Visual Efficiency

Purpose. This test is a check on Test 3b (Slide DB-2) of the basic Betts Ready to Read Tests. The dots in the signs have been rearranged to forestall guessing.

Normal performance. A score of 90 to 100 per cent is normal for this test.

Procedure. Follow the same procedure as outlined for Test 3b (Slide DB-2) of the basic Betts Ready to Read Tests.

Interpretation. For Test 2 the dots on the signs are in the following positions:

	Position of sign	Per Cent A.M.A.	Position of dot
Reading	1	20	Bottom
from	2	30	Left
near	3	40	Top
target	4	50	Center
to	5	60	Right
far	6	70	Bottom
target	7	80	Center
	8	90	Left
	9	100	Top
	10	105	Right
	11	110	Top

See "Interpretation" section of Test 3b (Slide DB-2) of the basic Betts Ready to Read Tests for interpretation.

Test 3—Right-Eye Visual Efficiency

Purpose. This test is a check on Test 3c (Slide DB-3) of the basic Betts Ready to Read Tests. The dots in the signs have been rearranged to forestall guessing.

Normal performance. A score of 90 to 100 per cent is normal for this test.

Procedure. Follow the same procedure as outlined for Test 3c (Slide DB-3) of the basic Betts Ready to Read Tests.

Interpretation. For Test 3 the dots on the signs are in the following positions:

	Position of sign	Per Cent A.M.A.	Position of dot
Reading	1	20	Left
from	2	30	Top
near	3	40	Center
target	4	50	Right
to	5	60	Bottom
far	6	70	Center
target	7	80	Right
	8	90	Top
	9	100	Right
	10	105	Top
	11	110	Bottom

See "Interpretation" section of Test 3c (Slide DB-3) of the basic Betts Ready to Read Tests for interpretation.

Test 4—Eye Co-ordination Level (Slide DB-6a)

Purpose. This test serves two purposes:

1. To re-check the score on Test 5 (Slide DB-6)
2. To test the eye co-ordination level at reading distance.

Normal performance. All individuals should score 100 per cent. It should be noted that 100 per cent on this test is not equivalent to 100 per cent on the tests used by specialists.

Procedure. Set the front of the slide holder at Reading Distance (this corresponds to 2.50_16 position on the 1934 model Telebinocular). Insert Slide DB-6a and proceed as with Test 5 (Slide DB-6) of the basic Betts Ready to Read Tests. It will be noted that on this test the test target in each row will appear to be recessed or farther back than the other targets.

Recording. Record the responses on the supplementary record blank provided with these tests. The score is the per cent of eye co-ordination level represented by the last target read correctly.

Interpretation. The following standards apply to this test only:

Row	Correct Response	Per Cent
1	Ball	10
2	Box (or Square)	20
3	Diamond	30
4	Cross	40
5	Star	50
6	Ball	60
7	Box (or Square)	70
8	Cross	80
9	Star	90
10	Box	100

See "Interpretation" section of Test 5 (Slide DB-6) of the basic Betts Ready to Read Tests for interpretation.

Test 5—Sharpness of Image (Slide DB-7e)

Purpose. This is a check on the tests of sharpness of image included in the basic Betts Ready to Read Tests. Every ball on this test slide contains three lines. This test is also valuable for the rapid testing of adults.

Normal performance. Three lines should be seen in each ball at Reading Distance and at .00_∞.

Procedure. Position 1. Set the front of the slideholder at .00_∞ and insert Test 5 slide (Slide DB-7e). Point to each ball and ask, **"How many lines do you see?"**
Position 2. Set the front of the slideholder at Reading Distance and repeat the procedure.

Interpretation. If the subject does not see three lines in each ball at both positions of the slideholder, he should be referred for a thorough eye examination. See "Interpretation" section of Test 8 of the basic Betts Ready to Read Tests for further interpretation.

APPENDIX E

Record Forms

Four forms are available for recording the data from the Betts Ready to Read Tests and other pertinent information:

1. *Kindergarten Form:*
   In this form space is provided for recording the scores on:
   a) Visual Sensation and Perception Tests.
   b) Auditory Readiness Tests.
   c) Visual Readiness Tests.

2. *Survey Form:*
   This form is used for recording scores on:
   a) Visual Readiness Tests.
   b) Auditory Readiness Tests.
   c) Visual Sensation and Perception Tests.
   d) Tests of Oculomotor and Perception Habits.

3. *Case Study Form:*
   This form is used for recording:
   a) Medical data.
   b) Reading Test data.
   c) Spelling Test data.
   d) Arithmetic Test data.
   e) Mental Test data.
   f) Visual Readiness scores.
   g) Auditory Readiness scores.
   h) Visual Sensation and Perception scores.
   i) Data on Oculomotor and Perception Habits.
   j) Eye Preference data.
   k) Hand Preference data.
   l) Observations by teacher.

4. *Secondary School Form:*
   This is a briefer form used for recording:
   a) Visual Sensation and Perception scores.
   b) Fusion Test scores.
   c) Agility of Fusion scores.

APPENDIX F

Report to the Doctor

The health specialist should be regarded as the ally of the teacher. Certain sections of the Betts Ready to Read Tests were developed for the purpose of identifying cases requiring the help of a specialist. Forms for the reporting of cases to the health specialist selected by the parents are provided in small pads by the Keystone View Company, Meadville, Pennsylvania.

The following form is used:

To the Specialist

The following is a record of the Betts Ready to Read Test results. Your professional co-operation in correcting visual difficulties which might interfere with efficient reading will be appreciated.

NOTE: The left-hand column of test numbers refer to Betts' *Manual* and record forms.

Test No.	Pass	Fail	Doubt
1			
2			
3-a			
3-b			
3-c			
4			
5			
6			
7			
8-a			
8-b			
9			
10			

KEYSTONE STEREOPHTHALMIC SERVICE
MEADVILLE, PENNSYLVANIA

School ....

Date.................... 193...

To................................
(Parent or Guardian)

Dear Patron:

Our tests show that ....
should have a thorough eye examination at your earliest convenience. We suggest that you take this record form to the
specialist whom you select. We will gladly re-test your child
while you observe.

Yours sincerely,

APPENDIX G

School Surveys of Vision

Ideally, the school population should be tested annually. Until
the public is educated to support a thorough-going educational
system, compromises will have to be made. First, all who have
apparent reading difficulties should receive the attention made
possible by the tests. Second, in the light of other data, surveys
will be of maximum benefit if made of all entrants to

1. first grade,
2. junior high school,
3. senior high school, and
4. college.

These testing periods correspond very closely to certain
psychological and physiological maturation rhythms which might
be directly reflected in reading achievement. The onset of pu-
bescence is probably as important as the other developmental
periods mentioned. At these periods, the special attention given
will be exceedingly worthwhile from the point of view of pre-
venting visual disabilities.

APPENDIX H

Use of Stereographs[7]

Eye-training exercises with special stereographs are used widely for the correction of eye co-ordination difficulties. It is possible, therefore, that schools might endeavor to *prevent* some of these difficulties by the daily use of interesting and appropriate stereographs, especially in the primary grades. In addition to the obvious educational benefits to be derived from this important use of visual aids, children can profit physically by the incidental exercises and eye recreations which aid in developing and maintaining the co-ordinate functioning of the eyes.

School people, of course, should not go beyond their professional province by endeavoring to give directed eye-training exercises in the school, for such exercises should be prescribed and supervised by a qualified eye-specialist. Nevertheless, it is quite proper that teachers make maximum use of educational materials which are hygienically correct. The use of stereographs for building educational backgrounds is endorsed by thousands of educators. Primary teachers use them to bring meanings to words; geography teachers use them to bring distant lands into the classroom. Their hygienic value in addition to these educational values now has the endorsement of outstanding doctors.

---

[7] Betts, E. A. and Wagner, Guy W., "Visual Characteristics of Good and Poor Readers," *Educational Screen* (April, 1936).

GLOSSARY

TERMS USED IN THIS LITERATURE

ability, capacity plus training.

accommodation, the act of adjusting the lens of the eye to keep a sharply focused image on the retina.

accomplishment quotient (A. Q.), ratio of educational age to mental age.

acquired aphasia, loss of established language ability.

acuity, sharpness of "vision"; visual power.

agraphia, disorder by which an individual forgets how to write.

alexia, loss of memory for process of reading, caused by a pathological condition.

alternating vision, visual sensations alternating between the two eyes but not simultaneously.

amaurosis, blindness caused by a disease of the optic nerve or retina.

ambidextrality, facile use of both hands for unimanual activities.

amblyopia, a dimness of vision from lowered sensibility of the retina.

amblyopia exanopsia, dimness of vision in one eye caused by a lack of eye co-ordination.

ametropia, an error of refraction, such as farsightedness (hypermetropia), nearsightedness (myopia), or astigmatism.

antimetropia, a condition where one eye is nearsighted and the other is farsighted.

aniseikonia, ocular images of different sizes and shapes.

antitropic, reversed symmetry; opposite of syntropic; opposite in function.

aphasia, sensory or motor language disability believed to be caused by lesions in the brain.
> auditory, word deafness.
> grapho-motor, (writing) agraphia.
> visual, word blindness.
> voco-motor, (speaking) aphemia.

apprehension, a low level of mental organization permitting understanding.

ascending letters, letters that ascend to the upper shoulder of the type body, as *d, b, h, l,* etc.

astigmatism, an irregularly shaped refractive media. A term applied to an eye whose refraction is not the same in all parts, causing the eye to focus the light at different points.

asymmetry, absence of bilateral functioning.

atavism, reappearance of a character supposedly outgrown by the race.

audiometer (or acoumeter), instrument for measuring auditory sensitivity.

audition, hearing.

auditory acuity, level of sensitivity, keenness of hearing ability.

auditory discrimination, ability to discriminate between sounds of different characteristic frequencies.

auditory perception, mental awareness of sounds.

auditory span, memory span determined by use of auditory stimuli.

blend, the fusion of two or more sounds in a word without loss of identity of either sound.

bimanual, two-handed.

binaural, simultaneous functioning of the two ears.

binocular, two-eyed.

binocular regression, right to left return of both eyes during reading.

bradylexia, lack of temporal orientation.

central nervous system, consists of brain and spinal cord.

cerebral dominance, the normal functioning of one hemisphere of the brain. (An explanation of laterality.)

chronological age (C.A.), calendar age or age since birth. Usually expressed in months.

congenital, innate, existing at birth, or inborn.

convergence, the act or power of turning the eyes inward from their normal position of rest so that the image of a near object will fall on corresponding parts of the retina in each eye.

cursive writing, longhand or script writing commonly used above the primary grades.

cyclopean eye, usually referred to as the resultant co-ordinate functioning of the two eyes.

descending letters, letters that descend below the type body, as *p, q,* etc.

dextrad reading, reading from left to right.

dextro-sinistrality, a condition in which a left-handed individual is caused to use the right hand.

differential psychogram, educational profile such as that made use of in the Stanford Achievement Test.

digraph, two letters representing one sound, such as *ea* or *ng*. There are consonant and vowel digraphs.

diphthong, two sounds that are so closely blended together that they give the impression of one sound, such as *oi* and *ow*.

dioptry, the unit expressing the refractive power of a lens. A one dioptre lens has the refractive power to bring parallel rays of light to a focus at a distance of one meter.

diplopia, double vision where one object appears as two.

disabled reader, one who is a non-reader or a very slow reader. Oftentimes, one who twists the symbols as he reads; that is, saying *saw* for *was,* etc.

distance seeing, viewing an object at a distance of twenty feet or beyond.

dynamometer, a device for testing the strength of grip.

dyslexia, a reading disability caused by a disease of the brain.

emmetropia, normally shaped eye with normal refraction.

entoptic, within the eye.

esophoria, condition of the eyes in which the visual axes *tend to deviate inward* when the extrinsic muscles are in a state of rest.

esotropia, condition of the eyes in which the visual axes positively and visibly turn inward.

etiology, causative factors of disabilities.

exophoria, condition of the eyes in which the visual axes tend to deviate *outward* when the extrinsic muscles are in a state of rest.

exotropia, an observable outward deviation of the eyes.

eye co-ordination, the co-operative functioning of the two eyes for the achievement of single vision.

eyedness, eye preference.

eye span, amount of material grasped during one fixation pause of the eyes.

eye voice span, range between the point where the eyes are and the voice is during oral reading.

face, the part of the type body which leaves an impress on the page.

facile, ease of performance.

fixation frequency, number of stops the eyes make per line when an individual reads.

fixation pause, the length of time required for the eyes to fix on a given part of a line in reading.

foot candle, the arbitrary unit of intensity of illumination.

fore exercise, a pre-test or preliminary exercise for the purpose of familiarizing a pupil with the testing technique.

fovea, a small depression on the macula lutea.

fusion (binaural), combination of auditory stimuli into a single impression.

fusion (visual), the mental blending of the right- and left-eye images into one composite image.

grouping, the process of classifying individuals according to their levels of achievement for instructional purposes.

group test, any test developed for administration to several individuals at one sitting by one examiner.

handedness, hand preference for unimanual or bimanual tasks.

hierarchy, a complex of habits which includes those of the next lower order.

horopter, the field of binocular vision when the eyes are fixated on a given area.

hyperope, one who is far-sighted.

hyperopia, far-sightedness. *See* hypermetropia.

hypermetropia, far-sightedness. Image formed behind the retina.

hyperphoria, the condition in which one of the eyes deviates upward.

illusion, a normal error of perception.

image, a mental reconstruction of sensory experiences. Three levels: after images (A.I.), eidetic images (E.I.), and memory images (M.I.).

imagery, collective mental images—visual, auditory, kinaesthetic, gustatory, olfactory, pain, or thermal.

individual test, a test, such as the Stanford Revision of the Binet, developed for administration to a single individual.

informal test, a test made by the classroom teacher; also subjective appraisal of an individual's achievement level derived from observation of daily performance.

intelligence quotient (I.Q.), ratio between mental age and chronological age; mental age in months divided by chronological age in months.

interlinear space, the vertical distance between the bottom of a short letter on one line and the top of a short letter in the next line below.

inter-pupillary distance (P.D.), distance between the pupils of the two eyes.

kinetic reversals, confusions of directional sequence, such as "left" for "felt."

lateral imbalance, a tendency of one or both eyes to deviate inward or outward from their normal position.

leading, spacing between the lines; interlinear spacing.

levosymbolic, right to left reading tendency.

levotropism, left lateral reactions.

levoversion, movement of both eyes directly to the left.

levography, (Strack) mirror writing.

macula lutae, the clear vision area (approximately two millimeters in diameter) which surrounds the fovea.

manuscript writing, "printing" or lettering by a free hand process in which the letters are not connected as in common longhand or script writing. Recommended for use in the primary grades by both teachers and pupils.

maturation, growing up plus training.

memory span, memory power or level; usually measured by presenting a number of items which the subject is asked to reproduce in correct order.

mental age, mental development or intelligence age of an individual measured in terms of the chronological age of the average individual of corresponding mental ability.

methodology, a study of methods used for teaching a given activity.

mirror reader, one who tends toward right to left reading for words, letters, or whole sentences.

mirror writing, handwriting which appears as ordinary handwriting would in a mirror.

mixed dextrals, right-handed, left-eyed individuals.

mixed sinistrals, left-handed, right-eyed individuals.

monocular regression, right to left movement of one eye during reading.

myopia, nearsightedness. Image is formed in front of the retina.

neologism, coining new words.

neural, nervous.

neurasthenia, an unspecified nervous disorder.

neurology, science of the nervous system.

nystagmus, short, jerky movements of the eye.

ocular dominance, preferential use of one eye for such fixation actions as sighting.

oculomotor, pertaining to the movements of the eye.

Oculus Dexter (O. D.), right eye.

ophthalmology, a study of the function and diseases of the eye.

orthoptic training, exercises for the development of eye co-ordination.

orthophoria, normal muscle balance.

Oculus Sinister (O. S.), left eye.

Oculus Unati (O. U.), both eyes.

pathological, diseased; functional inadequacy caused by an organic disturbance.

pause duration, length of time the eyes are focused upon a given part of the line during the reading process.

perception, mental awareness and integration of sensations.

perception span. *See* Eye span.

perimeter, an instrument for measuring the field of vision.

phonetics, the science of speech sounds.

phonics, the science of speech sounds as applied to reading.

phonogram, a letter or group of letters forming a speech sound.

phoria, tendency.

phorometer, an instrument for measuring muscular imbalance.

phobia, abnormal fear.

photophobia, light fear; intolerance to light.

pica, a size of type equal to twelve point. Standard of measurement for leads and for width and length of pages. Six picas are equal approximately to one inch.

point, a unit of measurement for a size of type. A point represents approximately one seventy-second of an inch. For example, twenty-four point type is cast on a type body one third of an inch high.

psycho-therapy, treatment of disorders through suggestions, psychoanalysis, etc.

pure dextrals, right-handed, right-eyed individuals.

pure sinistrals, left-handed, left-eyed individuals.

rapport, harmonious and understanding relationship between two individuals.

reading span, the number of words that can be repeated after a controlled time exposure of the reading material.

regressive eye-movements, right to left return of one or both eyes during reading.

regression frequency, number of times the eyes tend to re-trace or review portions of the line being read.

retarded reader, one whose reading age is blow his mental age.

retina, nervous and sensitive layer of the eye.

return sweep, the movement of the eyes from the end of one line to the beginning of the next.

reversal tendency, the tendency of immature children or of children who have practiced immature habits to reverse letters and word forms.

saccadic, discontinuous eye movements during reading.

schizophrenia, personality disintegration.

sinistrality, pertaining to leftness.

sight word, a word that is memorized or recognized as a whole.

somatic, bodily or physically.

spacing, lateral spacing between words, sentences, or columns and paragraph indentions.

static reversals, confusions of single letters similar or identical in pattern but differing in spatial orientation, such as "bad" for "pad."

stereopsis, depth perception.

strabismus, an inco-ordinate condition of the eyes.

suppression, psychological blocking or ignoring of vision in one eye.

suspenopsia, short periods of non-seeing in one or both eyes.

syndrome, a number of symptoms which characterize a disability.

tachistoscope, an instrument for controlled time exposure of visual materials.

trauma, injury or wound.

type body, the piece of metal on which the letters are cast.

type size, vertical size of the piece of metal on which the type face is cast; it has no definite relationship to the size of the type face.

unimanual, one-handed.

vaso-motor, muscular changes in the veins or arteries.

vertical imbalance. *See* Hyperphoria.

visual acuity, keenness of vision.

visual span, memory span determined by use of visual stimuli.

word blindness, inability to interpret words due to a pathological condition. (In recent literature the term is used only infrequently.)

INDEX

Aberrations, emotional, 231-232
Agraphia, 58
Alexia, congenital, 58
Allen, Conner, and Hildreth Metropolitan Achievement Test, 92
Ames, A., 159
Anderson, Walter A., 68, 195
Aphasia, 58
Art and reading, correlation, 208
Ashbaugh, Ernest, 272-273
Association
  disorders of, 58
  tests, 106
Astigmatism, 155-156, 301, 347
Attitudes, of remedial teacher, 234-235
Audio-frequency range, 192-193
  test for, 322
Auditory acuity, 192
  test for, 322
Auditory analysis, 208
Auditory discrimination, 194-195
Auditory fusion, 194
  test for, 320-321
Auditory perception, 194
Auditory readiness tests. *See* Betts Ready to Read Tests
Auditory span, 193
Auditory training, 195-197
Ayres, Leonard P., 68

Bachman, Frank P., 72
Bennett, C. C., 131
Berens, Conrad, 328
Berry, Charles S., 68-69
Betts, E. A., 254, 383
Betts Check Test on Reliability of Report, 374-375
  eye co-ordination level, 378-379

left-eye visual efficiency, 376
right-eye visual efficiency, 377
two-eyed visual efficiency, 374-375
Betts Fusion Tests
  administration of, 365-373
Betts Ready to Read Tests, 86, 88-89, 99, 161
  Auditory Readiness Tests
    administration and interpretation of tests, 318-322
    Auditory Acuity Test, 322
    Auditory Frequency Range, 322
    Auditory Fusion Test, 320-321
    Auditory Perception Test, 194, 321-322
    auditory span measured, 193
    Auditory Span Test, 318-319
    complete battery, 161-167, 310
    fusion slides, used in tests, 157-158
  Oculomotor and Perception Habits, 350-364
    purpose, 350-352
    sample, 167
    slide DB-20, 357
    slide DB-21, 357-358
    slide DB-22, 358-359
    slide DB-40, 359-360
    slide DB-41, 360-361
    slide DB-60, 361
    slide DB-61, 361-362
    slide DB-80, 362-363
    slide DB-81, 363-364
    slide DB-82, 364
    summary of tests, 352-353
    uses, 166
  report to the doctor, 381-382
  Visual Readiness Tests, 311-317
    administration and interpretation, 311-317
    Letter Form Tests, 311-313
    Letter Recognition Test, 317
    Phonetic Elements Test, 316-317

395